SAVAGE!

Robbie Savage retired as a professional footballer in the summer of 2011. He is now a full-time broadcaster and pundit for the BBC and ESPN, having won the prestigious Sony Rising Star award in May 2011.

Janine Self is a sportswriter with 20 years' experience working for national newspapers. Football has been her main beat, and first love, but she has also covered Wimbledon for the last decade, Formula One Grands Prix, the Olympics, the Commonwealth Games, the Ryder Cup and speedway. Janine met Robbie shortly after he moved to Leicester City and has reported on his controversial exploits for club and country ever since.

SAVAGE!

THE ROBBIE SAVAGE AUTOBIOGRAPHY

ROBBIE SAVAGE
WITH JANINE SELF

MAINSTREAM
PUBLISHING

EDINBURGH AND LONDON

This edition, 2011

Copyright © Robbie Savage with Janine Self, 2010
All rights reserved
The moral rights of the authors have been asserted

First published in Great Britain in 2010 by
MAINSTREAM PUBLISHING COMPANY
(EDINBURGH) LTD
7 Albany Street
Edinburgh EH1 3UG

ISBN 9781845967161

The authors have made every effort to clear all copyright permissions,
but where this has not been possible and amendments are required,
the publisher will be pleased to make any necessary arrangements
at the earliest opportunity

A catalogue record for this book is available
from the British Library

Printed and bound by
CPI Group (UK) Ltd, Croydon, CR0 4YY

3 5 7 9 10 8 6 4

To Mum, Dad, Jonathan, Nan, Sarah, Charlie and Freddie.
Without family I am nothing.

ACKNOWLEDGEMENTS

Writing a book is a bit like playing football: it's a team effort. I would like to thank Bill Campbell of Mainstream Publishing for giving me the platform to tell my story, Alex Hepworth for editing it and Kate McLelland for designing the book cover. Thanks too to Cliff Butler, the stats man at Manchester United, for his invaluable assistance and to Ryan Giggs for taking the time and trouble to write the foreword. I would also like to thank Paul Mace, Stephen Lownsbrough and Janine Self.

Robbie Savage

CONTENTS

FOREWORD

I have to say that I was really delighted when Robbie Savage approached me to provide a foreword for his autobiography. I've known him for a good deal longer than I care to remember, and the mere thought of him writing a book about his escapades is, at the very least, an interesting concept. I don't think I would get much of an argument from people in the game if I were to say that he is one of the most colourful and flamboyant characters football has to offer. We were juniors together at Manchester United for several years before he left the club to pursue his career at Gresty Road with Crewe and now at Derby's Pride Park, with one or two stops in between.

Robbie was an important element of the United side that defeated Crystal Palace to win the 1992 FA Youth Cup. That was a wonderful occasion for the club and an achievement that bridged a 28-year gap since the team that included George Best, Willie Anderson, Jimmy Rimmer and David Sadler, among others, last lifted the trophy, in 1964. I was proud and privileged to captain that side, which became known as 'the Dream Team' among United supporters.

It is now written in the history books that many of us were fortunate enough to go all the way and play first-team football at Old Trafford. Robbie departed from Old Trafford in order to pursue his dream, but it is to his eternal credit that he not only succeeded in carving out for himself an excellent career in the game but also established himself as an influential and colourful individual.

Wherever his travels took him, be it Crewe Alexandra, Leicester City, Birmingham City, Blackburn Rovers, Derby County or Brighton & Hove Albion, he quickly became a firm favourite with the fans, the backroom staff and the players. Robbie has an infectious enthusiasm for football. His never-say-die, non-stop, scurrying style has always endeared him to managers, coaches and supporters alike.

But it isn't only his insatiable appetite for hard work that has made him into an excellent professional footballer. Robbie has never been short on skill and has always looked supremely comfortable when in possession of the ball. I'm glad to say that his leaving Old Trafford didn't signal the end of us playing on the same pitch for the same side. Both Robbie and I were lucky enough to represent our country, and we played alongside each other, with the Red Dragon on our chests, on several occasions.

We had some great times travelling with the national side, but I cannot help but recall the wonderful days we enjoyed as apprentices at Manchester United. Incredibly, more than 20 years have passed since we all started out as young hopefuls. There was Gary and Phil Neville, Nicky Butt, Chris Casper, David Beckham, Simon Davies, John O'Kane, Kevin Pilkington, Keith Gillespie, Paul Scholes, George Switzer, Ben Thornley and others all under the guidance of Eric Harrison and Jimmy Curran at the Cliff training ground in Salford. But the memories of those wonderful days are still fresh in my mind, and I'm sure it is the same for all the lads. We had some terrific times together, and Robbie Savage was always at the centre of the wisecracking and larking about. There was never a dull moment when Robbie was around, and that's one of the reasons why it has always been an advantage to have him in your dressing-room. I don't doubt for one moment that all of the managers he has played under would echo my sentiments.

Football autobiographies are commonplace these days, and many of them, to be honest, are bland and predictable. I can assure the reader that this book will definitely not fit into that category.

Ryan Giggs

1

ONE DAY YOU WILL COME BACK TO HAUNT ME

The words whirred round and round in my head, making nearly as much noise as the ambulance siren. *Not good enough, son. Not good enough.* Five years of hope and a lifetime of dreams destroyed in a couple of sentences from the greatest manager in the world. But as I sat, trapped in the wreckage of my little Fiesta, I was more frightened of Mum and Dad than the fact that I couldn't feel anything in my left arm or that my little finger was clearly broken. My injuries were physical, but my pain was all mental.

Robert Savage, professional footballer with Manchester United. *Sorry, son, not any more. Not good enough.* I was now Robert Savage, out-of-work teenager. More to the point, I had just managed to total my pride and joy in a head-on crash that was all my own fault and had left an old guy badly hurt. The ambulance was on its way, and soon I would have to look Mum and Dad in the eye and confess to them that their boy had let them down.

I don't remember who pulled me out of the window of my white 1.1 Fiesta, bought for £900 as a present by my proud parents when I passed my driving test, but I can still smell the smoke and see the devastation as I sat on the side of the road and waited for the ambulance to come. What was going to be harder? Telling Mum and Dad I'd crashed their present or admitting to them that I had not made the grade at Manchester United?

My father, Colin, who was then a European sales manager for a canning company, was my biggest supporter and my biggest critic. I still have the letter he wrote to me on the day I left home in Wrexham to become a full-time apprentice at United.

Dear Rob,

Just a note to say what I find difficult to say in words to your face. I have been a lucky man. As well as having been lucky enough to have found a woman like your mum, I have been the luckiest man in the world to have had two boys like you and Jonathan. You now have an opportunity that millions of other young men would give their right arm for. Please don't waste it. You have a God-given gift, so use it, and remember, HARD WORK SUPPLIES ITS OWN REWARD. Take my advice, and remember to be very wary of the workmates that forever moan about everything under the sun. You usually find that the ones that moan are the ones that don't like hard work. It goes without saying that, no matter what problems you have when you're in Manchester, no matter how big or small, your family – Mum, Jonathan and me – are always here to help. We will all miss you, but most of all Mum. She will miss you like hell, so try to ring home as often as possible. Finally, never stop believing in yourself. We know you are the best, so believe that yourself. There is a great deal of difference between self-confidence and being a bighead. Fortunately, being a bighead has never been a problem with you, so be CONFIDENT. I love you lots, the best of luck, and work hard.

Dad

The letter means even more to me now, if that's possible. Dad has developed Pick's disease, a dementia-like condition that affects the frontal lobes of the brain. He is getting steadily worse, and there will come a time when he won't know who I am or that I played football or even that he is a grandfather. He has been the biggest influence on my life, and to see him fade away emotionally like that is truly horrible. My mother, Valerie, has to watch the man she loves turn into a shell, knowing he will soon depend on her utterly, even if he doesn't recognise her any more.

Dad never missed an international game, and he watched most of my club matches too. He would miss meetings, duck dinner, make every sacrifice for me. Now he is not half the man he used to be. He was clever until this disease affected him. To me he will always be a great man, but for him to be 63 and not able to hold a proper conversation is hard to take. I feel for my mother. She has always said that without him she is nothing. It is a testing time for both of them.

Lying in that hospital bed, I felt I had failed him. I'd failed Mum, my brother, Jonathan, and my grandmother Olwen. I waited for the family to arrive, and the tears flowed. Not even the grinning face of my best mate, Jamie Piper, could cheer me up. I grew up with Jamie in a little village called Bradley, just outside Wrexham, and he is still one of my closest pals.

It was Jamie whom I turned to on the day Sir Alex Ferguson called me into his office and delivered the news that United would not be offering me a new contract. I honestly thought I would get a 12-month deal, but that didn't stop the butterflies as I walked towards the manager's office. I sat down. I was so nervous I could feel my heart pumping and I didn't have any spit in my mouth. Ferguson was sitting behind his desk, wearing a red sweatshirt with 'AF' on it; I can see him sitting there now. He called me Robert: 'Robert, you've done fantastic since you've been here.'

And then I knew. He said there were better centre-forwards at the club. Oh yes, back then I was a striker. The shift to midfield would come later, thanks to Wales boss Bobby Gould, but in those days I was a forward and competing with the likes of Mark Hughes, Brian McClair, Dion Dublin and, in my own age group, Paul Scholes and Colin McKee. I didn't need telling that they were better than me!

'You aren't ready for here, but you will make it somewhere. One day you will come back to haunt me.' I never forgot those words, and over the years I think I have come back to haunt him a few times. So many players leave Old Trafford and simply fade away. If they make a living out of football, it is in the lower leagues. I am proud of the fact that I was a United reject who made good. David Platt is the other famous exception to the rule, and it's funny that we both started all over again at Crewe. I went on to play in the Premier League for 12 seasons, making over 350 appearances in the best league in the world, and win 39 caps for Wales. Having said that, I don't think Ferguson has ever lost any sleep over me. In the years since, he has said precisely three words to me – even though we were next-door neighbours for six months. 'Hello, Robert' were two of the words. 'No' was the other.

I can still feel my cheeks redden at the way Ferguson spoke to me the day I asked him for David Beckham's shirt. I've never been one for collecting shirts, but Becks was one of the kids I'd grown up with at United and we had always been good mates. I was playing at Old Trafford, up against Becks, and I asked him for his shirt. 'Of course,' replied Becks. 'Go and see Albert the kit man.'

I tracked down Albert and asked him for the shirt. 'Go and see the gaffer.'

I walked to the home dressing-room door and knocked. The great man himself was standing there. 'Hello, Robert,' Ferguson said. He'd always called me that.

'Becks has said it would be okay to have his shirt, and Albert has asked me to check with you.'

'No.'

Then he closed the door as my face burned up. It was as if any old Tom, Dick or Harry had asked. I don't think he treated me with respect that day. It wasn't as if I was going to stick it on eBay or anything. My plan was to get Becks to sign it and to put it on my wall with some other precious shirts. Given the way that meeting turned out, I suppose I shouldn't have been particularly surprised to find him equally remote when I moved in next door: when I joined Blackburn from Birmingham we rented in Cheshire for six months. We saw his wife, Cathy, who is a lovely lady, and I also spotted Fergie's sons, Darren and Jason, from time to time. I even had his brother, Martin, around for a cup of tea. But in the six months we were neighbours, Alex didn't speak one word to me, although he did complain about the dogs barking.

Meeting him again was the last thing on my mind as I stumbled out of his office as a 19-year-old reject trying to hide the tears. I was a popular lad, but I couldn't face the other players. I'd done fantastic. Fergie had said so. But I wasn't staying. Fantastic? Hardly. I headed straight to my digs near United's famous Cliff training ground to say goodbye to Brenda, who had looked after me from the age of 14. Next step: ring Jamie. 'I'm on my way home,' I told him. 'Let's go for a game of snooker.'

We met at a pub called The Wheatsheaf, and I broke the news. Typically, he told me not to worry. We decided to play snooker at the Gresford Colliery Club, which was a short drive away. To get there, we had to pass my old school, Ysgol Bryn Alyn, and drive down a long straight road with terraced houses either side. I was ahead in my white Fiesta, and Jamie was following in his blue one. I knew I was driving too fast, but my head was buzzing with Ferguson's words and the prospect of facing the family later. It seems overdramatic now, but at the time I honestly felt it was a death sentence, that my life was over.

I only saw the cat at the last minute and out of the corner of my eye. It might not even have been a cat, but I swerved to avoid something. My car was out of control in a street full of parked vehicles and with a little red Micra coming the other way. I was doing fifty and he was doing thirty, which is quite an impact for two little cars. I smashed straight into him. Jamie's face in the rear-view mirror was one of utter shock as he realised he had no choice but to ram into the back of me. Everybody came out of the terraced houses at the noise, and I realised I was trapped in a car that appeared to be close to blowing up.

My first concern was the other gent, who needed oxygen when the ambulance arrived. I nearly killed that poor guy, and the thought of what happened still gives me nightmares, even though, I am delighted to say, he made a full recovery. To add to the worst day of my life, my car was in tatters, my best mate's car was in tatters, I couldn't feel my arm, and Mum and Dad were on their way to the hospital. I wished my emotions had been numbed, not my left arm. I lay there dreading what was coming next.

Mum and Dad were absolutely brilliant, as they have always been. Like me, they were worried about the lack of feeling in my arm, but not because it might mean the end of football. They were concerned about me. Dad couldn't believe the mangled piece of metal that had been my car, either. Or, rather, he couldn't believe that I'd walked away with only minor injuries. I spent three days in hospital, but Jamie was fine. He laughed about it then, and he still laughs about it now. I wasn't about to start laughing, but as I lay in bed my mood changed from heartbreak to determination: 'I'm going to prove Alex Ferguson wrong. I am going to make it as a footballer.' I was promising my parents, but I was also making the promise to myself.

Home for the best part of three years had been my digs in Manchester. Now I was properly home in North Wales and ready to start all over again, back in my little box room in Pine Close, Bradley, where I grew up living and breathing football. You could just make out the Blu-Tack marks on the wall where my Liverpool poster had been: Graeme Souness, complete with '70s perm and wearing a Hitachi shirt – the very same Souness who was to chase me down the tunnel quite a few years later because of me and my big mouth.

This is a good time to make a confession. Over the years, I have been close to joining Everton on several occasions and have suggested each time that I am a lifelong fan. I lied. Goodison Park was not my stadium of dreams; Anfield was. I wore an Ian Rush Juventus shirt to my trials at Manchester United, and whenever I scored a header I'd always yell 'Toshack!' because of John Toshack, who was later to end my Wales career so famously. Strange world.

In the days after the crash, there was nothing big about me or my mouth. United sent flowers, and the club vicar, Father John, visited, which I thought was a lovely gesture. I just wanted to be fit again, especially as there was an offer on the table. Dario Gradi, manager of Crewe, had been on the phone. It was Crewe who had spotted me as a schoolboy and invited me to join their school of excellence. Gradi had always thought I was making a mistake when United came in, but that had not stopped him keeping tabs on me over the years. The grapevine had been buzzing, and Gradi didn't waste any time. 'I want Robert back,' he told Dad. 'Tell him to give me a call.'

Perfect. So many kids fall by the wayside when they are released from their clubs, especially clubs the size of Manchester United. Perhaps that is because of that horrible feeling of failure, or perhaps because of something inside a person. All I know is that players with far more talent than me have not achieved anywhere near as much as I have, and I sometimes wonder why. Then I look back at my childhood, my family, my upbringing, and the reason must be there, somewhere.

You would never think an ordinary guy from Bradley would make it. Just pulling on a Wrexham shirt would have been great, but to have played so many games at the very top is verging on the ridiculous. Sitting up in my bedroom and worrying about my future in football, I drifted into the past thanks to my scrapbooks, the first one started by me aged 13 and then continued by Nan and Dad. I gave Nan all my Wales schoolboy caps, and, over the years, she has acquired quite a collection of souvenirs from my career. I am so grateful now to have something to show to my sons, Charlie and Freddie.

My first scrapbook is dated December 1988, a month after I had been accepted as an associate schoolboy by United. Even then the press were getting it wrong! One of the cuttings said I had only been playing football for two years. Next to it I have carefully written, 'It is a lie about me only playing football for two years.'

When I think of all the publicity I have attracted since then, it makes me smile to see I was already grabbing headlines as a schoolboy and relishing every minute. A young, naive, trusting face stares back at me, and there is no clue that the kid in the photograph was to go on to become a magnet for so much attention – good and bad.

I still have my certificate, dated 21 November 1988, telling me that I had been registered as an associate schoolboy at United. Ten days before that I had received a letter from Ken Merrett, United's club secretary, telling me that there would be a two-year apprenticeship waiting when I left school at sixteen. Two years as a schoolboy, two years as an apprentice, then surely my first professional contract. As a kid, that wasn't just the future; that was the rest of my life. I was on my way, and nothing was going to stop me.

I've already mentioned Dad's letter, which fills me up every time I read it, and so does one written by Nan, the proudest grandmother in the world.

Dear Rob, enclosing £20 for you to go on Tuesday. We can only say three things – good luck, good health and God bless you and guide you on your way. That's all Nan and Taid can say. Just one more thing. Don't forget us, will you? Knowing you, I know you won't.

All our love always (we love you and Jonathan dearly),

Nan and Taid Xxxx

What had I done with their unconditional love? Failed at Manchester United. I was not going to fail again. Mum and Dad, Jonathan, Nan and Taid, my late grandfather: they all believed in me. They thought I was something special. Without them I was nothing, just as I would be nothing now without my wife, Sarah, and my boys. I had been given a second chance at Crewe, and I was not going to blow it.

The boy from Pine Close, Bradley, Wrexham, North Wales, was on his way.

2

IT'S NOT THE BOOTS;
IT'S THE FEET IN THEM

Whenever I go back to Bradley, I walk my boxer dog Tai round the fields where I once spent every spare second kicking a ball. One thing always strikes me as I gaze at the empty fields: kids don't play football any more. The pitches are deserted, but if I stop and concentrate I can still picture the jumpers we used as goalposts and hear the tantrums I used to throw when Dad came to haul me off to bed: 'Aw, Dad, do I have to?'

'Yes, Robert. It's getting dark, and your mother's expecting you.'

No one argues with my mother. Dad certainly didn't, and there was a very good reason for it. She goes off like a bottle of pop. It is one of several characteristics I have inherited from her, which is why we have been known to have the odd cross word. *Pop*. She's gone. *Pop*. So have I. Sometimes she gives me a look and I know just how she feels.

She smashed up the kitchen one day. We were sitting in the front room, Dad and I. She took every single cup, dish, knife and fork out of the drawers. I looked at Dad: 'Do something.'

'No point, son.'

We just sat there as she destroyed the entire contents of the kitchen. She was going through the menopause at the time and was one of those unlucky women who were really affected by it. Thank goodness it's not something that I will ever have to go through. Because we're so similar I really understood how she suffered, but underneath the fiery temper and the emotional outbursts Mum has a heart of gold and is the most incredible woman I know. She has been so supportive of me, and she has been a rock for Dad. Mum never wanted to move from the house she bought with Dad when she was expecting Jonathan. They bought it in 1970 for £3,000, and it's worth about £100,000 today. It is always immaculate, because Mum hates things out of place and dirty – and that included muddy sons. Maybe I was destined to make life difficult for her from the moment I was born.

Robert William Savage entered the world on 18 October 1974 at the Maelor Hospital, Wrexham, and managed to make a nuisance of himself from the word go. Mum lost four and a half pints of blood, and we were both in hospital for three and a half weeks before we joined Dad and Jonathan in Pine Close. Pine Close is an ordinary cul-de-sac in an ordinary village in an ordinary area. Dad spent a lot of his time travelling to Europe as a sales manager for Continental Can, while Mum had her hands full with Jonathan and me. Jonathan was the big brother, the one with the nicer room, the Atari, the Spectrum and the double bed. I had the little box room: rotting wood, ice on the inside of the window, single bed and black and white TV – but the telly only arrived when I was 13.

Bradley is a small place. There was a pub and a post office and, at the back of that, an off-licence. We had a Chinese restaurant too. It was nice growing up there. There was a council estate nearby, but there was not a lot of difference between the estate and the private houses. It wasn't like growing up in an inner city.

Best of all, halfway between Bradley and the next village of Gwersyllt there was a field. Out of Pine Close, left onto Beech Avenue, then a right turn onto Glan-llyn Road. Half a mile. I used to run all the way. That was where we put our coats down and played football. There were four football pitches, a bowling green and some tennis courts. I was good at tennis too. I excelled at most sports: cricket, pool, snooker. I was two-hundred-metres champion at the school sports day in 1987, and I won a local pool knockout five times. I play golf off 15 now, but football was my obsession from the start.

Now everyone knows me as Robbie Savage, but my parents still call me Robert or Rob. To everyone else in Bradley, I was Bobby. Look in my old scrapbooks and newspaper cuttings, and there it is: 'One of the best players in Wrexham is a boy called Bobby Savage.' I don't know where the Robbie came from. Robert, Rob, Bobby: everyone still wanted me in their team. In fact, the only people who were not carried away with the footballing talent of Bobby Savage were Mum and Dad. They were the strictest parents in the world. Now that I'm a father I can see where their discipline was coming from, but I wasn't quite so understanding then.

'You're going to be a footballer.' Everybody said it, and I thought it as well. We're going back 27 years, but I don't recall having any doubts. I think the gift came from my great-grandfather. Nan's father used to play for Wrexham. His real name was Johnathan Evans, but everyone knew him as Johnny Oxo. I had inherited the genes that meant my brother's mates wanted me in their team even though they were all three and a half years older than me. I would have been about nine. It wasn't about who could do homework. I was better than them on the football pitch, and that was what mattered. We played 13- or 14-a-side. There would be a knock on the door, and I'd bolt down my dinner – beans on toast, usually – in double-quick time.

My parents were really strict. I wasn't allowed to get muddy. I'd get a smack on my bottom. All my mates used to dive into sliding tackles, but if I got muddy I'd panic and start crying, 'Mum's going to be livid with me.'

All my older mates were allowed to play, play, play. There were kids with their new Nike trainers, and they would ruin them on the first day; we couldn't afford anything like that. And those Nike trainers would be filthy while I'd be worrying about grass stains on my knee. My first pair of boots were Panther Four Stripes, because Adidas ones were just too expensive. Mum bought them from Woolworths for £2.49. She must have seen my face, but she was quick to come out with one of her sayings: 'It's not the boots; it's the feet in them.'

Dad would come to the field to collect me. I'd scream and get a whack. I was always the first one called in, because I was so much younger than the others. That's my first memory: being the first one home and wishing I had been allowed to get filthy and stay out late. Bath night was Sunday. Every other night I was stood in the sink and washed. My dad would inspect my nails, and if I'd been biting them I was smacked. It was freezing in that sink.

I didn't ride bikes or do anything else. School was over at four in the afternoon, and everyone could set their watches by me. I would kick a ball against the wall of a house, because I wasn't allowed to go beyond the Pine Close sign: the two metal posts and the street name in between. I drove the neighbours mad by kicking tennis balls against the wall for hour after hour. We lived in a semi; there was the house on the end and then us. There were eight houses in all. I smashed Margaret's window on one side and Chris's on the other. John Smallwood was on the corner. If the ball went into his garden he wouldn't give it back. We'd have to sneak under the window, and if he caught you he'd go berserk as we trampled his plants trying to pick up loads of tennis balls.

John's a good friend of the family, and we often laugh about those days. I love going back, and when I see the Pine Close sign it feels like only yesterday. That cul-de-sac holds some precious memories. Mum would send me to the shop for cigarettes, and I'd have a ball or a tin can at my feet and run all the way there and back. At Christmas, no one ate the tangerines, because I had them on my feet, doing tricks. I played keepy-uppy in the back garden with the ball on my shoulders and head, and Mum would have to count. If she got it wrong, I'd make her start all over again. Mum calls me Peter Pan and says I've never grown up.

She stopped watching me play years ago, because she could not bear to see her boy abused by the fans, and she hates it when I get into trouble. I have never sworn in front of her, and I'm sorry for some bad language in this book, but footballers do occasionally swear, Mum. She also had another favourite saying: 'It's nice to be important, but it's more important to be nice.'

Most important to me was my family: Mum, Dad, Jonathan. Jonathan has never been jealous of me. We're chalk and cheese. I'm a bottle of pop, and he is completely laid-back. He liked being in his room with his books and computer games and left home to go to Bristol University and do an engineering degree. He looks nothing like me. He was always chunky with short hair while I was long-haired and skinny like a piece of wire. Jonathan was knocked down by a lorry one day. I was in the third year at school, and he'd just started as an apprentice at Dairy Crest. My godfather Chris came to collect me from school, so I knew something was up: 'Jonathan's had an accident, but he's all right. He's been hit by a lorry.'

He was rushed to hospital, lost all his teeth and had a six-inch gash slashed across his face. It was a really sunny morning after rain; there was reflection off the road, and the driver didn't see Jonathan as he was rounding some cable. Jonathan was pushed 20 yards, and we thought we'd lost him. He got over it, but he still has a huge scar and false teeth.

Then there was my Nain and Taid – Dad's parents, Doris and Craddog – but they died when I was young. Nain and Taid are the Welsh words for 'grandmother' and 'grandfather'. I'm ashamed to admit I can't speak my own language, but Dad is fluent. Mum's parents were William Till, who was Taid too, and Olwen, who is my beloved Nan. Bill Till was a POW in the war and escaped over the Alps and ate grass to survive. It's an incredible story. Taid was a brave man. He had Parkinson's, and Nan nursed him for 13 years until he died.

Nan loves her football. As I was growing up, and even when I went to Manchester United, she would put £5 into an envelope for me every week without fail. I'd wait three or four weeks and then pick up the envelope. The day I signed schoolboy forms for United I went back to Taid, who was bedbound by this time. I showed Nan and Taid the photos of Alex Ferguson with me, and they were so happy. When I won my first Wales cap at Under-14, I called in on the way home to give Taid the cap. He never saw me play. They lived in Moss Valley, known locally as the Moss, which is near Bradley. Nan became quite a celebrity. She presented prizes, opened fairs and was on ITV's football highlights programme, and she loved every single minute of it.

In one of my scrapbooks, I have a programme for the Parish of Broughton Summer Fayre, held on 10 July 1999. Admission 20p. And at two in the afternoon Mrs Olwen Till, grandmother of the Welsh international footballer Robbie Savage, officially opened the fayre. She'd walk round Sainsbury's and say to people, 'Do you know who my grandson is?'

I couldn't wait for Saturday nights. Mum and Dad liked to eat out, and we'd stay with Nan and get away with murder. She had a pensioner's bungalow with a hall. It was absolutely freezing, with one of those snake draught excluders. We'd roll up a paper ball, Jonathan and me, and we'd play football with the cabinet as one set of goals and the door the other. We'd beat the hell out of it. She didn't care.

Dad sometimes had a treat for me too. He used to take me to the pub round the corner, The Queen's Head, because he was friendly with the people who owned it. He had his own seat and was really well respected. We'd have a game of pool, and my treat was an orange juice. I took on the other men and won; I was good at pool. Dad always insisted that education came first. He said that was the most important thing and that I should pass my GCSEs. He never lost his temper with me, but one day I was caught practising autographs and the teacher brought me to the front of the class. I always took my report home and showed it to Dad. He didn't raise his voice but said he was disappointed, and that was enough for me. I got my head down after that.

School was okay. I wasn't stupid, and, best of all, I was very, very good at football. I had also grown out of a speech impediment by then, although I was still sleepwalking. There have been a few scary moments with that. I tried to climb into a fridge once, and years later, at Leicester, I woke my mate Graham Fenton because I was convinced a train was about to hit the building. Luckily I did learn how to say my Ss. Up to the age of six, I had a major problem, though. 'There's a wap on the window,' I once screamed hysterically, pointing to a wasp. All the kids used to make fun of me. I had a classmate called Claire Colley. We were playing with sticks one day when I said to her, 'Your dick's bigger than mine.' It probably was!

But to excel at football was the key to being popular – with the boys and the girls. My first school was Ysgol Y Gaer Infants, where, I believe, I was so shy I never put my hand up. Next stop was Gwersyllt County Primary, where I discovered a never-ending supply of Worcestershire sauce-flavoured crisps. I think fourteen packets was my record one day. Needless to say, it was thanks to my footballing skills: I was captain of the team, and everyone wanted to be on my side. I had quite a taste for crisps, and there was a tuck shop supplying them. 'Give me a packet of crisps and I'll pick you,' I told my mates.

Everyone tried to bribe me. Looking back, I suppose it was quite a nasty thing to do, but I didn't give it a second thought at the time. My great mate Jamie Piper still mentions it, though, which makes me think it wasn't something that went down particularly well with my school pals. I have one other overriding recollection from my junior school. I was in the third year and thought I would slide down the banisters of an iron staircase, as you do at that age. I fell and hit my head on the iron stairs, and this big lump came up on my leg. It put the fear of God into me, because I thought I wouldn't be able to play football. It was a greasy banister, really old, rock solid.

Having survived that scare, I moved on to Ysgol Bryn Alyn, where I diced with death once again. Yes, the career – not to say the life – of Robert William Savage could so easily have been cruelly cut short by an effing Fruit Sensations sweet. I couldn't tell you what flavour, either, as I never even tasted the bloody thing. I was in the fourth year of school at the time, and a teacher – I think it was Mr Randall – literally saved my life. I choked on the sweet. I honestly thought I was a goner; then a teacher grabbed me, turned me upside down and banged me on the back. I threw up all over his shoes, in front of 150 kids – Fruit Sensations and all. We had an area that linked one building to the other, which we called 'the Chicken Run'. There were 15 stairs up to the next building, and I was running when the sweet slipped.

Mr Randall and Mr Williams were my PE teachers, and Mr Williams was also my form teacher in the fourth and fifth years. Mr Watson was my form teacher before that. I went back to school a few years later, and Mr Watson was in a wheelchair. I hope they are proud of me. I was polite, well spoken and well mannered, and I had respect for my teachers. I only ever had three fights at school. One was with a friend called Patrick Griffiths, when I called him 'Fatty'. I wasn't the biggest around, but I'm proud to say I never lost a fight. The fact that I was so good at football meant I could get away with a little bit more too. It was also at Bryn Alyn that I met someone who would become a lifelong friend – and the reason I have seven GCSEs to my name.

I owe my exam results to my mate Jim Whitley. His family came from Zambia, and being one of the first black kids at school was hard for him. He was different from what people were used to. In those days, you just did not see many people from different ethnic backgrounds in Wrexham. He was about 11 when we first met. When the Whitley family turned up at school, there were comments made behind their backs because they were different, and I was not having it. I became friendly with Jim straight away, and I think that helped him settle in. I was friends with his brother Jeff too. His father was called James, and I think there were about six or seven kids, all their names beginning with J. Jim and Jeff were also fantastic footballers and would go on to play for Manchester City. Jim and I struck up a great friendship. Most importantly, he would let me copy his homework. At exam time, we had these single desks three feet from each other so no one could peek. I used to cough, and he'd turn his paper over so that I could see the answers. I've cheated in my career, and I cheated there.

We have stayed in touch over the years. He was getting nowhere with his football, and I wrote to Manchester City for him when I was on the books at United. He went for a trial and signed. He had a bad time, because he was innocently caught up in a robbery and served time for it. I wrote to him every week while he was in prison, and City stood by him too. He finished his career at Wrexham and was forced to retire with a knee injury. I was jealous of him. He was a fantastic footballer, a fantastic artist, a scratch golfer, clever, played in a band – and he was well endowed!

Dad always used to drum it into me that schoolwork came before anything else, but all I dreamed about was playing football. I played for the school team two years above me, and everyone would watch. I felt the buzz even then. All the girls wanted to know you. It was brilliant to be good at what you did. If you're a footballer, everybody likes you, even if you're not very well educated. We weren't rich either, so I was not spoiled in terms of money, even though my parents did everything they could for me.

I love my clothes and have always had an eye for nice gear. So, despite the fact I was last in the queue, I could boast that I owned a pair of Adidas ZX500 trainers – even if they were hand-me-downs and almost falling apart by the time I could afford to buy them eighth-hand. Catalogues were a big deal back then, and we were all so envious when Alan Shaw, a lad at school, ordered a pair. They cost about £130. When Alan decided he'd had enough wear out of them, he sold them on. The next boy sold them on again. And again. I was last, but I didn't care.

FIFA stickers were popular too, and one guy nicked £40 from his mother's purse to buy them. I confess to stealing penny sweets from the off-licence, and I know that was wrong, but I would never have thought about going into Mum's handbag. Mum and Dad used to drum into me what was right and what was wrong. It was why I was never tempted down the path of drink and drugs as a teenager. I'd always hated cigarettes, because Mum smoked heavily. It's something I hate now. So it was easy to say no when my mates started experimenting. I chose another path.

Having a close family helped too. We did things together. Our holiday nearly every year was at Pontin's in Prestatyn when the snooker tournament was on. I used to enter and so did Dad and Jonathan. The likes of Terry Griffiths, Tony Meo and Joe Johnson all played. Holidays abroad were few and far between, although 1982 stands out, as that was the time I was invited to join a game of football – but only if I took off all my clothes first!

Dad had an old brown Cortina with cloth seats. I still remember the registration: UTU 525R. It got us to the south of France. We went with Timmy Oldland and his family, who had a brown Granada. Timmy, who was two years older than me, lived in Pine Close too and was a very accomplished footballer. I modelled myself on him. I was usher at his wedding, he was usher at my wedding and I'm godfather to his son. The Oldlands and the Savages went in convoy, and we took the tents with us. Next to our site was a nudist beach. Timmy and I went to the local shop to buy some bread one day and walked past a pitch with a football match going on: ten versus ten and every one of them totally naked. 'Can we play too?' we asked.

'Of course,' came the reply. 'But only if you take off your clothes.'

I must have been about eight at the time. The World Cup was on, and we watched that amazing 3–3 semi-final between France and West Germany when keeper Harald Schumacher somehow avoided a red card and then saved crucial penalties. Timmy and I had World Cup fever, and we wanted to play football. But not naked. We turned and walked away.

When I was a little boy, the south of France had seemed miles and miles away, but years later I did the drive to Antibes in 17 hours, with plenty of help from my satnav. I wasn't in a brown Cortina either. I don't mind Cortinas, but . . . *brown*? And I mean brown! This time I was in a Mercedes S65 AMG, six and a half litres. Every hour we had to stop for petrol, all the way from Manchester. The car did about nine miles to the gallon!

My childhood memories are happy ones. A loving, supportive family at home, good neighbours, great mates at school and, top of the list, football.

3

IF ONLY I HAD
MARK HUGHES'S THIGHS

At the age of 13, my friends started going out and getting drunk. Me? I was drinking a pint of Guinness a night too. Bizarre as it may sound, this was Dad's remedy to beef me up, and it was much worse than taking medicine. Chickens had bigger legs than me. There is not a lot to me now, but my one overriding fear growing up was that I would be too skinny to compete against adult men. I have always found it hard to put on weight. I ran everywhere, I played for the school and boys' teams, I bolted down my beans on toast so that I could go outside and play football, and I inherited Dad's slim physique. He had read somewhere that Guinness could build you up, and we had stocks of the stuff in the garage because he worked for Continental Can. Every night I had to down a pint, and I hated every mouthful. I've never been a drinker, and I detest beer, so I was very glad when he decided it was not working.

I might have been puny, but I was still wanted by the boys' clubs in the area. Jonathan played for a club called Llay United, which was about a mile from our house, and I often watched him. John Thomas, manager of the Under-12s, invited me to come along for a training session. I didn't need telling that I was doing well. I was taking everyone on, for a start. I think we won eight or nine nil and I scored about six. People were asking, 'Who is this kid?' My pal Timmy Oldland, my holiday companion in France, was at Llay. Our pitch was at the naughty boys' home. It was like a borstal. I got to know some of the kids, and they were nice.

Llay's biggest rivals were Brickfield Rangers. We played against them once, and Andy Moore, who would go on to represent Wales in rugby, was in goal. They beat us 14–1, and that one was the best goal I ever scored. I collected the ball from the keeper and took on the whole team before beating Andy. I scored something like seventy-three goals in one season, eighteen games. It was a record. It might still be a record. I took all the player awards.

'That kid has got something special.' Everyone was saying it, and I was finding it incredible. The natural progression was to be picked for Wrexham and District to play against other district teams like Chester and Crewe, which is where my first big break came. We played Crewe and lost 7–2, but I scored the two in front of the director of Crewe's school of excellence, Barry Burnell, who ran it jointly with first-team boss Dario Gradi. My two goals swung it. I was asked to join the school of excellence just before my 13th birthday.

This meant Dad driving me over there every Monday night. I still have my end-of-season report in my scrapbook. Straight As for control, passing, dribbling, running with the ball, shooting, heading, winning the ball, small-sided games and attitude. 'Outstanding boy in the group. Very gifted boy who is lucky enough to have a pleasant nature and a competitive streak. Will find it harder in the next few years physically, but should be okay eventually.' Signed by Dario Gradi, 21 June 1988.

Underneath the report I have written, 'My favourite one out of all of them was dribbling, because I like taking people on and then to go on and finish with a long-range shot.'

Six weeks later, I was having trials at Manchester United, and I don't think Dario has ever really forgiven me for leaving. Crewe's set-up was exceptional, and I was looked upon as one of the best. It was the first real taste I had of being in football. You had your own kit and had to clean it. There were lads there like Danny Murphy, who was destined for great things at Liverpool and England, and Dele Adebola, who was as big then as he is now. On Sundays, we played in the Liverpool League. The Scousers were hard, they were dirty, and they knew every trick in the book, but the Crewe lads used to out-football them. Dario was very clever. We won the league hands down, and some of the battles were amazing, but we got used to the physical side. Technically we were better, and it taught us to be more aggressive.

Dario was the manager of the first team. I stayed at his house loads of times. One night, I was not at all well. We had bunk beds, and at two in the morning he got up and gave me a Lemsip. He looked after the kids. That was Crewe. The Under-10s, Under-16s and the first team were all treated the same. I disagreed with the way he treated me when I went back there as a professional, but I have nothing but praise for the way he ran the school of excellence.

It was also at Crewe that I had to make my first major footballing decision. I had the opportunity to go to Barmouth with my mate Carl Zanellan for a weekend of fishing, so I rang Barry to tell him I couldn't play on the Saturday. I was told that, if I did that, the door would be closed at Crewe. 'What do I do?' I asked Dad, in tears.

Dad was great. He didn't believe in pushing kids – not like parents now – and he told me that it was up to me. I went to Barmouth, and on the Monday Crewe rang and asked me to come again. I don't think I should have been put under so much pressure, and I thank Dad and Mum for leaving it up to me.

By this stage I was totally consumed by football. My best mates at school were Jamie Piper, Carl Zanellan and Matthew Jones, who were all as sporty as me. Carl's now a painter and decorator and a big Wrexham fan, and I have already mentioned Jamie.

My pals had started going to Wigan Pier. I was at home and scared of girls and scared of messing up. Looking back, I was quite ugly too, which is difficult to believe when you see me now! Girls would come knocking on the door, because they knew I was a footballer, but I was too shy to do anything about it. I'd be hiding in my room and whispering down to Mum, 'Tell them I'm not here.' Mum would say I wasn't in and send them away.

I did have one big crush, on a girl called Claire Bryan. I kissed her once – the first girl I ever kissed – and I really thought I would marry her. But one kiss and that was that. I wonder if she ever thinks of me? Sorry, Claire, you had your chance. I bet she's thinking she made a big mistake!

While my social skills with the opposite sex were sadly lacking, I was coming on in leaps and bounds at the football. I moved on from Llay because Dad set up a team, Bradley Youth. I had Crewe too. Bradley caused a storm because players were supposed to come from within a three-mile radius of Wrexham, and Dad recruited a couple of my Crewe teammates. Mike Earl was from Manchester and Nicky Pay from Buckley, way beyond the Wrexham boundary. Mike and Nicky were two excellent players who were probably better than me but didn't go on. It's hard to play for your Dad, but I was an automatic pick anyway. We were runners-up in the league, and we won the cup.

That was the season I was spotted by Manchester United scout Hugh Roberts. Even after I joined United as a schoolboy I still played for Bradley – until Dad gave it up because of the stress. He was reffing a game once and didn't book a player for an offence, so another player's mother came up to him and slapped him. When he packed in Bradley – I would have been about 16 – I moved across to the enemy, Brickfield Rangers, and we won the league and cup. It wouldn't be allowed now, but I was also playing for a men's team, Lex XI, in the Wrexham Senior League. I was skinny and small, but I could handle myself.

At one point I was playing for Brickfield in the week, Manchester United's B team on Saturday morning and Lex men on Saturday afternoon. One morning United beat Everton 1–0, and I scored with a header. That afternoon I turned out for Lex at the Llay British Legion and got kicked in the air by a 35 year old. Then I had a chip butty while they all drank pints! That was what life was about then, but you couldn't do it today. I was in the school team as well.

Coming from Wrexham, I thought that playing for my home team would be the pinnacle of my dreams. Liverpool was my team, because it wasn't cool to support Wrexham, but I still went to watch Wrexham when I could. I was there the day they drew with Real Zaragoza 2–2 and went out of Europe on away goals. They had a really good side, players like Jim Steel and Barry Horne. One of Wrexham's favourite sons is Mickey Thomas, who will be forever worshipped for that amazing free kick that helped knock Arsenal out of the FA Cup in 1992. I'm great friends with Mickey now. He's a bit of a rogue, like me, and he's given me plenty of advice. One tip was to make sure I wasn't paid in £20 notes. I would never have dared go up to the likes of Mickey to ask for an autograph, though. It's why I know how kids feel now when they come up to me. I'm still bad at things like that. My missus has to ask for the bill when we're out.

To play for Wrexham would have been unbelievable. Manchester United? No way. Not a skinny kid from Bradley. But I have the photo, taken by Dad on 12 October 1988, six days before my fourteenth birthday: Alex Ferguson sitting at his desk, smiling, and me standing next to him and shaking with fear. My scrapbook is full of cuttings with me holding up my associate schoolboy contract. Thank you, thank you, thank you, Hugh Roberts. It was Hugh who spotted me playing for Bradley, and I didn't even know he was watching.

Hugh, who became a grandfather figure to me, went up to Mum as she was getting tea ready for the post-match refreshments. 'Excuse me, I'm looking for the Bradley manager,' he said, not knowing then he was talking to the Bradley manager's wife.

'Sorry, he's busy sorting the kit,' Mum replied. Can you imagine? Someone from Manchester United was standing there having just seen me play an exceptional game, and Mum sent him away in that no-nonsense way she has. Luckily for me, Hugh left his card between the teacups. You should have seen Mum's face when she realised. One quick phone call and a few days later the letter arrived in the post. I was invited by the youth development officer, Joe Brown, to join United for a week in August. I was 13 and turned up in my Ian Rush Juventus shirt.

We stayed at the halls of residence at Salford University – thirty-three of us – and only three were picked. I was a bag of nerves. We had training sessions; then we played a game. Ferguson was watching, and I had a nightmare. I was so nervous I couldn't do anything. Dad was watching too. I was in tears; I thought I'd blown it. I went home and couldn't eat. Mum and Dad couldn't eat. The next day Hugh rang to say that Fergie had seen something he liked. I couldn't believe it. Manchester United offered me a deal. The biggest club in the world with the best manager in the world and they wanted me. I was invited over to sign two-year schoolboy forms and a two-year apprenticeship.

The next four years were mapped out. It was an incredible feeling. I went straight to Nan's house to tell her. I had to inform Dario at Crewe. He said it was the wrong thing to do. That was that. I eventually started my League career at Crewe, and for that I have to thank Dario, but I also believe he held it against me when I turned my back on him to choose United. But what else could I do? This was something beyond my wildest dreams. Mighty Manchester United were knocking on the door, and I was hardly likely to say no to a club like that. My life was never going to be quite the same again.

Every school holiday, I travelled to Manchester and stayed in digs with a lady called Brenda Gosling, who lived just opposite the famous Cliff training ground. At half-term, Christmas and Easter, Dad would drive me across. Sometimes I'd play for the B team on a Saturday morning against the likes of Liverpool, Everton or Manchester City. If you were deemed good enough, you could play with the first-year apprentices, and I was good enough.

Brenda's house was two turned into one, a terrace. One side belonged to her, and the other side was where the players lived. She had a dog of about 17 who was blind and deaf. I loved my cups of tea, but the kitchen was a no-go area. We weren't allowed in there at all to make toast or anything. I used to go to the shop for food. I moved in 24/7 when I signed my apprenticeship, and it was at United that I met David Beckham, Keith Gillespie, Lee Sharpe, Mark Bosnich, Shaun Goater, Colin McKee . . . The list is endless.

For a schoolboy, it was boring. We'd go to the pictures. I had only a small room, and it was a case of training then sitting in your room. I got homesick. I also had Osgood-Schlatter disease in the right knee – growing pains to the layman. Dario Gradi thought at one stage it would hinder me, but it didn't. I was progressing at United, and I was progressing on the Wales front as well.

At Under-15s, I won seven caps. I played three times for the Under-16s and twice for the Under-18s. I won five caps at Under-21 level before I moved up to the seniors, where my record is thirty-nine caps and two goals. I played for Wales schoolboys as well – against England too. At 15, I was in the Under-18s side and scored in the 2–2 draw against England at Gloucester's rugby ground. I also represented the Under-16s against Northern Ireland at Rhyl. I was playing five times a week, and I couldn't get enough.

When you sign for Manchester United at 14, all the girls – the schoolies – think you are cool. You begin to think you are going to make it. But my biggest fear was how skinny I was. I was so insecure about it. I once wore two pairs of jeans and two jumpers at a school disco just to make myself look bigger. I shot up to the height I am now – six foot – but did not put on weight. 'If only I had Mark Hughes's thighs,' I used to think.

On the face of it, though, I'd arrived. The boys and girls at school were all over me, and I was making it into my local paper in Wrexham on a regular basis. Everyone wanted to know me, but I was a bit wary. I have only a few close friends, and I would trust any of them with my life. They like me for what I am and not who I am. I am a lot older now, and there are some who would argue that I'm not much wiser, but I treasure my friendships.

I have six really good friends. If I were stuck on a desert island, they'd be the guys I would choose to have with me. There's Jamie Piper, the loveliest guy in the world. Jamie has never missed any of my debuts: Crewe, Leicester, Birmingham, Blackburn, Derby. He even drove down to Brighton when I was on loan there in the autumn of 2008. It was Jamie whom I phoned when Ferguson showed me the door, happy, smiling Jamie who would make the perfect son-in-law if only he could find a wife. He looks a bit like me, although not as good-looking, obviously. Sometimes he needs a rocket up the backside. Go get yourself a bird, Jamie. He has a normal job in Wrexham, and we still enjoy games of tennis, pool and golf. He is a very good tennis player.

Then there's Nutty: Martin Edwards. When I was a kid, I used to stay with my pal Carl Zanellan, and where he lived there was a row of council garages. We played football in front of the garages, and one of them belonged to Nutty. He chased us down the road and was quite aggressive. He threatened to kill me once. Nutty was a local footballer, and everyone called him 'Egg on Legs' because of his shape. He was a centre-half and the dirtiest player you've ever seen. At first I thought I could never be friendly with this guy, but he has got the biggest heart of gold. I became pally with him when I was at Crewe. He is 13 years older than me and a taxi driver. He would do anything for me. I sometimes watched him play for Bradley men's team in the afternoon. He still drives me around now.

Tuffy – Adam Tuff – is like my big brother. He was best man, with my brother, at my wedding, and he gave one of the worst speeches you've ever heard – only joking, Tuffy! But there was loads of applause to encourage him to finish early. I met him when I signed for Leicester. He's got the worst breath in the world. Every Christmas I buy him Listerine, toothpaste, the works.

Paul Hollinshead is sometimes 'Hollo' and sometimes 'Bruce', because his chin is rather large. He is married with two lovely kids. He's better than me at golf, but he never beats me, because I can get into his mind. I totally destroy him, and then he has a tantrum when he doesn't win.

Tony Quaglia is a more recent friend but a very good one. He was the Wales kit man and nutritionist when Mark Hughes was manager, and went on to be kit man at Manchester City. He knows everything there is to know about food and nutrition. He looks a bit like Rocky and has to be the only 50-year-old man I know who has dark hair.

Finally, there is my mate Jim Whitley, whom I grew up with in Wrexham and who is now an amazing artist. On the walls of my house I have portraits of myself, Sarah and the boys, and they are quite stunning.

Every year, Jamie, Nutty, Tuffy, sometimes Hollo and I go somewhere sunny together. We head to Marbella or Malaga for a few days of laughter, banter and sunshine. My treat. We tell Jamie it's time he found a bird. Nutty has three teeth in his mouth and always orders steak. He's the only man I know who sucks steak. We sit there and slag off each other and all the people walking by. I'm 'Big Nose' for some reason. Can't work that one out. They used to have a go at my crooked teeth until I had them done. Tuffy and Nutty look like the Mitchell brothers. We sit there and cane people as they walk by. We wonder what people are saying about us. The lads reckon people think I'm a C-list celebrity with my designer gear, hair, tan and teeth. Jamie is a bloke in search of a wonderful woman, and Nutty and Tuffy are out of the cast of *EastEnders*. The fact that they look like bouncers can be very helpful in certain situations.

Generally, people who used to hammer me now want to be my best mate. Deep inside, I don't forget. I want to tell them all to get lost. It's just jealousy. Sometimes there are people who fancy a bit of trouble, but they think twice when Nutty and Tuffy are around. They have been tempted to punch someone for me before, but it will only get them into trouble. We've had fall-outs, but we have great times together. This is what keeps my feet on the ground. They are the ones who mean so much to me, my real friends. You get so many hangers-on in this game, but I can be myself with these guys. If people heard us, they'd think we were rude. But if I picked up the phone in the middle of the night, they would be there for me, and I will always be there for them.

As the years have gone on, I have been able to value the friendship of these guys. As a 16 year old about to leave home for the first time, I was looking forward to making lots of new friends.

4

BETTING SLIPS, SUNTANS AND SHAG-THE-BED

Betting slips, suntans and Shag-the-bed. Ask me what springs to mind from my Manchester United days and that's what I would come up with: my room-mate, Keith Gillespie, surrounded by betting slips; going head-to-toe under the ultraviolet rays in a quick and cheap attempt to get a tan; and some of the most extraordinary initiation ceremonies you could imagine.

Not that I knew any of this was waiting as Mum and Dad dropped me off at Brenda Gosling's house. I'd spent half-terms and holidays there, but this was to be my full-time home now. It was a new world. I was a young lad from Wrexham going to Manchester United, carrying a small Nike bag with a few belongings. Mum was crying, and I warned her that I wouldn't be looking back as I walked into my digs. There was no way I could have kept it together because my heart was breaking too.

My GCSEs were in the bank, thanks to the brains of Jim Whitley and my ability to copy from him. I had my qualifications, just as Dad had demanded. It was time for an education of a very different kind, and I could not wait. Schoolwork went out of the window. Since the age of six, all I'd wanted was to play football. Here was a new challenge, a huge challenge and one that would mould me as a footballer and as a man, a man – okay, teenager – who was rubbing shoulders with the likes of Bryan Robson, Mark Hughes, Steve Bruce and Ryan Giggs.

Maybe rubbing shoulders is a bit of an exaggeration. The first-teamers did not give us a second glance until they fancied a laugh. In this day and age, what went on then might be regarded as bullying, and it certainly wouldn't be allowed now, but I loved every single minute of it. Generations of footballers must have gone through the same thing, and it didn't do anyone any harm. The pranks were thought up by the first-year pros for the new boys, but the seniors enjoyed watching. As far as I was concerned, it was a chance to be noticed. Alex Ferguson was never anywhere to be seen, so either he didn't know or he chose to ignore it.

We were 16, and there can be quite a difference in size and physique at that age. I was skinny, a late developer, a virgin. I did not shave until I was 22, and I was dead envious of the apprentices who already looked like men. It makes me cringe even now to think how embarrassed I felt. I would come out of the shower with a towel wrapped round me, and a few of the older apprentices would stand there and wait for me to get changed. I knew they would do it, but what could I do? It would either make me or break me.

Looking back, everything that happened *made* me. We had all sorts of dares, and if we didn't fulfil them there were punishments. We were the special ones. I wasn't quite as special as David Beckham, Paul Scholes, Nicky Butt, Chris Casper, Gary Neville, John O'Kane, Ben Thornley or Keith Gillespie, but I was part of a group that was always destined for great things. Our reputation as prospects did not help when it came to handling the demands of the dressing-room, though. I didn't mind the dares at all, but some of the lads used to hide in the kit van. They even found it hard to concentrate on training because of the thought of what was going to happen next.

What *was* going to happen next? Well, if you didn't fulfil the challenge then it was forfeit time. The Manchester United logo was rubbed onto your naked chest with a wire brush and boot polish. Or you could be put into the tumble drier, which was turned on. The 'bongs' weren't great either. A ball would be wrapped in a towel and the towel twisted round to create a hammer. We'd drape another towel over our heads and the hammer-towel was bounced on our heads. *Bong.* Playing naked golf was almost a relief.

Those were the punishments, but some of the lads thought they were preferable to the dares. Not me. I was up for anything, even Shag-the-bed, although I was a virgin and didn't actually have a clue what to do.

Some of the lads were petrified, but it was part of being a footballer. That was what it was all about. If I saw a first-team player, I would go red and try to disappear, but when it was time for a challenge I was first in the queue. Pick Sav. He's up for a laugh.

Shag-the-bed. It makes me squirm just thinking about it. It worked like this: an apprentice was selected, in this case, me. I was ordered to wait outside the changing-room while it was 'prepared', whatever that meant. 'Right, Sav, we're ready,' came the call from the other side of the door. I walked into a dark changing-room. Someone was standing by the light switch, flicking it on and off to mimic the flashing lights of a nightclub. 'Chat up the mop,' I was told.

The mop was upside down in a bucket, a coathanger attached to represent shoulders while the mop head looked like long hair. 'Chat up the mop?'

'Yes,' came the answer. 'You're in a nightclub, you're dancing and you spot this girl. Show us your moves.'

I was 16. I didn't have any moves. When the switch flicked off, there was darkness. When the lights came back on for that split second, all I could see were a lot of white teeth from smiling faces. It seemed like every player at the club was there. They were waiting. What the hell! There was no music, no *thud-thud-thud* of the bass, but my heart was doing a pretty good impression of a beatbox. With a bottle of water in my hand – a beer in this strange pretend scenario – I shuffled around the dance floor, all the time edging closer to the mop of my dreams.

'Hi,' I said to the mop. 'I'm Robbie.' Not the best chat-up line in the world, but I'd spent most of my school years hiding upstairs in the bedroom when girls called, so I wasn't exactly experienced at that sort of thing.

'Why, hello,' squeaked a voice from the darkness. I still don't know who it was.

'Do you come here often?' What a killer question.

'Yes,' replied Moppie. 'Do you?'

'It's my first time,' I answered as I shimmied closer and draped an arm over her shoulders, the coathanger. 'Do you want to dance?'

'Ooh, yes please.'

I picked up the mop, stepped onto the dance floor and we slow danced. I don't think I'd even done that before – with a girl, I mean. I definitely had never danced with a mop. 'Would you like to come back to my place?' I asked. An invitation that was only ever going to have one answer.

'Ooh, yes please.'

So we went back to my place: a treatment table with a hole in it. I climbed onto the table, and there, in front of a room full of spectators, I pretended to have sex. It was guesswork as I grunted and made various other noises at what I deemed to be the right time. How I made the earth move for that mop! Maybe not, but I swept her off her feet. Actually, I suspect the mop didn't fancy me at all, so it says a lot about my pulling power that I didn't get the brush-off! It sounds obscene, but it wasn't. I was fully clothed at all times, and it was purely simulation. Everyone was in hysterics, and it was quite a laugh.

We had Funny Movements too. A member of the first team would play music, and we had to dance for a minute, stupidly. My Funny Movements were renowned. Ask Gary Neville or Paul Scholes. I was legendary. I looked like a puppet on a string.

'This is ridiculous, it's nothing to do with football,' you think at first. But, looking back, it was hilarious. I had to pretend to have sex, and I didn't have a clue, as I was a virgin. People I had only ever seen on the telly were sitting there and killing themselves. I couldn't even look at a first-team player without reddening up, but I had no problem doing Shag-the-bed. I was even happy to dress up as Snow White in front of them.

My first Christmas at United, the apprentices put on a play for everyone. We sang Christmas carols too, and it was a really special time. Sadly, this is where it has all changed. You're not allowed to do things like that any more, but I'd bring it back. *Snow White* was the panto. Long-haired and baby-faced, I was born for the part! I didn't mind at all. I was in a dress performing in front of Fergie and the first team. Physio Jim McGregor wrote the script. I thought I looked quite good! Ben Thornley was Prince Charming, and I suppose I must have kissed him. No tongues, though. Everybody had a part to play, even Becks, although I can't remember who he was supposed to be.

It was the hardest apprenticeship you could imagine. If you could get through that then you had a chance. That's why we went on to do so well.

There was a little guy called Owie – he was tiny, smaller than Scholesy. The older guys put him in the kitbag, tied it up and put him on the bus because he wouldn't do a dare. When they got to Old Trafford and took out the kitbag, there was Owie. There was another punishment: lying down on the treatment table where I nailed the mop, you had to drop your head over the edge and someone would have three shots at kicking the ball at you. It caused a few nosebleeds. The lads who got through it became the best players the Premier League has ever seen.

Despite being homesick and the constant nagging worry that I was not strong enough to make it, I was loving every minute of my new life in Manchester. I also liked my roomie, Keith Gillespie. I shared a room with Gilly for three years. He was one of eight who were given four-year contracts. They were the *really* special ones. My biggest memory of Keith was of a room full of betting slips and placepots: that's all he used to do. After training he'd go to the bookies. There were these little pens all around the room. I did the odd coupon, but I have never been that way inclined.

I didn't earn very much, and neither did Keith. Every Friday he had to go to the bookies for some of the staff and senior players. We're talking £800 or £900 in cash, all rolled up, to do a coupon. Seeing all this money from very famous players did not help him. It was supposed to be harmless fun, but Keith got sucked in. One time he told me that a horse had no chance so he was not going to place the bet. The horse won, and he had to go to the bank and get three or four thousand quid of his own money to pay it.

I might not have been into gambling, but I was definitely into sunbeds. It was a passion. Most of us headed down nearly every night to the swimming baths. We couldn't afford it on our own, so a couple of us lay on the sunbed together. We were that brown it was unbelievable. Everyone knows now it's so bad for you, but we were on it all the time: five days a week for half an hour a time. We all used them, apart from Gary Neville and Paul Scholes.

Keith made his debut in the first team very quickly and got all the press. He was exceptional once, scoring against Bury. I was pleased for my roomie, but I was jealous. There he was on the back page of all the national papers. He had a stack of them the next day, and I was nowhere near that level. Keith was a very quiet guy, but he had a habit of nudging people. He'd nudge them and nudge them and nudge them again until he went too far. He'd just tap you very slightly. Nicky Butt warned him not to try anything, but Keith nudged him in the shower – and Butt spanked him. Keith's nose was splattered everywhere, and he cried his eyes out.

We had a long weekend free every four weeks: Saturday, Sunday and Monday. Keith came home with me sometimes, and Mum would make us beans on toast. He was a fantastic player. He and Nicky Butt were the two to watch. Keith was even ahead of Becks. He had pace and power and was regarded as the next George Best. I couldn't have asked for a better room-mate. Looking at team photos of the time, the array of talent was quite staggering, but we didn't think too much about it. Our most immediate worry was to keep on the right side of Eric Harrison, the man who would run our lives for the next two years. Eric was in charge of the youth set-up. His word was law.

Eric is a close friend now and someone whom I regard as a mentor. He went on to join Mark Hughes in the Wales management, and the rapport between us was there again immediately. He believed in me and thought I would make it. When I was eventually shown the door at Old Trafford, he wrote me a lovely letter, which I still have. He was and is a gentleman, but I was pretty frightened of him at the age of 16. I wonder what he made of us, the class of 1992. We were already being labelled the new Busby Babes outside United: the Fergie Fledglings. Within the club no one mentioned the Busby Babes, even though we had a paid-up member of Matt Busby's European Cup-winning team working as a coach. Brian Kidd sometimes took us for sessions, and, again, you couldn't find a nicer fella.

So, Eric, what did you think of us all? No one would have believed then that Becks would become the world superstar that he is now. At one point, I was ahead of him in the ratings, but he had the best jeans, the best shoes, the best belt and the best hair products. He was always immaculate. I got on well with him, but he came from London and I came from Wrexham – there was a huge difference. Everybody liked him. He was in different digs from me. He was a central midfielder alongside Nicky Butt. What I do recall is the way he used to stay behind and practise his free kicks. His passing range was amazing, and he had that bit of style too. He bought Giggsy's red Escort, so he had the best car from the start.

Butty was Butty. He was a proper hardcore Manc. You didn't mess with him. Gillespie did and got his nose splattered. Paul Scholes was a cheeky chappie with a really dry sense of humour. He was tiny like me, but he had great technical ability. That was the biggest fear for him – his size – but his awareness was unbelievable. The worry was that he wasn't going to grow. Gary Neville – Nev – was always busy but in a nice way. He came to Gwersyllt one day to play cricket, and I think he scored seventy from twenty balls. He was always methodical but a very funny guy.

Becks is regarded as the sexy superstar now, but when we were kids it was Squeaky who attracted the girls. Ben Thornley, my panto Prince Charming, had a high-pitched voice: Squeaky. He was the pin-up, and, to make us even more jealous, he played for the first team in the Milk Cup. All the girls fancied him and not Becks. He was the good-looking lad in a group that included me and Scholesy! Every away trip, the girls were waiting, and Squeaky got all the fan mail. He was the guy who matured, and he had hair everywhere! Under his arms – everywhere. We'd have girls hanging around The Cliff too. There must have been a school nearby, because they would all turn up in long socks and short skirts.

Chris Casper was very highly rated, but injuries meant he never fulfilled his true potential. He always wanted to make it, because his dad, Frank, had been a player and manager. Casp was probably more advanced than Gary Neville at centre-half, and everyone thought he was the better player. He was also one of the ones who signed four-year pro contracts in the second year of their apprenticeships.

We all had our own traits: Gary Neville was busy, I was the comedian, Butt was the hard one and Scholes was the cheeky one. That's what made us so good as a group. There were no superstars, and we were all on a similar level. Fourteen of us started as apprentices, and all of us were kept on as professionals, which is an outstanding achievement.

All we wanted was to be footballers. There was no drink, no women, no smoking, no sneaking birds into digs, nothing. We were that scared of getting chucked out. Football was the be-all and end-all, and the competition was so great you couldn't afford to do anything wrong. Our days fell into a regular pattern. We reported for training at nine. My chores were to clean Mark Hughes's and Bryan Robson's boots. After that, the first-team showers and toilets needed a scrub. Someone else had the task of doing the manager's office, and someone else made sure the balls were pumped up. Everyone had their jobs.

My peg in the dressing-room was always in the corner, because I was shy. As an apprentice, I had the wall and Scholesy as neighbours, and when I became a pro I was next to Joe Roberts. Becoming a pro was light years away though. Adapting to a life outside school and away from Mum and Dad was the first test. Having done the chores, we would change and then catch the bus at about ten in the morning. Our training ground was Littleton Road, even though we were based at The Cliff. We had double sessions, a shower, then the gym. There was a triangle of ground at The Cliff that we called Little Wembley, and we would go out after lunch to practise shooting or whatever.

We had to wait for Eric to dismiss us. He'd come down the stairs and make sure the jobs were done to his satisfaction. Then, at about four, we were free to go to our digs. There was absolutely nothing to do. It was a case of boredom. I can understand why Keith went to the bookies. He was not the only one. They could go and watch the races. All we had to go back to was a small room with a telly and video player.

I was eating like a horse. At the age of sixteen, I was having a three-course meal at The Cliff and a two-course meal at night at Brenda's, and I still didn't put on any weight. There was also the shop round the corner. Weights in the gym didn't help me either; I've never really done weights in my career. We had to wait until the first team had finished before we could eat. There was a sports scientist at the club called Trevor. I used to wind him up. He had me pinned up against the wall once; I can't remember why. He just snapped. Even then I was winding up people.

I never even thought about winding up Eric Harrison. He was like a headmaster. The last thing you would ever do was answer back or say a bad word to him. He was such a big influence, and you were too frightened to misbehave. Eric instilled a discipline in us. When we played at Little Wembley, he watched from a big window overlooking the pitch. If you did something wrong, all you could hear was the banging at the window.

Look up and he'd have disappeared. He was on his way down to give you a bollocking, and your concentration levels were gone in an instant.

We all had the technique to be there in the first place, but it was Eric's job to make sure we were fit too, and Becks and I were the two fittest. On a Friday morning, Eric would walk down the stairs and pin up the A and B teams on the main noticeboard. All the lads would be nervous. In the very first game, I was the only first-year apprentice in the A team: the only one out of a class of fourteen that included Beckham, Scholes, Neville and Butt. No kidding. As I have mentioned, I was a striker. In that game, I played up front against Tranmere with Colin McKee. It was great to make the A team, because you'd get first-team players like Bryan Robson or Lee Sharpe playing as they came back from injury. So there I was as a teenager, playing in the same team as Bryan Robson. I'd tell all my mates at home that I'd had dinner with Mark Hughes or Steve Bruce. I was playing more A-team games than anything, and I felt I'd arrived.

I celebrated my 17th birthday at Old Trafford, which meant another step on the ladder to becoming an adult: learning to drive. I had seven lessons, passed first time, and my reward was the beloved white Ford Fiesta that I was to write off a couple of years later. Crashing cars and Manchester United: they became synonymous. One day, as I was following Ben Thornley into training, he slammed his Fiesta into a car and I rammed him. Right by the entrance of The Cliff too, which made it all the more embarrassing.

Being able to drive meant I was designated chauffeur for our weekly trip to Accrington. All the apprentices were required to further their education as part of our two-year deal, and there were two options. The brainier lads, including me, did a BTEC in business studies in Accrington, and the rest went to Manchester College. Our course was supposed to be more intense. Becks and Scholesy were doing swimming and gardening in Manchester. Only joking, guys!

Nev, Keith, Casp and I went to Accrington to be taught by a lady called Trish. One day, Keith and I couldn't be bothered. We were a bit naive and pretended that we were there when we weren't. How on earth we thought we were going to get away with it, I don't know. Of course the club were going to find out. They did, and we were in so much trouble. The fear was of being chucked out, and I had risked that by doing something incredibly stupid. We were warned not to do it again – and we didn't.

One day we were travelling back from college. Gary Neville's father, Neville Neville, worked for Bury at the time, and we were heading over to see him. Gary was in his Peugeot, and I was driving my Fiesta with Keith a passenger. We came up to a set of traffic lights, and some guy pulled in front, so Keith gave him the V-sign. The next lights turned to red, and two huge men climbed out of the car. They smashed the window on Keith's side and tried to pull him out. I couldn't press the lock down, so one of the guys opened my door. 'Fuck,' I thought. 'I'm dead.'

Then, to my complete relief, he realised he didn't want me, slammed the door and moved round to Keith's side. The lights changed again, and they jumped back into their car and disappeared – but not before booting my Fiesta, so it was a wreck. The doors on both sides were kicked in and a window smashed. We went halves on the repair bill. It was a scary moment, but I was to have an even scarier one when I was mugged in Manchester.

To beat the boredom, we loved heading to the shops in the city centre. One day I went in with a lad called Gary Twynham, who was also Welsh. He came from Rhyl and later played for Darlington. He was my main sunbed partner. It was my birthday, and I had £140 in my wallet. We caught the bus from Priory Avenue, Salford, to the Arndale Centre. Two guys boarded the double-decker. We were upstairs, about halfway down the bus. One moved behind us, and the other sat in front: 'Hand over your money.'

I looked at the knife in the mugger's hand then glanced at Gary. As well as the birthday money in my wallet, I had a £20 note in my pocket. Could I bullshit my way out of this one? Gary handed over his eight quid. 'Listen, mate, I've only got £20,' I said.

I reached into my jeans and fished out the note. They snatched the cash and legged it. And there, making a very obvious bulge, was my wallet. I shudder to think what would have happened if they'd asked me to empty my pockets. But that was my mentality, and it still is. I didn't report it to the bus driver, but I told the club the next morning. The muggers were a lot older than me, with a knife, and I was 17 and from Wrexham. But I was growing up fast.

5

FLYING WITH THE FERGIE FLEDGLINGS

Ryan Giggs was always destined to lift the FA Youth Cup. Giggsy: so good he was already in the first team but young enough to qualify for a competition every club in the country rates highly. He was the obvious choice to raise the trophy when the Fergie Fledglings matched the Busby Babes and won the Cup – for the first time since the George Best team of 1964. Unfortunately for me, he took my place.

Giggsy was – and still is – extra special. It was a great privilege to play with him as a youngster at United and to pull on a red shirt and perform alongside him for the Wales national team. I have been on the same pitch as some wonderful players, but there is no one to touch Giggs for that special aura. He was in and out of the first team while the rest of us were a million miles away, but he still changed in our dressing-room, which meant we saw plenty of him. When I first met Giggsy, at Under-15 and Under-16 Wales trials, he was known as Ryan Wilson and stood out then. The name changed, but the star quality didn't. He lived up to all the hype, and I am honoured to call him a friend.

But I was still gutted when I played every single match of the 1991–92 Youth Cup campaign only to be dropped for the second leg of the final against Crystal Palace. It was my first big kick in the gut. Ryan was on a different level; he was called upon when needed. With a 3–1 first-leg lead, you could argue that he wasn't needed, but Eric Harrison picked him, and I was the one who gave way. To show how far ahead Ryan was, he reported for senior Wales duty afterwards.

The Class of '92: that's what we came to be known as thanks to that Cup success. Kevin Pilkington in goal, John O'Kane, Gary Neville, Chris Casper, George Switzer, Keith Gillespie, Nicky Butt, Ben Thornley, Colin McKee, Simon Davies and Robert Savage. The boy from Wrexham was ahead of David Beckham, who only broke into the side at the semi-final stages. Scholesy was nowhere to be seen until the following year.

In the weeks and months leading up to the start of the Cup run in November, I was beginning to feel very settled and happy. Fergie didn't have a lot to do with us at all. He did tell me to get my hair cut, but instead I'd gel it so it wouldn't look so long. I wanted the long hair to hide the fact my nose was so big! More often than not I was selected for the A team while the other first-year apprentices were in the B team. Being a full-time footballer was everything I had imagined. The group was tight, even though we were all competing against each other. I'd known these lads since signing schoolboy forms at 14, but there was a big difference between meeting at half-term or school holidays and spending every minute of your lives living, eating and breathing together.

I was sometimes homesick, but I was always skint. The basic pay was £29.50 a week plus a tenner for the bus fares. I spent it on sweets, crisps and chocolate from the shop round the corner from my digs. Music and films didn't interest me. In the second year, we were paid £39.50 a week. First-year pros earned £90 a week. When I got to that stage, the lads like Nev, Butt, Scholesy and Becks were offered four-year deals and jumped to £400 a week, which seemed an absolute fortune. The first-teamers were on £8,000 a week, and as I watched them drive through the Cliff gates in their Mercs I wondered how they could spend that sort of money every week. It's not a question I ask myself now!

I didn't have a pot to pee in. Clothes have always been one of my passions, but fashion is expensive and my budget didn't stretch to anything fancy. If I wanted a jumper or a pair of jeans, then it was a case of saving up for it. My pride and joy was a white Naf Naf jumper that cost £68. I wore it every day and dreamed of being able to afford Lacoste. An appalling red-and-white Nike tracksuit was another buy. It wasn't as if we were going out much to need lots of clothes.

Over the years, I have become quite well known for my love of designer gear, and Becks leads the way in looking cool with his clothes, hairstyles and so on. So picture this scene: me, Becks and the rest of the boys on the bus to the Arndale Centre in Manchester, where we all piled into . . . Marks & Spencer! I can hardly believe I'm revealing this, but £9.99 jogging bottoms from Marks & Sparks were so comfortable that we all had them, even fashion icon Beckham.

When I was really strapped for cash, Nan would come to the rescue. She continued to put a fiver for me into an envelope on her mantelpiece every week. When I went home for a long weekend, I'd pop in and pick up my pocket money. Nan never forgot, and I will never forget what she did for me. Those fivers came in very handy, as did my snooker skills. Salford Snooker Club was a regular haunt, and I'd play for cash. Becks, Gary and Keith went there too. Sometimes I'd win £20 or £30, which doesn't sound much but was around a week's wages.

There was another way to make money. We were entitled to two tickets for first-team matches, and they were always sought after. Either a guy at the snooker club or one of the first-teamers was always willing to buy them for £40 a pair: an offer too good to turn down. It's not as if we could use the tickets, because we played on Saturday too, and the cash could be the difference between putting petrol in my car and not visiting the family.

We fell into a routine at United that revolved around the next game. There were the usual A and B team fixtures and, starting at the end of November, the FA Youth Cup. We came into the competition at the second-round stage, and the first hurdle was Sunderland at Roker Park. Eric Harrison's side included six first-year apprentices, with me up front. It never occurred to anyone that I was anything but a striker.

The team that won 4–2 that night was Kevin Pilkington, Mark Gordon, George Switzer, John O'Kane, Gary Neville, Keith Gillespie, Nicky Butt, Simon Davies, Colin McKee, Robert Savage and Ben Thornley. David Beckham came on as sub for Butty, and Chris Casper stayed on the bench. I scored a header during the brilliant first half, in which McKee grabbed two and Gillespie the other. We were 4–0 up and cruising, then allowed Sunderland back into it. Eric was quoted afterwards as saying, 'They took me to the heights and depths, both on the same evening.'

Pilkington, known as Doofer, was a quiet lad in the same digs as me. He went on to play for the first team. Mark Gordon was called Sheepy because of his curly blond hair. Left-back George Switzer was a year older than me and looked like Scholesy. George was cheeky, a real prankster. I've read somewhere that he works as a mechanic, but when United released him he joined Darlington. John 'Scon' O'Kane lived in the same digs as Becks. He was a good-looking guy from Nottingham, a cultured centre-back who played for Everton. I have no idea why we called him Scon.

Simon Davies picked up the nickname Shaky because of Shag-the-bed. He didn't want to do it, so he was made to hold a cup of water. His hand was trembling so much that most of the water spilled out, and after that he was known as Shaky. He was a midfielder who also played for the first team and Wales, but his career petered out in the lower leagues. Colin McKee, my strike partner and two years older than I was, gave me a hard time because he thought his place was under threat. Raphael Burke was a tricky winger who played one or two games in that run. He came from Bristol and had so much ability but didn't produce it every week.

Burke wasn't the only one who had more ability than I did but failed to go on to make a decent living out of the game. Switzer and a lad called Joe Roberts were tipped for great things. Joe was also a forward, and I played alongside him a few times. I believe he finished at non-league level. When I look at the likes of Burke, Switzer and Roberts, I wonder how it was they did not fulfil their potential while I probably overachieved. There was another guy, called Adrian 'Doc' Doherty, who was tipped to be the next George Best. He was too old for the Youth Cup campaign that year. Doc played his guitar in the room next to mine and, years later, accidentally drowned in Amsterdam.

In 1991, we were a bunch of lads full of optimism and dreams with the world at our feet. Striker Savage was on a bit of a roll too, scoring in the 2–1 third-round Youth Cup win over Walsall. Ben Thornley netted the first. The tie was at Old Trafford, the Theatre of Dreams. It's an imposing sight for any footballer, and this was our first taste of stepping out onto the famous pitch in our traditional red shirts. It didn't matter that there were only 5,000 or 6,000 fans there. The hair was standing up on the back of my neck. Walsall gave us a decent game, and we were hanging on at 2–1, so Eric Harrison replaced me with Giggsy to see us through.

Manchester City away: the fourth-round trip to Maine Road drew a crowd of 15,000 and introduced me to a big-match atmosphere for the first time. It was always going to be tasty against the neighbours. United won 3–1, thanks to O'Kane and Thornley, but my claim to fame was setting up the first goal. I beat the offside trap, the keeper clattered me, and Scon scored from the rebound. Giggsy may have been very much part of the first team, but I am sure he felt honoured to partner me up front against Tranmere in round five. Ryan scored both goals in the 2–0 win.

Giggsy's double meant we teamed up again for the semi-final first leg against Tottenham at Old Trafford. Spurs were the clear favourites, with a side full of second-year apprentices and first-year pros, which makes quite a difference at that age. Sol Campbell, who was to become one of the best centre-halves in England, was a centre-forward. Darren Caskey and Andy Turner were also in the team.

It was a Saturday afternoon, and our run had captured the imagination. There were 20,000 people watching as we thrashed Tottenham 3–0. Ryan was again the hero, with two strikes, and the other was an own goal. The job was completed a couple of weeks later without Giggsy: Nicky Butt and Ben Thornley scored for a 5–1 aggregate victory, and United were in the final for the ninth time.

Becks started to make his presence felt from the moment he came on as a sub in the first leg of the semi. He was a starter for the last three matches in the campaign. Worryingly, I was taken off at White Hart Lane. Joe Roberts replaced me and then did it again in the first leg of the final against Palace. Time for the Savage alarm bells to start ringing.

We travelled to Selhurst Park on a wet Tuesday night in April. The rain was teeming down, but we were all singing in it when Nicky Butt beat goalkeeper Jimmy Glass after 17 minutes. Five minutes later we were splashing around in joy again when Becks sent a twenty-five yarder pinging past Glass. Palace scored a couple of minutes from the end, but Butty restored the two-goal lead straight away, so we were in the driving seat for the second leg. By that stage, I was off and Joe was on. Admittedly, I hadn't played brilliantly.

The second leg of the FA Youth Cup final was supposed to be the pinnacle of my first full-time season at United. Everything had gone so well. I was popular with the lads, I was up for all the dares, I trained hard for Eric Harrison, and I'd played every game in the run. Surely Mum and Dad could be confident of seeing their son jog onto the Old Trafford pitch as part of a team that, arguably, had the greatest crop of talent any youth system has ever produced at one time. 'Robert.' It was Eric Harrison calling me over for a word. 'I'm sorry, Robert. Giggsy is playing against Palace.'

Sorry? Not half as sorry as I was. I'd played in every single game and felt I'd made a decent contribution. Fair enough that Giggsy should play: he was the star of the side. But instead of me? I have rarely been a sub in my career, and the fact I went on to play in the final the following year didn't make up for the disappointment. Some of the lads reckoned Eric was acting under orders from Ferguson, but I have no idea whether it was true or not. It didn't really matter who had decided I wasn't playing.

There is a picture from that Friday when we beat Palace 3–2 (6–3 on aggregate). Both Becks and I were pretty ugly, but thankfully I've blossomed since! The photo is a reminder of a miserable night that was to become even worse. Replacing Simon Davies for the last 20 minutes was a slight consolation, and I almost scored.

At the final whistle, I didn't feel part of it, although I was as entitled as everyone else to the £40 bonus, the medal and the framed photo. For the record, the goals were scored by Thornley, Davies and McKee and ended United's long wait.

I trudged to the players' bar to see Mum and Dad, except Mum wasn't there. Dad and a neighbour were sitting together, and my heart sank. Mum never missed a game. 'What's wrong?' I asked, rushing straight over to them.

'Don't worry, son.' Why is it that people always say that even when there is clearly something to worry about? 'Mum's had a funny turn and has been rushed to hospital.' That was when all my disappointment disappeared. Football means nothing when something's happened to your family. Mum was ill, and she needed us. Luckily it turned out to be just a scare and nothing serious, but we didn't know that as we jumped into the car and raced down the M56 back to Wrexham. It was also one hell of a way to effectively end my first season at United.

Year two should have been another stepping stone in my development as a footballer. It was certainly a stepping stone in my development as a man: I had my first girlfriend. It might seem difficult to believe, but there have only been two serious relationships in my life: Hayley Lloyd and my wife, Sarah. Hayley was from Wrexham, so I was travelling home as often as possible to see her. It was my first experience of having a girlfriend, and I thought it was wonderful.

Not quite so wonderful was my progress at United. Twelve months earlier, I had been ahead of lads like Becks and Scholes. Approaching the second year of my apprenticeship, they had all been fast-tracked and offered professional contracts. I was up to £39.50 a week, and they were earning £90. They left the rest of us behind. It was heartbreaking not to be one of the special ones who were now involved with the first team in the League Cup. That was the first sign of the group breaking up. It didn't change the way we were, but I wondered what was going to happen.

I was still playing in the A team, but Becks and company were in the reserves. I could run all day, but I was weak as piss. Monday and Thursday afternoons were spent in the gym, and I am the first to admit I hated weights. There was one particular machine where I had to sit and reach for a bar above my head and then pull it down as far as I could. When I relaxed, the bar shot straight up and pulled me out of the chair! The lads killed themselves. I wasn't the only one who didn't have muscles. Scholes was tiny, and Becks was hardly a strong man, so I can't put my finger on what was going wrong. My attitude was the same. Perhaps it was because I was a striker, because it is fair to say I didn't score enough goals. Half the time I'd shut down the corner flag!

There was a familiar pattern to the season, however: another Youth Cup run all the way to the final – although I didn't figure in all the matches this time. Different lads came through. Some were from my group but hadn't been good enough the year before, and the others were new boys who faced the same Shag-the-bed baptism we had.

Richard Irving was a new arrival that season and ended up taking my place. He was a year younger than I was and came from Halifax, just like

Eric Harrison. I believed Eric liked him because of that, which I realised later was a stupid thing to think. He was a promising youngster, but he didn't make it. Richard became a pilot and is now in property management near where I live in Cheshire. He's put on a pound or two as well!

Scholesy stepped up into the Youth Cup side, as did his mate Steven 'Rizor' Riley. Right-back Rizor was just like Scholesy, and they caused havoc together. Darren Whitmarsh, who was from Northern Ireland, replaced Pilkington in goal. And there was another Neville to contend with. Phil was still a schoolboy, so everyone thought he had a great chance. He had his brother to look after him, and Gary was always there. There was an Irish centre-half, Colin Murdock, who was really promising but finished playing in the lower leagues because of injury and is now a sports lawyer. Who says footballers don't have brains?

In effect, though, I went from being a year younger than everyone to not being able to hold down a place. They all had pace, but I didn't. Our Cup run started in December 1992 against Blackburn in the second round at Old Trafford. We had home advantage all the way through to the two-legged semi and final. Rovers were thrashed 4–1, and I should have been delighted, but it was difficult to get too excited. Blackburn had a player sent off after half an hour, and we were making hard work of it. Irving replaced me and grabbed two goals. Gilly and Scholesy scored the others. Great, just great.

I was quite surprised to be in the starting line-up for the third-round tie against Notts County. Richard Irving was in but at the expense of Joe Roberts. Irving scored again, along with Gary Neville and Scholesy. I missed the fourth-round victory over Wimbledon and was super sub for the next match, against York. Mark Rawlinson – Rawler – gave way for me, and I netted minutes after coming on. It was a 5–0 massacre, and the scorers were Gary Neville, O'Kane, Savage, Irving and Beckham. Rawler was a pretty boy. He looked like something out of the Chippendales, and he was also one of the worst players at United. We were all amazed when he was given a two-year pro contract – especially me, as I got only a year.

The boys negotiated the semi-final against Millwall without me, winning 3–2 on aggregate to set up a mouth-watering final against Leeds. Everyone knows about the rivalry between the Uniteds of Manchester and Leeds, so both matches were played in front of crowds of 30,000.

On a Monday in May we lost 2–0 at home with me coming on as sub for Becks. Three days later, I started in the second leg at Elland Road. The team was Whitmarsh, Phil Neville, Riley, Casper, Gary Neville, Gillespie, Scholes, Beckham, Irving, Savage and Thornley.

Leeds had some good players as well. Noel Whelan and Kevin Sharp spring to mind straight away. I played well, but something was nagging away at me: I wasn't destined to be a centre-forward. If only someone had thought to try me in midfield, then maybe my career would have been different. As it was, I was still a striker and could not prevent Leeds running out 2–1 winners in the second leg for a 4–1 aggregate victory. My consolation prize was a 12-month professional contract in my back pocket. Every single one of us was kept on. The special ones had four years, Rawler a two-year deal and Rizor and I got the one.

My money leaped from £39.50 to £90. Instead of saving for a jumper I was rich enough to go out and buy one. The last 12 months had been difficult, but now I was a professional footballer, and the plan was to make my mark and force Fergie into offering me another contract at the end of the season. What I didn't expect to have to contend with was an injury that would keep me out for four months.

How was I supposed to impress the greatest manager in the world when the medics couldn't stop green pus oozing out of a hernia scar? I do feel bitter about the way it ended at United, because I was never given the opportunity to show what I could do. My attitude was spot on; Eric Harrison would vouch for that. But I never caught up after all that lost time.

I started the 1993–94 season with a double hernia injury. It needed an operation, but it just wouldn't heal. There was an infection inside, and every time I started running it opened up again. The physios at United were Jim McGregor and Jimmy Curran, who used to be a singer called Jimmy Buchanan. They were like father figures to me, and a great support, but no one could work out what was wrong. It took four months, and I was beginning to worry. The special ones were playing in the League Cup while I was trying to make the reserves. I was fit for a couple of matches then out again. I scored a few for the reserves, including two against Wolves. Dion Dublin bagged the other one, and we beat them 3–2.

Dublin really dislikes me, and I have no idea why, as we were fine in those days. He headbutted me a few years later when he was at Aston Villa and I was at Birmingham. I was blamed for *his* red card, bizarrely. He has gone on record since to say he does not like me. Dublin is a TV and radio pundit now, like I am, and he has chosen that platform to attack me as a person. Criticise me as a player, Dion, that's what you are there for, but don't make it personal.

It's a fact in football that when a player is injured he might as well be invisible. I was no use to anybody, so there was no point in Alex Ferguson wasting his time thinking about me. Me? I had nothing else to do. The clock was ticking towards the end of the season, and I knew I hadn't done enough to impress, because of my four-month lay-off. Surely Fergie would take that into consideration, I said to myself about a million times a week. I'm a worrier, just like Mum, and I was doing plenty of it then. At the point I had convinced myself another year was in the pipeline, I received the fateful call: 'Gaffer wants to see you.'

The lads were patting me on the back and telling me everything would be fine. I was popular in the dressing-room, and I'm sure there was sadness when I left. Not that I hung around long enough to say goodbye. As Ferguson's words sank in, I felt physically ill, that feeling when you've had too much to drink and you lie in bed and the room starts revolving and you want to be sick as quickly as you can. That feeling. Perhaps it wasn't wise to jump straight into the Fiesta and head home, as I proved I was in no fit state to drive.

Smashing my car into someone else's car head-on at a combined speed of 80 is imprinted forever in my memory. That whole day is like pressing the slow-mo on the video. I have re-run it countless times through my mind, and it is only as I approach the end of my career that I have been able to put things into perspective: being released by United could actually have been the best thing that ever happened to me.

I wasn't ready to be a centre-forward at United. I was not good enough to be a centre-forward in professional football. But why, oh, why didn't a coach the calibre of Ferguson think about playing me in midfield? I was one of the fittest, I could run all day, my attitude was spot on and my technique had been good enough to be taken on in the first place.

It was a question I would soon be asking of Dario Gradi at Crewe.

6

ARE YOU A SURFER FROM ABERSOCH?

As a kid, I would imagine my League debut. The dream usually included a winning 30-yard wonder goal, a dazzling run past every opposition player and the inevitable sound of popping corks from the man-of-the-match champagne. At no point did it involve phone threats to Mum and Dad and dodging a full can of lager chucked at me in a bar.

I was 19, a Manchester United reject and a rookie who had just spent the summer recovering from a head-on car crash. I was also, apparently, a figure of hate – something I know all about now. Luckily there was nothing wrong with my reflexes as I ducked to avoid the can, which hit the wall next to my head and exploded. Imagine the headline: 'Robbie Savage Killed by Beer Can'. What a joke that would have been, especially as the welcome-to-football message was delivered in Wrexham. 'Robbie Savage Killed by Beer Can in His Home Town' – and all because I played for Crewe Alexandra.

Even though Wrexham and Crewe are separated by 29 miles and a border, there is still a rivalry between the clubs. In the last few years I have finally convinced the people of my home town that I have never snubbed the Robins: not when Crewe came in for me at 13, not when I joined United at 14 and not when Ferguson released me. It was Crewe boss Dario Gradi who picked up the phone as I lay in hospital after that car smash. I almost had an opportunity to join Wrexham as player-coach during my dark days at Derby, and I'm delighted that my last appearance there was a pre-season friendly when

I was at Blackburn and that I received a fabulous reception.

But in September 1994 there was only one conclusion to be drawn from my pending date at The Racecourse Ground: I was a traitor. In the run-up to the match, Mum took threatening phone calls, and we changed our number. I'd never attracted headlines before, but I was all over the evening paper in Wrexham. They were fanning the flames, building it up and up until everything was ready to explode. For the record, my League debut was a 1–0 defeat, and I was subbed. So much for the Dom Pérignon and the 30-yard worldie. Still, it was a milestone that deserved proper recognition, and I headed into Wrexham to celebrate with a bunch of mates. We were in a place called The Wine Bar – great imagination – when the beer came flying through the air. I hate beer. Always have done, from the time Dad gave me a sip of lager and orange after Tottenham beat Manchester City in the 1981 FA Cup final. It was an over-the-top reaction to a situation that was actually very low-key. But at least I could now call myself a professional footballer.

When Dario phoned Dad while I was in hospital, I thought my prayers had been answered. The benefit of hindsight is a wonderful thing, but I look back now and ask why he wanted me back. Perhaps it was the challenge of turning a United reject into something special, to prove that the Crewe way was better than the Manchester United way. David Platt was Dario's shining example. But Dario never forgave me for turning my back on his centre of excellence in the first place. I was not one of his boys, and when I wanted an arm around me it wasn't there. I needed to be loved after what had happened at United. At first, I thought I was loved. Crewe gave me a three-year deal paying between £190 and £210 a week, and I received a £5,000 signing-on fee. Even then I remember going to the club secretary for an advance. It was a major rise on my United pay packet of £90 a week, though.

I had kept myself fit through that summer, because I wanted to be right for starting at Crewe. I knew a few of the boys from when I'd been there before, but now I was a man. I was going to play in the Football League. I was training with men, and my mentality needed to be different. I was not aiming to get into B teams or A teams or even reserve teams. I was aiming to get into Crewe's first team. The irony was that I hardly played that first season.

The first day at Gresty Road was strange. My technique and ability to pass had disappeared, and Dario commented on it. He was surprised and felt I'd gone backwards and lost all my skill. My report as a kid under Dario had been all As. If he'd done the same report again, it now would have been all Cs. But if I'd played the Crewe way at United I don't think I'd have been given a pro contract there at all. The whole mentality was different. At United, it was all about five-a-sides and having fun. At Crewe, the training was as boring as I've ever experienced. It was all about the team, the 11, the team shape. Training was stop–start.

My progress was stop–start too. It took until September to make my League debut, and I only played six first-team games that season. We finished third in Division Two and lost in the play-off semi-finals to Bristol Rovers, but I did not figure at all. My aim when I signed was the first team. The reality was that I spent most of the season turning out for Crewe A under Neil Baker, who has never had the recognition he deserves. I don't know if Dario held a grudge against me.

I played for the A team at Burnley, and I scored the best hat-trick of my career: a left-foot, a 30-yarder and a right-foot volley from a corner. I chested it down and shot top corner, and we won 6–2. Dario still did not say well done. It was weird. My first League goal was at Oxford's Manor Ground. We lost 2–1, and I played up front with Ashley Ward. Most of the time I was on A-team duty on a Saturday morning in the Lancashire League, just like at Manchester United. I even played against Rawler once.

There were familiar faces at Crewe and one even more familiar sight: the chippy opposite Gresty Road. They've still got my photo in there. I'd go in for my dinner: fish and chips, sausage and chips, whatever and chips. Everyone went to the chippy, because there was no advice about diet at all. It was the same chippy that had served Dad and me so well when I had been a schoolboy at the club. Strangely, there was no real social life at Crewe. I went out with Danny Murphy in Chester sometimes and with Murph and Neil Lennon to Nantwich occasionally. It was on one of those nights in Chester that I would eventually meet the missus.

We didn't go for a drink after training; we just went our separate ways. There wasn't a drinking culture as such, because the lads lived in Manchester, Liverpool, Chester, Wrexham and so on. Christmas parties were different: we'd book strippers and a comedian. We'd have lap dancers, the works. It certainly opened my eyes, some of the things that I saw.

Every morning, I drove to Gresty Road. We changed, walked the mile to the training ground and caught the bus back. We passed a pub, and one day there was a Cortina parked there with a different-coloured door. It was actually Neil Lennon's car. If you were late, you could be sneaky and drive your car and hide it in the car park, and Dario would never know. I was in a different world, back on the first rung of the ladder. We took our kit home – in my case to Hayley's house – to be washed.

The relationship with Hayley Lloyd was still on but beginning to turn a bit rocky. We had met in a pub when I was a United player, and I spent lots of weekends at her house. When I came home, I moved in. We went out for four years, which I look back on as four lost years. I was in the Wrexham papers, and the girls were after me, but I had a girlfriend. I missed out, to be honest. I was a prisoner. I finished with her on several occasions but kept going back.

I knew it was going to end, but I was in such a routine that I kept putting it off. I had a laugh with her two younger brothers, and we had a dog called Casey. I'd always wanted a dog, but Mum had never let me. It was easy to go back to Hayley's house, with a big family and dogs, rather than home with Dad away in Europe and Jonathan at university. I'd spent every day of the last three years with thirteen other lads, and I needed company. I did eventually finish with Hayley, and Mum also let me have a dog, Naz. I love boxers. They're friendly and boisterous, a bit like me. They don't stay still for a minute, and they never stop running, also a bit like me.

I loved my dog, and I needed to be loved by Crewe. But I knew that if I had one bad game I would be out of the team. I wonder whether it would have been different if I'd stayed as a schoolkid. I was one of the best prospects that Crewe had ever had, but we just couldn't rekindle it when I went back. Gareth Whalley was Dario's favourite. He could have the worst match in the world, and he would still play the next one. The doubts were beginning to overwhelm me. I weighed ten stone. I was not strong enough, not quick enough, not big enough – and I didn't score goals. I'd gone from playing with Giggsy and Becks to struggling to make an impact in Crewe's A team. A lesser character would probably have given up, but there was a turning point and it came in the 1995–96 season, when I became a midfielder.

My second year at Crewe started fantastically – as a striker. Gradi picked me seventeen out of the first eighteen games, and I scored seven League goals in fourteen matches, including five goals in seven. *Bang.* I'd arrived. I was in a rich vein of form, and the press were saying that I was the next big prospect from Crewe. Except after that I found myself back on the subs' bench or, even worse, not involved at all. People think I'm brash, but I didn't knock on Dario's door. I would never have made it as a centre-forward. I had two twigs for legs, and Dad was quicker than me. I didn't have anything, but I could tackle and I could keep the ball. And it was Bobby Gould who first thought about me as a midfielder.

To be Welsh and to play for your country is the ultimate honour. I am hugely proud of the fact that only two people have played for Under-15, Under-16, Under-18, Under-21 and the national team. Robert Page is one, and I'm the other. It was also while wearing a Wales shirt that my career took a very important detour. I joined up with the Under-21s for a match against Germany, and coach Brian Flynn pulled me after training: 'Bobby Gould has been asking questions about you.'

Great! In training, I played everywhere, and Gouldy, watching from the sidelines, apparently liked what he was seeing. 'Try Sav in midfield against the Germans,' he suggested.

I was incredible. I was making an impact and smashing the Germans all over the pitch with my tackling. Then I was pulled off after 70 minutes, along with Gareth Taylor, who was going to be promoted to the first team. Gouldy took me to one side and said, 'You were great, but I want Gareth's physical presence. Keep doing what you're doing.' Then he found Mum and Dad and told them, 'Your boy has a future.'

Presumably he picked up the phone to Dario too, because I returned to Crewe as a midfielder and never looked back. Alex Ferguson and Dario Gradi saw me as a centre-forward, but Gouldy, who took a lot of stick at Wales, was the one who spotted something else.

Crewe finished fifth that season and suffered play-off heartbreak again. This time I was part of the side to lose over two legs against Notts County in the semi-final. I was Crewe's number eight, playing in a midfield trio of Savage, Whalley and Murph, because Neil Lennon had already gone. It was incredible, the best midfield that Crewe has ever had, although Lennie might disagree! Every match, 30 or 40 scouts would be there to watch. Everyone thought they were going to be the next one out of the door. It was the Crewe way.

By the time the 1996–97 season kicked off, I was one of the first names on Dario's team sheet. It was also time to talk about a new contract, with my original deal due to end after my third year. I was offered £220 a week and another £5,000 signing-on fee, and I said no. It was barely a pay rise, and I was one of the best players in the team – plus, I had become a full Wales international.

Bobby Gould picked me for a Euro '96 qualifier in Albania in November 1995. I came on as sub in the 1–1 draw in Tirana and then figured in a 2–0 friendly defeat against Switzerland, again from the bench. In the summer of 1996, I replaced Barry Horne with nine minutes to go in a 5–0 World Cup thrashing of San Marino, thanks to my shin pad superstition.

Lots of players sit on the bench without their shin pads, but I am suited and booted for football from the moment I jog onto the pitch for my pre-match warm-up. As far as I'm concerned, I want to be ready to go if required. The habit gave me one of my thirty-nine Wales caps. Gouldy needed to make a quick substitution, because Barry was injured. He looked down the bench, and there I was, jumping up and down. 'Me, me, me,' I pleaded with Gouldy. He nodded. I was on.

Gouldy made it plain he rated me and thought I would be a good bet for a Premier League club. What's more, I would only cost about £400,000, as I was coming out of contract at Crewe. Dario hadn't liked me refusing the club's offer. That season I played every game, apart from when I was on international duty. Dario dropped me for the League One play-offs. Robbed of a Youth Cup final at United, robbed of a Wembley appearance at Crewe.

Luckily I hadn't known what was round the corner when the campaign started. Football was fun and so was my social life. I was single again. Bye-bye Hayley and hello to my boxer pup Naz and some nights out in Chester with Murph. I was still as nervous round girls as I had been as a schoolboy, but when I saw Sarah Element across the dance floor I fell instantly in love with her, even though she thought I was a surfer from Abersoch. Murph and I were in Brannigans in Chester one Thursday night when we bumped into Sarah and a friend. Because I was driving, I wasn't drinking. Murph introduced us, but she was going out with a golfer at the time and didn't want to know.

'Have I seen you somewhere?' she asked. I thought she must have seen me on telly at 1.30 a.m., when all the League goals were shown on the highlights programme. 'Do you surf?' was the next question.

'What?' That brought me crashing back down to earth. Long hair, fake tan, and I looked like a surfer. Sarah didn't have a clue that I was a footballer. All I knew was that I wanted to see this beautiful young woman again. 'Can I have your phone number?'

Even now I have no idea how I plucked up the courage to ask the question. To my delight, and surprise, she gave me her number. I was sure it was a con. Surely this stunning woman would not hand out her proper number. I have come to realise that ringing her parents at three in the morning to check was probably not the best idea in the world, especially as Sarah had gone for an Indian meal with her friend and wasn't even home.

'Er, excuse me, is this Sarah Element's house?'

'Yes. Do you know what time it is?' snapped her father.

Oops. But at least I knew her number was real and that she had willingly given it to me. It was just a shame that her father thought I was a complete idiot for ringing her at that time of the night. Sarah worked in Tessuti, the best clothes shop in Chester. She is an illustrator by profession but needed to earn some extra cash. I went in there all the time to the men's department, but she worked in women's fashions. Our paths might never have crossed.

Sarah wouldn't have anything to do with me, even though I kept phoning her. She never said no to going out, but then she didn't say yes either. One day I was at Chester races, and I saw her walking by the road. I pulled in, she stopped and we had a chat. I knew that she was the one, but it still took six months of chasing to convince her. Sarah went to Paris with her then boyfriend and said she would ring me. I just sat by the phone. She'd gone to France to do some research for a mural she was painting in a French restaurant in England. She found a phone box, called me for the first time and I knew I had a chance.

Sarah finished with her boyfriend shortly afterwards and was finally free to go out with me. I was a nervous wreck so asked my mate Nutty to drive me over to the Wirral. By that stage, my love affair with cars had started. In my three years at Crewe, I went from Nova SR to Vauxhall Calibra to silver Golf VR6.

My dating history was far less exciting than my car-buying history: hiding in the bedroom at home, a kiss for Claire Bryan at school, a slow dance with a mop at Manchester United and four years with Hayley Lloyd! Lack of experience is the only way I can justify what happened next. I cringe even thinking about it, and Sarah's dad has never let me forget it either. I can still see the expression of disgust on his face. If it's any consolation, I know better now!

Nutty pulled up outside the house where Sarah lived with her parents, David and Alice, and beeped the horn six times. I know! I should have walked up the drive, knocked on the door and politely introduced myself to the Elements before escorting Sarah back to the car. Instead, it was *BEEEEEEP.* The front door opened, and David stood there. I could see the scowl from where I was sitting – in the passenger seat of the VR6. It would be fair to say he wasn't very impressed with his daughter's choice of dinner companion. I'd already woken him at three in the morning to check Sarah hadn't given me a fake phone number, remember.

The date is memorable for two reasons – not that! It was the first time I drank wine, and it was the night I realised Sarah and I were going to be serious. The venue for dinner was The Clayton Arms on the Moss, near to where Nan lived. I asked Sarah what she wanted to drink. 'I'd like a glass of wine, please,' she replied.

Wine? I thought she was really posh. Mum didn't drink, Dad had an occasional beer, and I was virtually teetotal. I ordered a bottle to share between us, and two glasses later I was absolutely steaming! Sarah ordered spare ribs while I had chicken in a white-wine sauce, and we had a fabulous evening. My mate Nutty took me home and delivered Sarah back safely to her parents. Romance was in the air.

Things were going well for me at Crewe. As I mentioned, I was part of the senior set-up at Wales, although I was a nobody from the Second Division. On one of the first trips, I went out with the lads – superstars like Mark Hughes, Gary Speed, Dean Saunders, Ryan Giggs – and they attracted autograph hunters from every corner. These fans would look at me with questioning faces, 'Who the hell are you?'

I knew what they were thinking as they politely asked me to sign even though they didn't know my name, my position or my club. I even lied and told them I played for West Ham, because I thought that sounded cooler than Crewe. 'Yeah, I play for West Ham. My name's . . .' and I would mumble something. They'd be looking at my writing and trying to work out what it said. 'My name is Robbie Savage, and I play Second Division football for Crewe' didn't quite have the same ring about it when Giggsy, Sparky and Speedo were standing next to me.

Danny Murphy, Gareth Whalley and I played every other midfield in the division off the park that season. We finished sixth, and I missed five games because of Wales call-ups. I scored only one goal – the winner over Bournemouth – which proved again that I wasn't cut out to be a striker. The scene was set for a May trip to Wembley. Except that I was now a 'contract rebel', according to the headlines.

I didn't have an adviser at that point, so it meant I was getting little guidance about what to do next. Dario made up my mind for me. At half-time in the last game of the season, against York, I was substituted. Phil Charnock, originally a loan lad from Liverpool, replaced me, and I was absolutely furious. I jumped into my car and raced home. We drew the game, but I ended up with four points that day thanks to the speeding ticket I picked up as well. I was never involved again, and I didn't see Dario again. Charnock was picked for the play-offs, and I vowed never to sign a new contract with Crewe. I watched my pals overcome Luton in the semi-final but didn't even travel to Wembley to see them beat Brentford.

Talk about lightning striking twice. I played every match of the FA Youth Cup campaign at United and missed the final, and I appeared in every available game for Crewe and missed the play-off final. It was the last straw. I felt that Dario had let me down, and I still say that to his face now. I was 13 when we first met, and I will always be so grateful that they spotted me. The education at the centre of excellence was second to none. I also acknowledge that he was first on the phone to offer me a professional contract when United released me. But what should have been a time of celebration became a time of rows and unhappiness. I'd heard the whispers. I knew there were clubs after me, clubs who were prepared to offer me something slightly more generous than £220 a week, a tiny pay rise for three years' good service.

7

PINK FOR A BOY

The day I became a Premier League player I bought a pink Porsche. A few hours later, my shiny new dream machine blew up. It made one hell of a mess of the car and didn't do much for the white chinos or white shirt either. Oil everywhere. I went out to celebrate my move to Leicester City driving a high-powered sports car and came home on the back of an RAC tow truck. From big-time Charlie to feeling a proper Charlie!

But not even the sight of my beautiful pink Porsche, clouds of smoke billowing from it, could spoil the day. I was a Premier League footballer. How about that, Dario? How about that, Fergie? The boy from Bradley had arrived. Snubbed for the play-off final in May and now, just a few weeks later, preparing to play for the legendary Martin O'Neill. I couldn't stop smiling. It was incredible.

The summer of 1997 flashed by in a whirl. I was in love with Sarah and out of contract at Crewe. Malmo were interested in me and so were Leicester, Crystal Palace and Hearts. The transfer fee would have to be decided by a tribunal, because I was under 24, but that didn't stop me being wanted. I warned Sarah I might be off to Sweden and bought a locket and put a lock of my blond hair in it so she had something to remember me by . . . Then I signed for Leicester! She still has the locket and thinks it's very romantic, but I feel a bit of a tit.

George Urquhart was my agent. I came to look upon him as a father figure, and we were together for many years. I relied on him, and I opened up to him. He knew everything there was to know about me. I went to him because he'd done Lee Jones's transfer to Liverpool and I thought he would look after my best interests. Unfortunately, our relationship broke down after I joined Derby. It breaks my heart that we went from being inseparable to drifting apart. When I was at my lowest ebb, I felt I became a burden to him and he wasn't there for me.

Back in the Leicester days, our partnership was just beginning, and the future looked very rosy indeed. Everything sparked from a Wales game in Kilmarnock, of all places. We were playing Scotland in a friendly at the end of May, and I made my first senior start. We won 1–0, and my good mate John Hartson scored the winner. I played well – in front of a lot of scouts too. The other memory of the trip was Dean Saunders pinning me down in his hotel room and coming at me with scissors and clippers to cut my hair. I wriggled free and rushed straight to the barber to have it cut a bit and then gelled up. No one touches my hair without permission.

With the international fixture out of the way, I could begin to talk to the clubs who were chasing me. First we went to Hearts. George drove his Merc, and the journey took about nine hours. He made me pay for the toll road on the way, so it's true what they say about Scots! We stayed at his parents' house near Edinburgh, and from there I visited the club and met Jim Jefferies. As soon as I talked to him, I wanted to sign for Hearts. Palace next. I met Steve Coppell at a hotel near Heathrow Airport, and after I'd spoken to him I wanted to sign for him too. Finally, I went down to Filbert Street. Martin O'Neill was on holiday, so I saw assistant John Robertson instead. And I knew then, really knew.

'We came up to Crewe to have a look at Danny Murphy,' Robbo told me. 'And you caught the eye. We knew you were out of contract, and we've been watching you ever since.'

'I want to join Leicester.' The words were out of my mouth.

'Martin will ring you at home tonight,' said Robbo.

I drove home in a daze – a happy daze for a change – and sat by the phone. By seven, I was getting twitchy, because I'd promised to visit Nan, who wasn't well, to tell her how things had gone. I made the three-mile trip to Nan's house, and when I got home Mum said, 'Martin O'Neill's called.'

I was distraught. I thought I'd blown it. My prospective new gaffer had told me to wait by the phone, and I'd missed his call. Thankfully, an hour later he rang back and made me feel just as wanted as Robbo had. Then I nearly failed my medical. They discovered a split on my cartilage. It wasn't causing me any trouble, and for all anyone knew I'd been running around with it since I was a kid. But Leicester had to make sure, and they sent me for another scan the next day. It was a horrible wait for the all-clear. As soon as I was passed fit, terms were agreed. City gave me a three-year deal, worth £3,000 a week, and a £150,000-a-year signing-on fee. There were bonuses in there too. It seemed like a staggering amount of money after Crewe's final offer of £220 a week and a £5,000 signing-on fee. Ian Silvester was the club secretary. I think he was a bit surprised when I asked, 'Do you mind if I have an advance so I can buy a car on the way home?'

Armed with a banker's draft for £24,000, and the other £16,000 on finance, I headed home via a garage I drove past all the time. It was called The A41, and I've bought a few cars from there. I phoned my old Crewe mate Neil Lennon, who moved to Leicester before me, and told him about the Porsche. 'Don't tell anyone,' I instructed.

Lennie called the world, and I was getting seriously hammered as a big-time Charlie, but I didn't care one bit. The garage wanted to prepare the Porsche, but I wouldn't let them. Mum and the rest of Pine Close were about to get an eyeful of my new car, and, I have to admit, it was quite an eyeful, in a shade of pink melting into purple. Next stop: pick up Jamie Piper and go cruising in Chester.

I looked like Don Johnson out of Miami Vice. That, or the cover boy of *Gay Monthly*. I was wearing white chinos and a white silk shirt and sporting a fake tan. We growled our way into the middle of Chester, and, suddenly, there was a bang and a crack. We conked out in the middle of the road. I climbed out of the driving seat, and Jamie spilled out onto the road too. Together we pushed the car to one side.

'What a poser.' You could see that's what people were thinking. My white chinos had a black, oily sheen on them, and my fake tan was covered in a layer of soot. Where my face wasn't black, it was red with embarrassment. People stopped to stare, not because I was a footballer, as I was not at all well known then, but because I looked like some rich kid in his father's car. My big night out in Chester with Jamie and the Porsche came to an unexpected end on the back of a recovery van.

Over the years, people have worked themselves into a frenzy over my cars. I like cars. Fact. I have lost an absolute fortune on them – something in the region of £500,000. *Ouch*. It hurts to add up the figures, but I have never been into gambling or vintage champagne or jewellery, and I have earned good money in a long career. Love me or hate me – and there are plenty who hate me – no one can say I have ever given anything less than 100 per cent wherever I've played. Succeed at the top as a footballer and you are financially rewarded. I was a boy with a passion for cars, and I became a man who could afford to do something about it.

It was thanks to Martin O'Neill that the door opened to a very different world. Crewe were a small club with a small fan base and a reputation for grooming young players who would go on somewhere better. The tribunal ordered Leicester to pay £400,000 for me plus £250,000 after a certain number of appearances, and I played the required number of games, so Dario got a fair deal. I was like a kid in a sweet shop. Dad came down with me to the Hinckley Hotel, where I was staying, looked at me and said, 'You've made it, son.'

Too right. I was at a Premier League club, and they'd just won the League Cup. I was looking forward to European football and domestic trips to Old Trafford, Highbury and Stamford Bridge. And I was on serious money. First, I needed to settle in, which is difficult when you are living in a hotel. I shifted across to the Holiday Inn in Leicester, and Pegguy Arphexad was there too. He was a lovely guy and so laid-back. When we went to nightclubs, he used to stand in the corner, watch people and pout his lips – but keepers are crazy.

My first challenge was to impress in pre-season and discover what made everyone tick. I played well in a friendly at Preston alongside Garry Parker, and he just kept giving me the ball. I was skilful, I had a trick and I could pass. Robbo and Steve Walford, another loyal member of the O'Neill team, were there, and I felt like a king. But it was Martin you had to impress, and he never gave anything away.

I have been unbelievably lucky in my career to have played for some great managers. I never knew Brian Clough, but my experiences at

Leicester with Martin and at Derby with Nigel Clough have given me an insight into the legend that was Cloughie Senior. Martin had that aura about him. If you were with him, he would do anything for you. If you took on board what he wanted, he would back you all the way. Then, just as you thought you'd got close to him, he wouldn't speak to you for four or five days. I stopped for petrol once, and his wife was filling up her car at the next pump. We said hello to each other, and Geraldine suddenly said, 'Martin thinks the world of you, Robbie.' I felt ten feet tall. Actually, make that twenty feet.

Martin would come out for training with a stopwatch around his neck, and the work rate would go up 5 per cent. For him to have signed me, he must have had belief in me. When you had played well, he came over and squeezed you at the final whistle, and you'd feel fantastic. But there was nothing worse than him having a go at you. At Leicester, I had a new lease of life. We played five-a-side, and it was fun, laid-back and a different world from Crewe. I went from learning about the game to enjoying it.

Steve Walford – Wally – would be there with a fag in his mouth. Robbo wore a knee brace but could still ping a ball. No brash kid was ever going to say, 'Show us yer medals,' to two European Cup winners like Martin and Robbo. There was immense respect and a lot of laughter. The young 'uns played the old 'uns, and the worst player wore the yellow jersey: donkey of the week. No one wanted that yellow jersey.

On match day, Martin, wearing his trademark green sweatshirt, would come into the dressing-room about an hour before kick-off clutching a scrappy piece of paper. He read out the team. No one had a clue until that minute. Then he'd go out again, and you wouldn't see him until 2.40 p.m. In training, he'd come over and say, 'Thirty seconds to go round that tree.' Everyone would take off. It was not scientific, but it was fun and it worked. I was 'Big Nose' straight away. Wally took some stick for wearing cut-offs all the time. Seamus McDonagh, the goalkeeping coach, was great. He used to chase me around the training ground. When he played for Everton, he was known as Jim McDonagh and hated it. I called him 'Jimbo' and ran very fast. 'I'm going to kill you,' he would echo behind me as I made a dash to safety. Luckily he could never catch me!

They all went to Celtic together and then to Aston Villa, and I suspect they did it pretty much the same way. The gaffer took us away on trips. We'd have nights out together and went go-karting; it was unbelievable fun. Once we were travelling back from a match, and he stopped the coach at an off-licence and bought us some beers. The spirit in the camp was wonderful. There were so many jokers at the training ground, but Alan Birchenall topped the lot. The Birch. What a legend. He was part of that swaggering Chelsea side before I was even born, and I'm ashamed to admit I didn't have a clue who he was at the start. Birch was based down at the training ground and did the pitch announcements on match day. Birch always called me 'Lil', as in Lily Savage. Luckily he was on his own with that one.

Birch was a character. He was a lot like me, although older and uglier. Birch was also responsible for the strangest footballing injury I have ever suffered: a burn on my nose! Can you imagine if I'd knocked on the gaffer's door to tell him that I was a doubt because of a jacket potato? Birch lived on his own so was in the habit of taking his evening meal home with him. The canteen ladies wrapped up the meal in foil, and he'd keep it in his office. One day I nicked the keys while he was in the gym, sneaked into his office and tipped the contents of his plate into the bin before restoring the foil lid. Birch arrived home, peeled off the lid and there was nothing there. The next day, as I was eating in the canteen, he came up behind me and pushed my head forward in a playful manner, and this is where my big nose definitely got in the way. I found myself up to my nostrils in boiling-hot jacket potato. My nose was seriously scalded. I even had to see the club doctor.

Birch is Mr Leicester still. He played at the top when there was no money in the game. He could talk about the great days at Chelsea, but I was the one who climbed into a Porsche, even though I hadn't achieved anything yet. The charity work he does is unbelievable, and that's why he was rightly awarded an MBE. But I still haven't forgiven him for sticking my hooter into a hot spud! One of Birch's jobs was to host question-and-answer evenings for Leicester fans. One time, every ticket had been snapped up for a session at Jongleurs nightclub with Neil Lennon, Muzzy Izzet and me in the hot seat. It was the first one we'd done, and we were all feeling a little bit nervous. The problem was that training finished at lunchtime and we didn't have to be at Jongleurs until seven. 'Let's go for a drink,' one of us suggested.

As the afternoon wore on, the prospect of facing 400 supporters became more and more daunting. So we had another drink. Then another one. And one for the road. We turned up at Jongleurs absolutely steaming. Birch went berserk, but there wasn't a lot he could do, with a sell-out crowd waiting. The first half was a disaster. Lennie accidentally spat beer on one lady, and Muzzy fell asleep. Luckily we brought it back a bit after the interval. God knows what those fans must have thought.

Birch would have been a millionaire if he'd played 30 years later. As far as I was concerned, the money was unbelievable. I could give some to Mum and my brother. I bought a house quickly in a place called Glenfield, near Leicester. It was a four-bedroom new-build detached and cost me £90,000. Because I didn't want to live on my own, I could afford to pay a mate of mine, Mark Robinson, to move in and keep me company until Sarah finally joined me. At United and Crewe, I had shopped by price tag. Now I walked into Christopher Scotney, a designer clothes shop in Leicester, and if I liked it I bought it. It wasn't a problem to me. If someone asked me how much a pint of milk or a shirt cost, I wouldn't know. In a way, being a footballer is a fairy-tale existence.

Moving into my first house was a frightening experience. I'd only ever lived in digs, at home or with my ex-girlfriend's family, and I didn't have a clue. Luckily I met Tuffy. Dad first bumped into Adam Tuff in a pub called The Dominion just round the corner from my new house. They talked, and when Dad realised Tuffy lived a couple of doors down from me he asked him to keep an eye on me. Tuffy was a local butcher, like his father. He took so much stick for being my mate. I didn't have a lawnmower, and the grass was growing really long – the garden was no more than six metres by six metres. Tuffy offered to cut it for me, and when his friends saw him they taunted him and gave him stick for cutting a Premier League player's grass. I think it was just jealousy. He is one of my oldest friends and is godfather to my son Charlie. At my wedding, when he was joint best man with Jonathan, he worked himself up into a real panic about his speech. He stood up and cracked this joke: 'He's walked into a bar; it was an iron bar.' Then he told it again. And again.

Tuffy was my saviour, because I was hopeless at home. Sarah came down at weekends and wouldn't get into bed as it was full of dog hairs, because Naz would sleep with me in the week. We'd switch rooms, and she would scoop up the sheets and stick them in the washer. One week later and they would still be there when she came down again – with mould on them! Naz was my constant companion, even at the Holiday Inn before I moved.

My cousin Matt sometimes stayed. Matt is a Sergeant Major WO2 in the army and has been to Iraq and Afghanistan. Whenever he was in England, he lived with me. He is like a brother to me. His dad died of a brain tumour when Matt was only a few months old, and the army was the easiest route for him. I was best man at his wedding in April 2010, and now I've handed over the job of looking after him to his wife, Debbie. Because we're like brothers, we're really competitive about everything. One night he was at Glenfield, and we went out together. It was about three in the morning, and we were in the back of a taxi, and he said he could beat me in a race. So we asked the driver to stop, and we ran the mile and a half home. I beat him easily. Then he said he could get me on the floor in ten seconds, but he couldn't pin me down. We didn't speak for a week! But I proved I was the fittest and hardest in the family.

People think you're bigheaded when you earn big money. In Wrexham, they threw cans at my head. Dad and Jonathan were paid next to nothing, so I do know what it means. The first time I went out for dinner with Sarah, I had to borrow money from Mum and Dad to buy clothes. I didn't even own a suit when I signed for Leicester. At Crewe, we wore tracksuits. My first Leicester suit was lime green with a blue shirt and showed off the fake tan very well!

I took stick for it, the suit and the tan. The Porsche might have been mentioned too. Everyone saw me as daft, and I'm sure Martin O'Neill still does. I had a reputation for saying silly things, and the guys labelled them 'the Savisms'. I remember asking which train the Krays robbed. But I was enjoying the company. There were guys at Leicester like Steve Claridge, Steve Walsh, Matt Elliott, Muzzy Izzet, Neil Lennon, Emile Heskey, Steve Guppy and Garry Parker. Garry was the joker, the character. Beneath the banter, we had some very good players too.

Emile was unbelievable. He used to destroy defenders but was such a down-to-earth lad. When you saw his name on the team sheet, you'd be happy. He was the key.

Steve Claridge – Cleggy – was an absolute legend too. You should see him on the dance floor. He never drank, but he is one of the best dancers I've ever seen. As a player, he worked his socks off. He was a bit like me. He was a scruffy bugger, though. His car was full of clothes, and he'd have one sock up and one sock down. Cleggy was always late and didn't give a damn. He'd amble out with a cup of tea in one hand and an apple in the other, and he used to wind up Wally. I got close to Cleggy. Most of these characters had just won the League Cup, and Martin's team were being taken very seriously indeed. Not me – yet. I was the new boy, the big mouth with the big nose, the pink Porsche and unique suits, but I was not quite a Premier League player.

On 9 August 1997, that changed. My first touch in the top flight was from a throw-in. I got a foot to it. It was home to Aston Villa – a club I would enjoy many a battle with over the years – and Ian Marshall scored the only goal. I came on for the last seven minutes and felt twelve feet tall. I'd woken up that morning in the hotel. Sarah was there with Mum and Dad. They'd brought Naz down, so I even had my beloved boxer. I arrived in the city centre that morning as the invisible man. No one gave me a second glance. According to the local paper, I was in the predicted team. As it happened, I was sub and Stuart Campbell, a young kid, was ahead of me. I wasn't disappointed at all. I felt that I would get on.

Another sub's appearance followed against Liverpool the following week. Matty Elliott and Graham Fenton, my room-mate and a lovely guy, scored the goals to record a memorable win at Anfield. The next match was at home to Manchester United. United, the club that had dumped me as a kid. Now I was facing them as an equal. We were in fourth place, and Steve Claridge and I replaced Ian Marshall and Campbell. It was one of those 0–0 draws where Emile could have had a hat-trick and United hit the woodwork three times. Roy Keane and I both came out for a corner, and we were sprinting. I went past him, raced past Stevie Claridge, and Peter Schmeichel saved my shot. We had a free kick around the box, and I asked Garry Parker, 'Can I have it?' It clipped the wall. Afterwards, Martin O'Neill said, 'You were fantastic.'

I picked up the papers to read the reports and look at the ratings. I was given nine out of ten – star man – in one of them. Brilliant! I even entered one of those fantasy football competitions one year with a load of mates. It was the only place where I was guaranteed to be first name on the team sheet! I'd always go looking for the relevant reporter to check my mark. The London guys don't like me, but one or two of them would still make me man of the match, and for that I thank them all.

Eight of my mates had stayed in the Holiday Inn before the United game, including two of the hardest blokes in Wrexham. They were known as Hucci and Gucci and supported United. After the match, we went out for a meal, and it was quite useful having those two around, because I wasn't the invisible man any more! People were coming up to me; every Tom, Dick and Harry was after tickets. People who hadn't spoken to me in years were ringing. I was in a different world.

Keane one match, Patrick Vieira the next. And me with legs like twigs. I made my first start at home to Arsenal at the end of August in what was a memorable 3–3 draw. We scored three times in the last six minutes – take a bow, Emile, Matty Elliott and Steve Walsh. Dennis Bergkamp scored a hat-trick for the Gunners. My overriding thought was, 'Oh, my Lord, this is hard.'

For the first time in my life I was picking up national papers and seeing my name. I wasn't the infamous Robbie Savage; I was up and coming. I was going out in the town and getting recognised. When I arrived, people hadn't known who I was, but now they were asking for my autograph. I was even playing in Europe! Okay, slight exaggeration there. Leicester's success in the League Cup meant they had qualified for the UEFA Cup, but – Sod's law – they drew Atlético Madrid. I wasn't involved in the first leg in Spain, although I travelled, but I did get on as sub at Filbert Street for the last 25 minutes. I looked round the Vicente Calderón stadium and pinched myself. In 12 months, I'd made the journey from Gay Meadow and a fixture against Shrewsbury to Madrid. It was a wonderful feeling. We should have had three penalties too. Kiko was outstanding. Instead of calling for the ball, he whistled for it. We lost 2–1 there, and they beat us 2–0 at home.

Probably the biggest disappointment of the start of that season was going out to Grimsby at the first hurdle in the Coca-Cola Cup, when

Playing for Bradley, with manager Colin Savage (back left). I'm smiling, second from right in the front row. My pal Jim Whitley is standing in front of Dad.

Me and my big brother, Jonathan.

Putting pen to paper as a Manchester United schoolboy in front of Alex Ferguson. Scout Hugh Roberts and Mum and Dad look on.

Giving my Wales cap to Nan.

From my scrapbook. With Taid the day I signed for Manchester United as a schoolboy.

Today 12ᵏ October 88, Robert signed for Manchester Utd.

It's there in black and white. United club secretary Ken Merrett writes to offer me a trainee contract at Old Trafford.

THE ENGLISH SCHOOLS' FOOTBALL ASSOCIATION

C. S. Allatt, General Secretary:
4a Eastgate Street, Stafford ST16 2NQ. Tel: 0785 51142

This is to certify that ___ROBERT WILLIAM SAVAGE___

has been registered as an Associated Schoolboy with

___MANCHESTER UNITED___ Football Club

This regulation is subject to the terms of Football League Regulation 65

Registration Number

___14338/479___

Date of issue ___21.11.88___

General Secretary

My associate schoolboy certificate.

The iconic photograph in the United programme. The day that the Fergie Fledglings lifted the FA Youth Cup.
(© Cliff Butler, Manchester United)

My wage slip at United – told you I was badly paid!

Feeling ten feet tall. Being hugged by Leicester boss Martin O'Neill.
(© Raymonds Press Agency)

Every player's dream moment: the chance to strangle a ref. Luckily, Peter Jones saw the funny side in a testimonial match.
(© Raymonds Press Agency)

Danny Mills, then of Middlesbrough, shakes me warmly by the throat. He is in serious danger of messing up my hair, too.
(© Getty Images)

And the groom wore cream ... but was still outshone by beautiful bride Sarah.
(© Jane Hockey)

Surrounded by my friends on the happiest day of my life. From left to right: Jamie Piper, Darren Eadie, Paul Hollinshead, Richard Element, brother Jonathan, me, cousin Matt, Tim Oldland, Adam 'Tuffy' Tuff, Simon Element and Martin 'Nutty' Edwards.

The Savage family: Dad, Mum, me and Jonathan.
(© Jane Hockey)

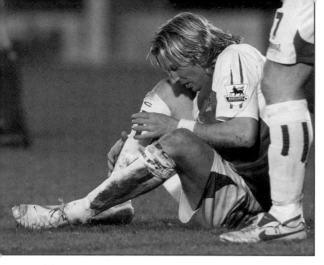

Breaking my leg at Watford. Just looking at the picture brings it all back.
(© Getty Images)

My two boxers, Naz and Tai. It broke my heart when we lost Naz at the start of 2011.

Sharing a joke with the gaffer, Nigel Clough, at Old Trafford. It was the start of my journey back.
(© *Derby Telegraph*)

I am the proudest dad in the world. My sons, Charlie and Freddie.

Spot the tattoo. Enjoying life as Captain Savage on the good ship *Elementary Sarah*.

My Derby turning point. The fans chanted my name as we beat Nottingham Forest 3–2 in an FA Cup replay, and I couldn't resist picking up that scarf and celebrating with them.
(© *Derby Telegraph*)

On the beach in Barbados renewing my marriage vows with Sarah in front of our two little angels.

Out for dinner with the gorgeous woman who is my wife. Don't we make a lovely couple?

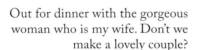

Keeper Robbie Savage's penalty technique is spot on. Shane Long couldn't cope with the Worzel Gummidge look.
(© *Derby Telegraph*)

Leicester were the holders. I played well, and Martin pulled me out in front of everybody and had a go at the rest. You were always so grateful when the gaffer praised you, because he certainly knew how to take you down a peg or two otherwise. I once had a bollocking from him at Sunderland. I tackled Stefan Schwarz and leaned over to shout at him as he lay on the pitch. 'Show the opposition some respect,' Martin told me in a tone of voice that no player wanted to hear too often.

October was a disaster for the team, probably because Martin was named manager of the month in September and the award often turns into a curse. We lost to Derby, Chelsea and Grimsby. I won't forget what Kasey Keller did to me either. I came on as sub at home to Derby, and there was a mix-up between us. Kasey should have clattered me as he went for the ball, but he stopped and blamed me afterwards. When I first signed, he was a friendly, straight-talking American, but he talked a lot of rubbish and I used to wind him up. Kasey couldn't take a joke and sneered that he earned more from his Nike contract than I did from Leicester. I didn't care. I was being paid a fortune, and I was coming face to face with the likes of Keane and Vieira.

December was even worse in terms of results though. We went five games without a win, although I was playing quite well. I also scored my first Premier League goal. Unfortunately, we lost the match 2–1 at Southampton. I received the ball on the right side and smashed it into the top corner with my left foot, beating my Wales room-mate Paul Jones. The manager singled me out for praise afterwards. Martin was a fantastic man-manager. He didn't often compliment me – his tactic was to joke about my lack of ability – but he tended to use different methods on different players. I remember once when Steve Guppy was awful. Martin told us we had all been shocking – apart from Gupps. The next game, Gupps was sensational.

We weren't exactly sensational as we rang in the New Year, but our fortunes improved. We had back-to-back draws against Villa and Liverpool and thrashed Northampton in the FA Cup. I scored and won my fourth successive man-of-the-match award. There was a bit of a buzz surrounding me. I could run all day. The joke was that if they opened the gates at Filbert Street I would run through them. At the end of January I had cause to remember Alex Ferguson's final words to me: 'You'll come back to haunt me.' Leicester went to Old Trafford and became the first visiting team to win there that season.

If only I'd scored! I had a hand in Tony Cottee's winner, and at the final whistle all my emotions were released. I was playing against my mates, and they were all lovely to me. There's a great picture of Ryan Giggs and me grabbing each other's shirts and going into the tackle.

There was one nagging worry at the back of my mind. Martin O'Neill saw me as a right-wingback in a five-man defence, and I wasn't totally convinced. As I've said, I could run all day, but I was a bit short on tricks and I never felt really comfortable there. Our results were a bit hit-and-miss too, and by the middle of March we'd dropped to 12th, which was the low point of the season. A couple of days later, we travelled to Wimbledon, where I looked really good on two counts: the white away kit brought out my fake tan, and I scored. But we lost 2–1.

The final game of my first season in the Premier League convinced me that I could handle myself. We lost only one in the last eight, and that was the final match, a 4–3 defeat to West Ham when we were both going for Europe. Villa beat Arsenal that same night to pinch the last UEFA Cup spot. That was where I smashed Stuart Pearce. I'd faced Keane, and I'd squared up to Vieira. Now for Psycho, a legend who had earned a nickname like that for a reason. He was playing left-back, his shorts rolled up tight. I saw him coming in, full-blooded. I just won the ball and caught him in the chest. I thought I'd killed him. He needed oxygen, the works. I was ten stone, wet through, and I remember thinking, 'I must be quite a hard man.'

We finished tenth at the end of that season, and when I picked up my wage slip there was an extra £60,000. 'What's this?' I asked.

'Your bonus for us coming tenth.' I didn't have a clue that sort of money was due to me. It made me realise what sort of rewards you could expect if you were a Premier League footballer. I loved every minute of that first season as a Leicester City player.

8

I COULDN'T GIVE A SHIRT

'I want you off the premises in 20 minutes, or I'm calling the police.' I couldn't believe what I was hearing. Bobby Gould, the manager of Wales, was threatening to call the cops if I didn't leave the team hotel. But we were playing Italy, I was in the squad and this was my breakthrough season; what had I done wrong? The thoughts raced through my mind as I looked at the unforgiving face of Gouldy.

It was five in the morning when the phone rang in my room. Effing 5 a.m. We weren't supposed to have calls put through, so my first thought had been my family. Mum, Dad, Jonathan, Nan. *Please let them be all right.* 'I want to see you. Now. In my room.' Gouldy sounded angry. Actually, he sounded absolutely furious. I woke my room-mate, Paul Jones.

'Jonah, something's wrong.'

'What?'

'Gouldy wants to see me. Now. And it's five in the morning.' Jonah was instantly awake and could see that I was in a right state already.

'Good luck, mate.'

I walked down the corridor of the very exclusive Carden Park Hotel, near Chester, to the manager's room and knocked on the door. I still thought something had happened to the family, despite Gouldy's angry tone. But if they were okay, I didn't have a clue what else could be wrong. It had to be serious to be woken up at dawn. Gouldy ordered me into his room. He was raging as he looked at me and said, 'You have shown complete disrespect to a fellow professional.' What? I was becoming more confused by the minute. Then Gouldy gestured at the telly and said, 'That stunt with Paolo Maldini's shirt.'

It was never supposed to be a stunt. It was meant to be a bit of fun. Me, walking along in front of the Sky cameras and tossing away legend Maldini's shirt as a joke in the build-up to our 2000 European Championship qualifier against Italy. Pete Colley of Sky had suggested it, and I was naive and went along with it. When the lads saw it that night on the TV in the hotel, they were all laughing about it. I thought it was funny too. I thought that Gouldy overreacted at the time, and, as the years have gone on, I haven't changed my mind. Disagreeing with him at that moment was not an option, though.

'You're out of the squad,' he informed me. 'We'll keep it in-house. No one needs to know, but I want you out of the hotel in 20 minutes, or I'll phone the police and have them escort you out.'

Drummed out of the Wales set-up in shame. I was the cheeky chappie. Everyone knew that. 'Hey, Robbie, toss that shirt away, will you?' It was a laugh. Wasn't it? Gouldy thought I'd overstepped the mark and that I was taking the mick out of one of the giants of the game. Paolo Maldini is a legend, and there was no way I was showing him disrespect. There was no malice intended at all. But the manager of Wales was resolute. I don't know how I got out of his room and back to mine. 'Jonah, he's thrown me out of the squad.'

I was crying by this time. We were playing the game in Liverpool while the Millennium Stadium was being built, which meant I was only a ten-minute drive from Mum and Dad. I drove straight over and still don't know how I kept my car on the road. My first task was to ring Martin O'Neill, and the gaffer tried to calm me down. I switched on the TV, and there I was, breaking news on Sky Sports.

'Robbie Savage has been thrown out of the Wales squad for his behaviour,' announced the newsreader. Behaviour? That made it sound like I'd been caught drinking or something. So much for keeping it in-house. Mum and Dad were looking at me, and I could see the expressions on their faces. Their boy was making news – and for all the wrong reasons. All week, Dad had been talking about going to Anfield, and now I was sitting on his sofa in the living room, tears running down my cheeks and feeling utterly humiliated. The phone was ringing off the hook. My teammates wanted me back. Gary Speed and Mark Hughes went to see Gouldy to ask for me to be reinstated. More players defended me, and Gouldy realised he was in danger of a major mutiny. He called me back into the squad. 'But you're not playing. You'll be sub,' he warned.

I went back feeling let down by the manager, but he was saying the same about me. All I know is that what should have been the highest point of my blossoming new international career had turned into a fully blown crisis that has followed me ever since. When people dredge up the past, the shirt throwing is always there on the crime sheet: things Robbie Savage did wrong. The consequence was that I sat on the bench for the 2–0 defeat at Anfield until the final ten minutes. It still turned into 'Robbie Savage Day' though, because the Italian fans booed me when I replaced Sparky. And the next day I had to sit and squirm next to Gouldy as he called a press conference. I felt degraded, and Bobby still knows that, even though we did not let it spoil our long-term friendship.

It was Gouldy who gave me my big break in international football and who spotted that I could be of value to a team as a midfielder. Without his input, I might have stayed as a centre-forward at Crewe, which would have been a disaster for me. Gouldy's biggest problem was his place of birth. Because he was an English manager of the Wales national team, there was always an agenda for some people. He took a load of stick from pundits and fans, not to mention from some of the players. From my point of view, he was generally good to me and is someone whom I have stayed in touch with over the years. I loved him. But some of the senior pros weren't having him at all. Dean Saunders is a great impersonator, and he'd sit in the back of the bus and take him off.

I'm sure Gouldy will be the last Englishman to coach the Wales national football team. Three Welshmen – Mark Hughes, John Toshack and Gary Speed – have managed the Red Dragons since, and I can't see that policy changing at the Football Association of Wales. The FAW liked Gouldy because he was prepared to do the job on a small budget. We flew on scheduled flights, we had a small backroom staff, and we even trained in a prison!

Seriously. There was an open prison near Usk that had a top-class training pitch, for some reason. Bobby knew about the pitch from someone who had served time there and thought it was the perfect venue. It made great publicity, all those inmates just feet away from multimillion-pound footballers. They were very friendly. The guards would wait for us to leave the changing-room and then lock it, just to be on the safe side. One day, we were all waiting for Gouldy on the pitch. There was no sign of him. A few minutes passed and still no sign. He was locked in the changing-room! We were in fits. Gouldy held his traditional pre-match press conference there too, and all the journalists had to wait in the canteen while the inmates finished eating. I wouldn't have minded seeing a few of them behind bars. The reporters, I mean!

The Wales set-up today is light years from what it was then. Mark Hughes transformed everything and persuaded the FAW to put their hands in their pockets for the first time in their history. Now the national team is based at the Vale of Glamorgan Hotel outside Cardiff, and the facilities are top class. The Wales rugby union boys and Cardiff City make use of the Vale too. I'm not having a go at Bobby Gould, but it was Sparky who persuaded the FAW to use chartered planes, and we had better hotels, better food, better everything. We went from being a pub team to an international team in the way everything was done.

Pulling on the red shirt of my country meant so much to me. Taid, my late grandfather, had all my caps, going back to Under-14. I would have loved it if he had seen me play just once. I often closed my eyes when the national anthem was being played before a game and thought of my grandfather.

In my scrapbook collection, I have a programme from an Under-15 English Schools' Football Association match between England and Wales, played at Filbert Street, where I would spend so many happy years as an adult. It is dated 31 March 1990. The England team included my United schoolboy colleagues Nicky Butt and Ben Thornley. A year later, I was playing against England again, for the Under-18s – even though I was still only 16. Each time I moved up, I inched closer to the day I would be part of the senior national side.

It happened when I was still at Crewe but after I had switched into midfield. I knew Gouldy was keeping an eye on me from what he had said when I had played for the Under-21s against Germany. There wasn't much glamour attached to a trip to Albania, but, as far as I was concerned, Tirana was the best place in the world to be in November 1995. We met in a Slough hotel convenient for Heathrow. I was so nervous. These were my heroes, players like Ian Rush, Dean Saunders, Mark Hughes, Neville Southall, Gary Speed and my old United Youth Cup teammate Ryan Giggs. At least Giggsy was a familiar face, and Sparky remembered me too. But what would they think of me? I played for Crewe. Who?

Walking into dinner that first night, my palms were sweaty and my mouth was dry. The closest I'd come to most of the guys was sitting on my sofa watching them on the TV. They were household names, confident, popular and a magnet for fans, while I felt an outsider, a nobody who played for Crewe. They were friendly and welcoming and introduced me to a drinking culture I had never known before. At United we were too young, and at Crewe the lads all lived so far away from each other that we didn't go out together very much, but Wales trips were all about drinking and clubbing – especially on home games. It opened my eyes. I still can't understand why people drink beer, though.

Bobby knew we went out, and he didn't mind. It wasn't the issue then that it has become. We didn't get into any trouble, and the press guys weren't bothered. Most of them liked a drink too, I recall! There was one occasion when the Wales boys were out at Brannigans in Cardiff and Vinnie Jones got on the mic and started to sing 'Mustang Sally'. Vinnie was absolutely brilliant with me. He took me in, looked after me and made sure I was all right. I was still thinking, 'What am I doing here?' The stars would be mobbed in nightclubs, and I'd be mobbed too, and then the fans would stop and look again because they didn't recognise me at all.

Back to Albania. My overriding memory is that it wasn't a particularly nice place: it rained all the way through the match, and we drew 1–1. Mark Pembridge scored. I came on as sub and could finally call myself a Wales international. Five months later, I was in the squad for a friendly against Switzerland in Lugano. Roy Hodgson, who has done such a great job at Fulham, was the Swiss coach at the time. I came on as sub when we were losing 2–0. John Hartson was up front on his own. Andy Legg played, and Barry Horne was captain. That was the day I lost all respect for Horne. I've blanked him ever since.

I made an impact when I was on the pitch. I tricked Ramon Vega, the ex-Spurs defender, and set up Harts for a chance. He didn't score, but it was a promising move. My passing was good, and Hodgson said some nice things about me afterwards. When we arrived back at the hotel, Bobby had a team meeting and talked us through the game. 'It's taken a 20 year old from Crewe to come on and show the big-time Charlies how it should be done,' he said.

'I'm not having that,' Horne replied. 'It's easy to come on and look good.' The captain of Wales was saying it was easy for me. I'd been in fear of them all, but I wasn't scared of Horne any more. I'd made a difference on the pitch, and this guy was being so harsh and unfair. Gouldy disagreed with him too. Horne talked about 'easy', but surely it would have been easy to say, 'Well done.' If I were the captain now, and a youngster came in like that, I would be straight over to congratulate the kid. What was his point? I still had the last laugh: he was finishing his international career while I was starting mine. Two months later, I replaced him from the subs' bench in the 5–0 thrashing of San Marino, the game when I was ready with my shin pads in place. Andy Melville, Giggsy, Pemb and a Sparky double saw us through that one. Two more friendlies followed, including the win over Scotland in Kilmarnock, before my move to Leicester.

It was only after I became a Premier League player that I felt I belonged with Wales. When I was in my last year at Crewe, Gouldy often said I was worth a chance at a bigger club. He was never in doubt, which was why he called me up for a World Cup qualifier in Turkey in August 1997. I was still only a few weeks into my time at Leicester, but I felt part of the national squad. From Gresty Road to Istanbul – now I was part of a bigger, better crew. Galatasary's notorious Ali Sami Yen Stadium awaited us, and I certainly didn't have a clue what to expect, although Dean Saunders could give us a few hints, because he'd spent a year playing there.

On the first night in Istanbul, we had a team meeting. Halfway through, my mobile phone started to vibrate in my pocket. And ring. I'd forgotten to switch it to silent. Every single member of the squad turned to stare, and I could feel Bobby's eyes on me as well. I tried to make the best out of a bad situation. I lifted the phone to my ear and said, 'Hello Mum.'

Everybody was in fits of giggles. Daft Sav had got them all smiling. I was laughing too, but 24 hours later I was gulping at the Galatasary ground. Fans were trying to get to the coach to push it over, and stones were being thrown. There were some angry Turks out there, and they wanted to get to us. When I went to Blackburn, I became very friendly with Tugay, and he's made me realise just how patriotic the fans are when they follow their football team. It was an unbelievably hostile place to go. Walking through the tunnel was like being in a prison cell – not that I've ever been in a prison cell! The canteen at Usk was the closest I'd come. There were stone walls on either side, and then you stepped out into a cauldron.

If there was anything to throw, the crowd threw it. Gouldy had to move back into his dugout as every object you could imagine rained down on him. Turkey had an outside chance of qualifying for France '98, which is why they were in such a frenzy. It was my first competitive start, and I marked it with a fantastic goal, a volley from the edge of the box after Giggsy's cross had been headed out by Alpay. It was one of *ten* goals scored on the night. Turkey 6, Wales 4. It sounds like a set of tennis, except there was no sign of fluffy balls. We were 3–2 ahead. Then we led 4–3, but we ended up losing because of the magnificent Hakan Sukur and his four-goal haul. Nathan Blake, Dean Saunders and Andy Melville scored the others.

Twelve weeks earlier, I'd sat at home as my Crewe teammates headed down to Wembley for their play-off success. How low I'd felt. Three months on and I was playing against a legend like Sukur in a smoky, noisy and packed Ali Sami Yen Stadium. And three days after that Manchester United were coming to Filbert Street. What a remarkable turnaround. I'm Robbie Savage, and I'm playing in the same side as Neville Southall, Gary Speed, Dean Saunders, Mark Hughes and Ryan Giggs. You let me down, Dario, but look at me now.

From that point on, I was always part of Gouldy's planning. We lost 3–2 in Belgium in the final qualifier, and Giggsy was quite sensational. In the summer of 1998 we went on a mini tour of Malta and Tunisia for a couple of friendlies just before the World Cup. I had a groin injury that was going to keep me out of the Malta game. But I didn't pull out of the squad, and we travelled to Valletta. Craig Bellamy had just come

into the set-up then, and he played against Malta. We won easily, and
Gouldy announced he would be sticking with the same team in Tunis.
'Hang on a minute,' I tackled Bobby. 'I've sacrificed my family holiday
to come away with Wales, and you're not going to play me?'

He changed his mind, and I was part of the team that lost 4–0. I
was playing right-wingback too. Afterwards, we were all invited for
drinks by the British ambassador to Tunisia. The whole squad went,
and Gouldy invited the journalists who were travelling with us to come
along. That's what it was like. Reporters and players could share a drink
and some banter.

The serious business of the Euro 2000 qualifiers started in September
with that fateful match against Italy. 'Maldinigate', I suppose you
could call it now. The knives were out for Gouldy immediately, but he
rescued the situation when we went to Copenhagen in October and beat
Denmark 2–1. Four days later, we saw off Belarus 3–2 at Ninian Park
– because the Millennium Stadium was still being built. The problem was
that Gouldy was only ever one result away from a crisis. Every pundit
in the country would have a go at him. He took some stick. The end
was still pretty dramatic, though. We lost 2–0 in Switzerland in March
1999. My roomie, Paul Jones, had a back spasm during the warm-up
and lasted 26 minutes. Gary Speed won his 50th cap that night, but
that was about the only thing to celebrate.

It meant the June double-header against Italy and Denmark was make-
or-break in terms of pressure on Gouldy. We travelled to Bologna, and I
was an injury doubt but still went with the squad. I didn't make it. The
Italians thrashed us 4–0, and that was enough for Bobby. He walked
into the dressing-room at the end, looked around and announced, 'I've
resigned. I'm not coming home with you. I'm flying back with Marge.'

Marge, Gouldy's wife, always travelled to matches and was a big
support to him. That was it. Neville Southall and Mark Hughes were
put in charge for the match against the Danes at Anfield, which we
lost 2–0. I missed that one too. By the time Wales played Belarus in
Minsk in September, Sparky was still in temporary charge. We won 2–1,
thanks to Giggsy's 86th-minute goal, but I was back in Leicester with a
groin strain. The final match of that European Championship qualifying
campaign summed up how far we had fallen. Just 5,000 people turned

out to see us lose 2–0 to Switzerland in Wrexham. To run out at The Racecourse Ground was a momentous occasion for me, but it was a dire night. The pitch was terrible, and our performance wasn't very good either. We finished fourth out of five in Group One, and we were pretty much on the floor. Little did we know then that Mark Hughes was about to take charge on a permanent and full-time basis and launch an era in which playing in front of 72,000 fans at a sell-out Millennium Stadium would be the norm.

9

RABID AFGHAN WITH BLOND HAIR

The 1999 Worthington Cup final will always be remembered for two things: me getting Justin Edinburgh sent off and my big nose. Or, more accurately, the snot dangling from it as I walked off the Wembley pitch followed by 78,000 pairs of eyes and dozens of TV cameras. That was the day I became a hate figure, the long-haired blond wanker who turned a showpiece occasion into 'The Robbie Savage Sideshow'. Martin O'Neill's Leicester versus George Graham's Tottenham with me on a mission to mark David Ginola out of the game. To be fair, I did keep him quiet, not that many people will necessarily recall it after that crazy afternoon in March. The world of football analysed every minute of the match, and pundits from all corners joined forces to have a go at me. All my mates slaughtered me too.

'Effing hell, Sav. How big is your nose?' These messages kept coming through, one after the other. Hang on a minute. I'd just been involved in a major controversial incident. Edinburgh sent off thanks to my reaction, verbal bust-ups with Steffen Freund and Allan Nielsen, Spurs fans baying for me to be dismissed – which is why I was substituted with a minute to go – and all my friends could talk about was the size of my nose. I've seen the footage since, and they are right. It was my most high-profile moment in football, and all the pictures show is me coming off the pitch with snot swinging side to side. Unbelievable. The timing could not have been worse. Just as the board went up with my number, I blew my nose. The cameras panned towards me and followed my exit. I go red thinking about it now.

Everyone saw red that day, even if it was only Edinburgh who was sent off. My first Wembley final and what should have been the perfect reward for making the breakthrough in my second season at Leicester had become a headline writer's dream – but not for the reasons I'd imagined in the run-up. When I look back at my career, there are moments that will stay with me forever. It's strange how the 1998–99 season provided two of them: the Paolo Maldini shirt incident and the League Cup final.

Martin O'Neill had already led Leicester to triumph in the Coca-Cola Cup before I'd arrived and would do so again in the Worthington Cup before he left. This is why I had signed. The gaffer was a winner, and I wanted to be a winner with him. In my first season at Filbert Street, I had established myself, slightly uneasily, as a right-wingback, and we'd finished tenth. Now we were preparing for another campaign, and I had every reason to feel full of hope and expectation. My home life was also entering a new and welcome phase. Sarah and I were living together.

During my first year, Sarah visited every weekend by train. Naz the dog and I would meet her at the station. One weekend, we didn't. I told her to catch a taxi, because I was knackered. She'd had three changes of train from the Wirral and was knackered too. We had our first argument, and I realised I was wrong. I'd come to take her for granted, and after that our relationship moved onto a new footing. Sarah agreed to move down to Leicester. Mum and Dad brought her, but I couldn't be there because of a pre-season friendly at Norwich. So I asked my mate Tuffy to help me out with a little surprise. Sarah arrived to find him waiting to let her in. She walked into the lounge with my parents. Tuffy nipped out, picked up a Vauxhall Tigra I'd bought for her and parked it on the drive with a big bow round it.

Sarah's a twin. When I first met her, I was praying it would be a sister! Only kidding, Simon. He's great, and I think I've finally won over the in-laws. I wasn't a Premier League player when we met, and she wasn't a groupie. You see so many women hanging round footballers now, and it's so difficult for the lads. I've been amazingly lucky with Sarah, especially as I'm not an easy person to live with. She gets on my nerves sometimes, like all women do!

The highlight of every week was the game. I'd drop Mum, Dad and Sarah off at a pub called The Key. Dad and Sarah enjoyed a couple of drinks, and Sarah would be laughing and giggling even when we lost – she hasn't got a clue about football. I wouldn't talk to her for two days. I rang her once on the way home from an away game, and she asked me if we'd signed a new player. 'No. Why?' I said.

'On Teletext it says that someone called Og has scored.' OG? Own goal. At least she bothered to look for the result. It must have been difficult for her leaving her job and her parents. Christopher Scotney in Leicester sponsored me, and he gave her a job in his shop, because she didn't want to sit at home all day. Sarah's not a typical wag. She has an art degree from Hull and is a very talented artist. One of her commissions was a mural for Steve Walsh's Chinese restaurant in Leicester.

With my home life in perfect working order, I prepared to tackle the new season. The first fixture was a mouth-watering one: away to Manchester United. I did think I would come back to haunt Fergie again, because I was brilliant, but unfortunately it didn't work out that way. Emile Heskey and Tony Cottee scored for us, and a dream result was waiting. Then I went to check inside Giggsy. He took the ball from me and played it to Andy Cole. They scored from the corner. To make matters worse, David Beckham equalised in the *seventh* minute of injury time. Martin O'Neill was raging, and I felt I'd let him down. I was crying my eyes out afterwards. Dad was there, ready to drive me home. He parked his car at the Trafford Arms pub, a short walk away, and I had to make my way through a crowd of United fans. Can you imagine that now?

Those tears at United gave Martin the ammunition to have a go at me. We were travelling to a match at Sunderland, and the coach was one of those where you had two seats facing each other and separated by a table. I was sitting opposite the gaffer, who loves telling stories. I acted as if I was asleep and started snoring. Martin immediately began to pretend to cry, like I'd done at United. He made me feel very small. That's when I realised that, even if you thought he liked you, it didn't mean you were getting close to him. I preferred his praise.

I tended to sit at the front of the bus on those trips. Down the back, some of my teammates were losing £5,000 in poker games. I've wasted a fortune on buying and selling cars, but I've never been a gambler and I'd be gutted if I lost £50 on a bet. The lads didn't play with limits, so a lot of money was changing hands. Again, it's not something you would see now, and it didn't upset the spirit we had. Everyone paid up quite happily. I watched sometimes and found it nerve-wracking as a spectator. It was quite the norm everywhere. Some of the guys liked to gamble on other things. I went to the toilet at half-time in one game, and one of the lads was in the next cubicle on his phone, putting a bet on the horses. The card schools helped relieve the boredom.

After a year in the Premier League, I was beginning to feel I belonged. But I wasn't utterly convinced about the right-wingback position. I didn't have a trick, Ian Marshall was quicker than me and I couldn't dislodge a midfield of Muzzy, Lennie and Parker. Still, I was in the team, and that was the important thing. Having given United a scare in the first match, we didn't build on it, and by the end of September we'd won only one of our first seven League games. Little did we know that beating Chesterfield over two legs in September would set us on the path to the Twin Towers. Gerry Taggart scored against Chesterfield. Taggs arrived from Bolton that summer, and he was hard. Martin liked his central defenders to be big and mean, lads like Spencer Prior. We joked that at 3 p.m. on a Saturday all the planes had to be diverted from East Midlands Airport because of Spencer's clearances!

Matt Elliott was huge too and a lovely guy. He was a ball-playing centre-half. Matt's wife, Kath, was a very attractive lady. She was queen bee among the wives. Kath opened a shop in Leicester and asked us along to do a fashion show. I think I modelled the gloves and balaclavas! Sarah always used to feel a bit left out of it all and that she was not part of the group. There were girls' nights outs, and Sarah wouldn't be invited. It was the same when Darren Eadie's girlfriend, Kellie, arrived a year later, although they did go on one night out to Nottingham. Kath organised a stretch limo for all the wives. There would have been about ten or fifteen of them. Sarah only had a couple of glasses of wine but would have been drunk on that. The conversation turned a bit racy, and the wives were talking about what they got up to in bed with their husbands. A certain sex act was mentioned, and one of the girls said, 'I've never done that.'

'Oh yes, you have,' piped up Sarah. 'Your husband told Robbie you had.'

That was the time that I decided to go down the tattoo route. Steve Walsh had an Armani logo done, and I liked it. I have about ten on me now and regret them because I'm going to have them when I'm old. I'm a real hypochondriac, but I didn't have a problem with the needles at all. All the tattoos together cost me £4.50! The only needle I get now is when I have acupuncture treatment. It's quite common in football. I injured my groin in the 2009–10 season playing for Derby, and the physio took one look and said, 'It's only a little prick.'

Back then, I was still waiting to make my mark on the Leicester side. October was good: we beat Leeds, Tottenham and Liverpool and drew at Villa when they were leaders of the Premier League. November wasn't quite so great. We didn't win in the League at all. Even worse, I ended up in hospital after the 4–2 defeat to Chelsea because I couldn't name the Prime Minister! It was a fantastic game, so I'm told. About ten minutes into the second half, Graeme Le Saux cleared the ball and it smacked into my face and knocked me out. I was lying on the pitch, and the club doctor came out to see if I was concussed. 'Who is the Prime Minister?' he asked.

'I don't know,' I replied.

'Robbie's got concussion. Get him off.' I was carted off to hospital. They kept me in overnight too. The next morning they asked me the same question, and I still didn't know! I was young, I wasn't interested in politics, and it was a stupid question. Why couldn't they have asked the name of the Cheltenham manager? However, I have made a point of knowing the name of every prime minister since then.

Martin must have been big friends with the Prime Minister, because he dropped me for the next match against Coventry! Andy Impey, a £1.6-million right-wingback, made his debut. I came on as sub and hit the side netting and was feeling the pressure. That nagging feeling at the back of my mind had been right. Martin didn't think I was up to the job, and he'd brought in someone else who could do it. I was upset, but I didn't sulk. It was hard, though, as I found myself relegated to the bench throughout December. But I was back in for the 1–1 draw against Blackburn at the end of the month, only to be stretchered off with a knee problem that kept me out of the next four League games. I'm a worrier by nature, and I was beginning to get very concerned. Things were going wrong.

The League Cup proved the turning point at Leicester. I can go back through my career and pick out crucial moments that set me on a certain path. The second leg of the semi-final was one of those. We'd beaten Sunderland 2–1 away – without me – but we were struggling in the second leg and at half-time were losing 1–0 to a Niall Quinn goal. Martin turned to me and said, 'You're going in the middle with Muzzy and Lennie. This is your opportunity.'

Muzzy – what a player. He followed me to Birmingham eventually and had to retire early through injury. He was one of the most talented players I've ever seen and a very generous guy. He had that X-factor. I always thought he should have played for England. He went on to play for Turkey and has a World Cup semi-final against Brazil in his locker. Lennie looked after me when I first arrived from Crewe, and he is someone I have huge respect for too. We fell out later when he joined Celtic and came back to play a friendly at Leicester, but I remember the good times.

With those two at my side, I produced my best forty-five minutes in a Leicester shirt, replacing Gerry Taggart and going four-four-two. I think some of the lads were surprised. No one had seen me play midfield before. At the final whistle, everyone came over and hugged me. Martin had his arms around my shoulders. 'Thank Robbie for getting us to the final,' he said to the others.

That was it. It was the best thing that had ever happened to me. We went out that night to an Italian restaurant called Baffone in Leicester. I'd never done karaoke before, but I was up there singing 'Simply the Best'. I'd just been doing a job up until then, but that was when I really made it. That was the day I became Robbie Savage, Leicester City footballer. I was accepted by the lads from that moment on, and I still believe we were the best midfield that Leicester has ever had.

Our League form wasn't great leading up to the final, but I couldn't wait for the biggest day of my career. We travelled two days before, staying at Burnham Beeches. We saw a show at the Palladium on Friday night and had Saturday morning to relax. There was a team meeting that day, and Frank Sinclair was late. He was thrown out of the squad, and I think he watched the game from a pub. You don't mess with Martin. As we boarded the coach for Wembley, I couldn't help but think about

Dario Gradi. He'd robbed me of my chance to go there in a play-off final, but here I was on my way to play at the famous stadium.

As a proud Welshman, I love the Millennium Stadium, but there is, and always will be, something very special about Wembley. That bus ride was an incredible feeling. We'd been to Christopher Scotney in Leicester to buy our suits – Armani or Boss. We were in all the papers. It was a surreal experience. My first memory of a major cup final was 1981 between Manchester City and Tottenham. Dad gave me a lager and orange that was mainly orange. It's probably why I hate lager!

The coach drew nearer Wembley, and you could see hundreds and thousands of Leicester fans waving and cheering. We walked onto the pitch in our suits, and I thought about how many times I'd watched this scene on TV. Now I was there, on the famous Twin Towers turf. I had the reputation of being someone who would work his nuts off and tackle people. I didn't score many goals, but you'd want me in your team. My instructions were to keep Ginola quiet. I went into him hard, and he didn't like it.

Then I tackled Justin Edinburgh. It was a fair challenge, but he objected. He swung his arm. He didn't touch me, but he did brush my hair. I fell down, claiming he'd caught me in the face. He was shown the red card by ref Terry Heilbron. Edinburgh had raised his arm, which is a sending-off offence, but I did make a meal of it. There were words said to Allan Nielsen and Steffen Freund. I didn't touch Freund, but he went down as though he'd been shot. I didn't like him. He had a big mouth. He thought he was hard, but he wasn't hard. He was useless. He probably thought the same about me.

In the 89th minute the board went up: *Robbie Savage off*. The game was heading into extra time. I sat down, and 30 seconds later Nielsen scored. It was a terrible way to lose a cup final. There were a few verbals after the game. The Spurs players were saying, 'See you next game.'

Unbelievably, the very next fixture was at White Hart Lane. Freund was accusing me of cheating and diving. Edinburgh wasn't very happy either. I got him sent off, and regret it, but he committed the crime of raising his arm. Death threats were sent to the club and my home address afterwards. You know the sort, cut out of newsprint and anonymous. This was a game of football, for goodness' sake.

That summer, Sarah and I were on holiday in Spain and went for dinner. We were sitting inside, and the blinds were down to shield us from the sun. As it grew dark, the blinds were raised, and sitting on the other side of us were Edinburgh and his missus! He didn't say anything to me, and I don't really blame him. I also had a holiday meeting with Ginola about four or five years later. He was such a lovely man. We had a good chat, and he kissed Sarah. She melted. I think she would have liked to snog him. Even I would have snogged him!

After the final, we went back to the hotel, and, Leicester being Leicester, the party started. Martin was brilliant, and everyone had a lot to drink. Having tasted defeat at Wembley, I wanted to go back and win something. I'd have been a whole lot happier then if I'd known that it would be only another year before I would. We did make a bit of money. I think we were on £10,000 to win it, which we didn't manage, but we picked up a few quid.

It's a strange quirk of the fixture list that often you are drawn against a club in a cup competition and then meet them the next game in the League. Leicester started the month of April with a visit to Spurs. There are times when players sit in the changing-room before a game and know they are going to win, and this was one of them. So much had been written in the run-up to the match. After the League Cup final, Jeff Powell of the *Daily Mail* called me a 'rabid Afghan hound with blond hair'. The London bias that has lasted all my career started then.

This wasn't a fixture that needed any more hype. George Graham appealed for calm from the fans, while Martin insisted he wouldn't be leaving me out. There was so much publicity. We clapped Tottenham onto the pitch, although I'm not sure whether that was meant as a gesture of respect. Every time I touched the ball, I was booed. In the very first minute, I went into a tackle with Edinburgh and got him, fair and square. Matt Elliott scored from a header just before half-time, and Tony Cottee made sure in the second half. Nielsen came over to shake my hand at the end. The hypocrite. Spurs had lost at home for the first time in six months, and we had our revenge.

The misery of March was forgotten as we went unbeaten in April. It was the month I scored my only League goal of the season too; it came against Villa. Over the years, I have enjoyed some fierce battles with

Villa. I went something like 14 games unbeaten against them while I was at Leicester and Birmingham. We came back from two goals down as well. Lee Hendrie and Julian Joachim scored, and then a long ball by Gupps was missed by Gareth Southgate. I spotted Mark Bosnich off his line and chipped him from 25 yards! Tony Cottee, who we knew as TC, scored the equaliser from a Guppy cross. I won man of the match, and my mate Tuffy still has the bottle of champagne. We went from the ground to the hospital to see Tuffy's wife, Nicky, who had given birth to twins, Morgan and Melissa. I tease the girls now and say that bottle of champagne is as old as they are.

We had made ourselves safe, but the season ended disappointingly. We lost to Southampton, Derby and Nottingham Forest, with a 2–0 win over Newcastle sandwiched between the defeats. Muzzy and TC scored against the Geordies. Tony was a real character. Martin had rescued him when he was playing in Malaysia. He had these little stumpy legs, but he'd keep scoring. He had a great partnership with Emile. Ask anyone who has ever played with Emile, and they will say that he was worth 20 goals a season, because he dealt with all the buffeting. He's had stick for his scoring record, but he made goals for his teammates. Like TC. That season, Cottee finished on sixteen goals and Heskey on nine. Meanwhile, I was beginning to become a cult hero as far as the supporters were concerned.

I had a fan club. It was run by a friend, Morag Clark. We had five hundred members at one point, and we'd send out monthly newsletters and publish calendars. I sometimes brought a fan back to the house to eat with us. Morag's husband, Gary, was also a friend. He was a taxi driver. I'd ring him and say, 'Gaz, can you go to the chippy?' I couldn't be bothered to leave the house. It would cost me £28 for a bag of chips!

I even switched on the Christmas lights with the actor who plays Roy Cropper from *Coronation Street* one year. He's a massive Leicester fan. He told me that the script had a bit of leeway and he'd try to get me a mention. He managed to do it, so I've been talked about on Corrie!

Loved at Filbert Street, hated in London, doing well for Wales. I was nicely settled down with Sarah and Naz and about to help Leicester to an even better season.

10

WEMBLEY WINNER

Match of the Day was due to start. Friends and family crowded round the telly. I couldn't wait. Leicester 2, Liverpool 2 – and I'd been fantastic. I knew it but still wanted the sofa pundits to confirm it to the millions who tuned in every week, not to mention my packed front room. There was the gaffer, trademark tracksuit, waiting to be interviewed. 'Well, Martin, you must have been delighted by the performance of Robbie Savage,' said the reporter with the mike.

Martin O'Neill brushed his hand across his face, licked his lips and looked straight into the camera as he reduced me to a heap of jelly. 'Robbie lacks just one thing,' said Martin. 'Ability.'

Noooooo. I sat there going redder and redder. It was September 1999. We'd pinched a draw with mighty Liverpool, and I had played a major part. Tony Cottee scored two minutes in, Muzzy Izzet grabbed an equaliser about three minutes from the end, and Michael Owen hit two in between. Frank Sinclair was sent off, David Thompson was sent off, and Gérard Houllier was not at all happy afterwards. Did I mention I'd been fantastic?

The gaffer pulled me in first thing on the Monday morning. 'Did you watch *Match of the Day*?' he asked.

'Yes.'

'Do you play every week?'

'Yes.'

'As a manager, I look for things. Ability is not everything. What's better? Having all the ability in the world with no heart or desire or having no ability but lots of heart and desire?'

'The second one, Gaffer.'

'Right. And you're playing every week. Now get out.'

Martin O'Neill. Master motivator. He had the knack of taking you to the heights then dumping you in the gutter. That's why I wanted to play for him: for the highs. There was a player called Arnar Gunnlaugsson at the club who had incredible ability but wasn't picked that often. I never forgot what Martin said. He was selecting me because he knew what he was getting. I was someone who did as he was told, kept it as simple as possible and was there for the team. That season, I played virtually every match, and we finished eighth in the League, won the Worthington Cup and reached the fifth round of the FA Cup. Martin helped turn me into a winner.

People often ask me whether I'd swap my medal for £1 million. I usually joke, 'Of course,' but I am very, very proud of it. I spent a lot of years playing for teams who were never going to challenge for titles or FA Cups, and my first priority was to earn enough to look after the family. Yes, I love nice cars, designer gear, holidays abroad and all the other perks of being a well-paid footballer, but it is more important that Charlie and Freddie have a good education. The boys were not yet on the horizon, although Sarah and I were engaged. Once again, I showed my romantic side to propose to her!

Everything was planned to perfection. I had a ring made and, when it was finished, booked a table at a lovely 'olde worlde' place called The Grey Lady, in Rothley, near Leicester. The meal was fantastic, and the setting was wonderful. Suddenly, the lights were dimmed, and a musician playing a violin came towards our table, followed by a waiter carrying a tray, and there, on top of a mountain of ice, was the engagement ring. The ice made the ring sparkle. The place was packed, so every eye in the restaurant was on us by this time. I picked up the ring, went down on one knee and asked Sarah to marry me. She was crying as she said yes – thank God she said yes – and the other diners were clapping and cheering.

A few months later, my mate Paul Hollinshead – Hollo – thought he would do the same thing. All four of us were in Spain on holiday. Hollo popped out to the toilet to give the ring to the waiter and told him to bring it in on a tray of ice. We had the starter. No sign. Then the main course. No sign. Hollo was getting a bit twitchy by this time. Finally, we saw the waiter approaching – with a tray of mint ice cream! Hollo had to fish out this ring covered in sticky green ice cream. One of us could have swallowed it by mistake! It was hilarious.

Sarah and I also moved house. We bought a £260,000 new-build in Stoughton to celebrate my new contract. My £3,000-a-week wages had doubled to £6,000, but the £150,000 signing-on fee remained the same. The house was on a small estate. Darren Eadie and his girlfriend, Kellie, lived a couple of doors down, and Jockey became my first big footballing mate. Darren and Tim Flowers were the two main arrivals in the summer of 1999, and both were great additions to the squad as players and as people.

Tim came from Blackburn and sometimes struggled to get out of his car because of his hip. He was still one of the best keepers I've ever seen. I have the video of the day we knocked out Arsenal on penalties in the FA Cup that season. Davor Suker broke through in the last few minutes and smashed it four yards out. Tim made an unbelievable save. 'It's me against Davor!' he yelled. Great stuff.

Sarah and I often went out with Darren and Kellie. One night, we were going home in a black cab and pretend fighting in the back. We got the girls' knickers off. The next morning, I looked out of the window and could see Sarah's knickers hanging over a lamp post – and we lived in a really posh road!

Darren and I bought mini motorbikes. His was normal size for him! Now you know why his nickname was Jockey! We loved racing round the streets near the house, but our adventures came to an end when the dog-sitter decided to have a go on mine and the neighbours complained to the police. I needed the dog-sitter because Naz hated being on her own. I came home one day and honestly thought I'd been burgled. What the hell had happened? Then I realised Naz had torn the sofa apart. She'd ripped through the leather, and there was foam everywhere. So my mate Ashley came round to keep her company for £50.

Just outside the posh estate, there was a big field near the main road. It was my dog-walking route. There were sheep in the field and a buzzing fence surrounding it. I didn't have a clue it was electric. Naz got away from me one day, spotted the sheep and tried to dash through the fence.

By the time I caught her, she was still shaking from electric shock after electric shock. Grabbing her was probably not the best thing to do. I got a big shock too. Naz was too petrified to walk past the field, and, from that day on, I had to pick her up and carry her about 100 metres past the fence.

Electrifying off the pitch and pretty steady on it. That was the only way to describe me at the start of the season. I also managed to add Chelsea fans to the growing list of London supporters who hated me – and this time I was completely innocent. We played them at home in the first week of the season and drew 2–2. We'd lost at Highbury a week earlier, and I had said I thought the Gunners were a better bet for the title based on the two matches. 'Savage brands Chelsea a bunch of softies and says they haven't got the bottle to win the title,' screamed a couple of the papers.

I had not said it. The gaffer went ballistic and threatened to fine me two weeks' wages. I was going to appeal through the PFA, but someone convinced Martin that my comments had been twisted. I was now beginning to realise that everything I said was fair game, especially when it involved a London team. I've always had a pretty good press from the Midlands guys, because they've understood what I'm about, but it hasn't extended to the south. Chelsea fans sent me death threats, to go with those from Tottenham supporters from the year before.

As far as I was concerned, the only person I had to please was Martin. We were doing okay, challenging near the top of the table. At the end of September, we played Villa and beat them 3–1. The match was memorable because Gareth Southgate was sent off and Villa boss John Gregory accused Emile Heskey of falling over like a sack of spuds. Four months later, just before we played them in the semi-final of the League Cup, he was telling the world he wanted to buy Emile.

We were pretty much on fire at Filbert Street but were picking up vital away wins too. The most satisfying was in October, when we won 3–2 at White Hart Lane. Muzzy scored a couple, and Gerry Taggart the other, and Emile had a bust-up with Nielsen at the final whistle. A few weeks later, I elbowed Ryan Giggs in the face! It was a complete accident, and I know that Ryan accepted it. We went to Old Trafford and lost 2–0. Andy Cole scored from a bicycle kick. I'd moved my arm and given Giggsy a thick lip. I've never deliberately elbowed anyone in my life, and I just caught him. Having lost to United, we bounced back by beating Wimbledon and Coventry and were beginning to feel a bit more buoyant.

December was a peculiar month as we beat Leeds on penalties in the fourth round of the League Cup, struggled to get past Hereford in the FA Cup and lost all four of our League matches. Arsenal, Derby, Leeds and Newcastle combined to push us back down to seventh. Martin picked me out for praise after we drew 0–0 against Hereford at Edgar Street. One of Martin's favourite words is 'sensational', and he told the whole changing-room I was sensational that day. It had been three months since the Liverpool *MOTD* moment. Time for me to feel ten feet tall again. We eventually needed extra time to win the replay 2–1 at our place. I set up Muzzy for the winner in the 104th minute.

That Christmas, I went to our party dressed up as Neil Lennon! We went to Nottingham for the do, and I walked round the town with a mask and a bright-red wig. I used to take the mickey out of Lennie. But I did get some funny looks that night.

The start of a new millennium, and we had fixtures coming thick and fast in January: eight matches, including two meetings against Chelsea, two against Arsenal and two more penalty shoot-outs. That was where I became a figure of hate for yet another London club, but I hold up my hands here – I gave Arsenal plenty of ammunition. It was the fourth round of the FA Cup, and the match ended 0–0. Somehow, I stayed on the pitch. The ball broke, and I went for it. But Kanu arrived just before me. I stepped on the ball and got his leg with the downforce of my studs. If I'd followed through, I would have broken his leg. I could easily have been sent off, and when I saw it again on the TV I apologised.

The replay was ten days later. Thierry Henry did me, but Arsene Wenger didn't see that, did he? He only ever sees what he wants. That was the game when Tim played a blinder against Suker but had to go off in extra time with a knee injury. Pegguy Arphexad replaced him and was our penalty hero. He saved from Gilles Grimandi, and we were through to the fifth round. Stefan Oakes had a penalty saved by David Seaman that night, and I went to put my arm round his shoulder afterwards and told him not to worry. His mum rang me the next day to say thanks.

The other penalty shoot-out came in the match between the two Arsenal games. We drew 3–3 with Fulham, where I showed that my big mouth does not always connect with my brain before I open it. Geoff Horsfield played for Fulham, and I'd read somewhere he had been a builder before he became a footballer. The Hors scored for Fulham but missed in the shoot-out, which we won 3–0. 'After you miss, come back to mine and build me a patio,' I whispered in his ear just before he took it.

He was virtually the first person I bumped into when I signed for Birmingham, and I was pretty nervous after what I'd said. Luckily, he saw the funny side. What a top guy – and he still spent his summers building patios!

The longest January in history was still not over. We went to Villa for the first leg of the League Cup semi-final. The game ended 0–0, and Villa boss John Gregory revved it up beforehand by saying he'd like to buy Emile Heskey. He also made a comment that we didn't get over the halfway line at their place, so, to celebrate the 1–0 second-leg victory, we all rushed up to the halfway line and pretended to trip over it. I never had much to do with John Gregory. He came across as suave and sophisticated, and he loved the limelight.

That was also where my feud with Lee Hendrie began. I hated him, and he hated me. I thought he was arrogant. He wasn't involved in the first game but played at Filbert Street and nailed me. Whenever we faced each other on the pitch, we'd have a problem. Years later, we were to become teammates at Derby, and he phoned me before he signed. 'Let's just not talk to each other,' I told him.

Then he came on as sub for his first Derby game, and we were in the same team. So I changed my mind about not talking to him, and now I think he's a decent lad. I admit that Lee had the ability to wind me up. Ken Bates seemed to have the same effect on the gaffer. Martin was absolutely fuming when the Chelsea chairman accused Leicester of negative tactics on the day of our FA Cup fifth-round tie at Stamford Bridge. We'd drawn the League game there a couple of weeks earlier, so I don't know if it was sour grapes. The Cup tie was mayhem. Steve Walsh and Dennis Wise were sent off, John Robertson had a bust-up with Luca Vialli and Martin called Bates a 'cretin'. Unfortunately, we lost 2–1.

Three days later, Matt Elliott scored the only goal against Villa, and we were on our way back to Wembley. Stan Collymore also arrived. Stan's a mate of mine, a very good friend. We are both columnists for the *Mirror*. When I was at Crewe, my teammate Jamie Moralee was Stan's great pal. Jamie and I went for a night out in London once and bumped into Stan, and he really took care of us. Stan looked like a gangster in his leather jacket, though! He's a lovely, kind, generous person, and I will never forget hearing the crunch when he broke his leg playing at Derby.

Stan had fallen out with Gregory at Villa and wanted a new start. But if any manager could handle Stan, it had to be Martin. He walked through the door and had this presence. And even though he was not eligible to play in the Worthington Cup final, he will always be remembered for the major impact he had on our pre-Wembley bonding session. La Manga: two little words, so many headlines. And all because Stan let off a fire extinguisher in the lounge bar of our very exclusive hotel at four in the morning.

I had bailed out at about two-thirty, and not because I was a goody two-shoes. I was pretty much full of Smirnoff Ice at the time. But on the way back from an Irish bar, one of the lads had peed in a flowerpot outside the main door of our very exclusive hotel, and I could see all these people looking at us in horror: men in white tuxedos, women in smart evening dresses. As the lads headed for the piano bar, I took the route to bed. At nine the next morning, there was a bang on the door and the instruction to pack. Our jaunt had lasted 24 hours!

The idea to go to Spain was a good one. Martin thought we could relax before the League Cup final against Tranmere. He didn't come with us, and that was the reason things happened the way they did. We started drinking as soon as we boarded the plane. Robbo was on Bloody Marys. Some members of the Leicester team were big drinkers, and they could handle it. We arrived at La Manga and piled into reception. The floors were marble, huge chandeliers were hanging from the ceiling, and the whole place was very expensive, very exclusive and very up-market.

'Where's the fucking bar?' shouted a broad Scouse accent. Ian Marshall, the joker of the changing-room, wasn't wasting any time. In the bar, we found Gary Lineker and his brother and had a bit of craic with them.

The beer was flowing. So was every other alcoholic drink you could name! Norwegian club Rosenborg were staying there too. All the players were in tracksuits and flip-flops and shaking their heads as they muttered, 'Lager louts.' The Rosenborg coach asked us to keep the noise down. We were like a pub team.

We took the hint, left the hotel and found an Irish bar. We carried on drinking. And drinking. At one point, Robbo told us it was time to go to bed, because we had a curfew. Ian Marshall asked Robbo for an extension, and he said, 'You'd have to ask the gaffer.' So Marshall rang Martin back in England, at whatever time it was in the morning, left a message and told the rest of us that we had a couple of extra hours. Robbo's tie was round his neck by now. We were all in a state. We were in a very different state a few hours later when we realised we were being thrown out. What happened? Stan had let off the fire extinguisher in scenes of carnage, according to the lads who were there. And the incident had been reported on Sky News already.

Marshall was petrified. Even the lads who hadn't done anything were frightened at the prospect of facing Martin. Twenty-four hours after flying out of East Midlands Airport, we were jetting back in. Photographers and cameramen were waiting to capture the looks on our faces. I boarded the coach and took a window seat. Later that day, the Sky footage showed me making V-signs at the camera. It wasn't me! Muzzy was sitting next to me and thought he'd have a bit of a laugh. We weren't laughing when we arrived at the Sketchley Grange Hotel for the meeting with Martin. He was fuming. We'd dragged the name of Leicester City through the mud. Finally, he turned to Marshall and ordered, 'Don't ever leave a message on my phone again.'

I suppose the least we could do was win the Worthington Cup for him. We followed the routine of a year earlier: we travelled to Burnham Beeches, saw a show and had some leisure time. Matt Elliott scored both goals as we beat Rovers 2–1. Referee Alan Wilkie made history when he became the first official to be stretchered off at Wembley. He hurt his calf. I played right-back, because Martin couldn't drop me. I didn't have an impact on the game, but that didn't matter at the final whistle.

The scenes were so emotional. We had champagne in the bath, and the lads were singing and shouting. To go to Wembley two years running was amazing, but to leave the Twin Towers with a medal in my pocket was unbelievable. We were in Europe. Our bonus was something like £15,000, but this was about glory not money. All my mates came to the party, and Sarah asked the gaffer for a dance. The *gaffer*. I nearly killed her! I was livid and embarrassed. I don't think he accepted her cheeky invitation. There was an open-top bus tour of the city, and I was wearing sunglasses – at night. The streets were packed as the fans came out to cheer us. I have some special memories of that night. When the coach arrived back at Sketchley Grange, I knocked off a policeman's hat.

Stan, having made plenty of headlines with La Manga, needed one game to show just what he could bring to Leicester on the pitch. His home debut against Sunderland was out of this world. Stan grabbed a hat-trick, while the other scorers were Emile and Stefan. It was to be Emile's farewell: he joined Liverpool for £11 million a few days later. If we'd kept those two together, we'd have had a strike force as good as those of Manchester United or Liverpool. It was inevitable that Emile would go. He was our best player, and it was only a matter of time and deciding which was the right club.

We always used to take the mick out of each other. Emile had this Mitsubishi 3000, and I had a purple Merc. They were the two worst cars but also the two best ones, if you know what I mean! Like me, he loved his cars. Emile was a quiet lad and kept himself to himself, but when you got to know him he was funny. All the players at Leicester knew if they performed they would move on. It was the same with Martin. He was giving the club such success, but it made him a wanted man.

Stan looked a pretty decent replacement, but a month after the hat-trick against Sunderland he broke his leg in a 3–0 defeat at Derby. I was near him, and I heard the crack. I saw the agony on his face. It was such a tragic thing to happen. He turned on the pitch, and his ankle went the other way round. That was the beginning of the end for Stan. I went to see him in hospital and felt really sad for my old mate. He'd found a manager who trusted him, who could put his arm around him and get the best out of him. Even after La Manga.

April was also notable for two other reasons. I scored my only League goal of the season – at Newcastle – and Lee Hendrie sparked a mass brawl when we played Villa in the League. First, the goal. We won 2–0 on Tyneside, and it was one of my best games in a Leicester shirt. Stefan played a through ball, and I beat Shay Given. Dad and Nutty were sitting in St James's Park somewhere, but I couldn't see them because they were so high up. I came off a couple of minutes from time to an O'Neill hug.

The 2–2 draw at Villa Park must have been a nightmare for Graham Barber to ref. Hendrie went straight through me. I couldn't understand why. If there was going to be a brawl, I had Gerry Taggart, Steve Walsh and Matt Elliott to help! Hendrie didn't like me. He antagonised players behind their backs, and he did it to me in the Cup semi too. That's where our dislike started. Villa were in the lead twice that day, through Alan Thompson and Paul Merson, but we were their bogey team, and Matt and Muzzy brought it back each time. To give credit to Gregory, even he said Hendrie's tackle was a reckless one.

As the season drew to a close, it became clear Martin would also be on his way. As soon as we knew Celtic were in, that was that. There is only so far someone can take a football club. Martin took Leicester to three major finals in four years. I was sad when I heard. He was like a second father to me, and I would have loved to have gone to Celtic with him. He bought Lennie, and he tried to sign Matt. I would have followed him too, but maybe he felt he couldn't take everyone from Leicester. Just before Martin left, Steve Guppy had been offered a new contract, but he hadn't signed it. I think that's why Martin went for Gupps too – because he'd promised to look after him. Martin has always been loyal to the players who were loyal to him. He was different from most managers, just like Brian Clough was. He made me cry one minute, and he convinced me I could conquer the world the next. He was a very special man to play for.

11

SMARTIN' AFTER MARTIN

Panic. That's the only word to describe what happened at Leicester after Martin O'Neill joined Celtic. Martin left behind a club in Europe, £11 million in the bank from the sale of Emile Heskey and a squad of players who were in demand. The board were petrified we'd all disappear and decided they needed to keep stars like Matt Elliott, Muzzy and me at any cost. And it was at *any* cost. The phone rang while I was on the golf course. 'We're offering you a new contract. How much do you want?' It was Peter Taylor, the man with the hardest job in the world: following Martin as Leicester manager.

'I'd like £1 million a year, at least,' I replied, not expecting to get it.

'I don't know if I can do that,' Peter said. Half an hour later, he was offering me £17,000 a week and a £250,000 signing-on fee, which took me to £21,000 a week – just over £1 million a year. Unbelievable. I'd seen Lennie and Muzzy get much bigger new contracts, and there was speculation about me going to Newcastle. The club eventually couldn't stop Lennie linking up with Martin again, but they were determined to do what it took to keep their other top players. And I was a top player, an important figure in the dressing-room and among the fans. I signed that contract in double-quick time.

I liked Peter Taylor and count him as a friend now. He came from Gillingham and was completely different from Martin. Peter was approachable, a bit like a mate. In the end, I think it was his downfall. That first summer, we were in Marbella and he was in the bar at two in the morning doing his Norman Wisdom impressions. He was so funny.

I couldn't believe what I was seeing. He had Colin Murphy with him, and Murph was a character too. He was a big thinker, and he would love to test me: 'There are three birds in the tree, and the farmer takes his shotgun and shoots one. How many birds are left in the tree?'

'Two, Colin.'

'Wrong.' I'd look at him as he laughed at the expression on my face. 'None.'

'What?'

'No, the farmer kills one, and the other two fly away in fright.'

Definitely very different from Martin, Robbo, Wally and Seamus! Things were changing dramatically, and in the dressing-room too. The Heskey money and more was spent on players like Ade Akinbiyi, Trevor Benjamin, Junior Lewis, Matt Jones, Dean Sturridge, Simon Royce, Callum Davidson and Gary Rowett. I think Peter spent £25 million in his 14 months in charge, and he will probably look back now and accept some of that spending wasn't very wise. Part of the problem was that selling clubs also knew Peter had a lot of cash, so the prices went up and up.

Ade was an example of that. I felt really sorry for him, because Leicester paid Wolves £5.5 million, and when he struggled the fans had a go. He'd been fantastic for Wolves, and the fact that he cost so much money was not his fault. Trevor came from Cambridge in a £1.7-million deal. He was a decent enough player, but he wasn't improving the squad. The signings didn't inspire me. Trev's eyesight was pretty poor – yes, we signed a striker who couldn't see! He wore glasses and used contact lenses to play. At Leicester's training ground, we could either turn left into the canteen or right into the laundry room. One day, Trev wasn't there; he'd gone for dinner in the laundry room!

Junior Lewis followed Peter from Gillingham and was a lovely, lovely guy. Peter told Muzzy and me that he was bringing in this kid. 'If you or Muzzy are under pressure, just give it to Junior,' Peter told us. Muzzy and I looked at each other.

Simon Royce came in as Tim Flowers's number two. He couldn't take a joke. We all knew that Roycey loved his food. He would spend ten minutes getting himself settled down and everything set up just right. One pre-match meal, I undid the tops of the salt and pepper while he wasn't looking. Everyone watched as Roycey sat down, picked up the salt and tipped it upside down over his beans on toast. *Whoosh*. Salt everywhere! The lads were killing themselves, but Roycey didn't see the funny side. He tipped his dinner all over my suit. We nearly came to blows over it. I had to change into a tracksuit, and the manager wasn't happy.

Looking back now, it is hard to imagine a better start for Peter. We were unbeaten in our first eight games of the 2000–01 season, topped the table, and our manager was put in caretaker charge of England for a friendly against Italy in October. It was the game in which David Beckham was handed the captaincy of England. Peter told me, 'Sav, if you were English, I'd give you a cap.'

As a proud Welshman, I didn't quite know what to say, but I took it as a great compliment. The only downer was going straight out of Europe, although the wives and girlfriends did enjoy their trip to Vienna! It was typical Peter to ask the club to put on a plane for families. We were actually drawn against Red Star Belgrade but played the UEFA Cup away tie in Austria because of the political situation. I'm not so sure the wives and girlfriends would have been quite as keen on a trip to Belgrade!

The autumn also saw the beginning of the end for Stan at Leicester. He recovered from his broken leg and even scored in the 2–0 win at Chelsea in September, but he was involved in a bust-up with Trevor in a reserve match and left later that season. We also knew that Lennie would be on his way to Scotland, because his body language showed his heart wasn't in it any more.

Beating Chelsea summed up the start of the season. Martin's leaving had been almost like a death in the family, but Peter breezed in and made us all laugh. I man-marked Gianfranco Zola out of the game that day – it was the first time I'd ever man-marked anyone. I thought, 'Right. I'm not going to let you run away from me.'

A couple of weeks before that, I added a fourth London club to the fans-who-hate-me group: Tottenham, Arsenal, Chelsea and now West Ham. Darren Eadie scored the only goal of the game at Upton Park, and Igor Stimac was sent off for a foul on me. Stimac had a pop at me afterwards, and Harry Redknapp chipped in too. They were just bad losers. Having done a job on Zola against Chelsea, I did exactly the same to Paul Gascoigne when Everton came to Filbert Street the following week. I never left Gazza alone for a minute.

We lost our first League match of the season on 14 October, when Manchester United came to Filbert Street and won 3–0. I was wearing a new pair of Puma boots after signing my first kit deal with them. My legal adviser, Stephen Lownsbrough, arranged it. There wasn't a lot of money involved, but Mum, Dad, Sarah and I were all wearing this Puma stuff. We looked like trolley ladies! The Puma contract was proof that I was in demand and doing well. I was in demand for autographs too. The strangest request came when I was out with Darren and our girlfriends one night. This girl came up to me and said, 'Can you sign these?' She'd taken her knickers off! I couldn't even look at them.

'See that blonde lady over there?' I said to her. 'Go and stick your knickers in her face, and I'll sign them for you.' I never actually thought she was going to do it. Sure enough, this girl walks across the room, goes up to Sarah and sticks her knickers in my girlfriend's face. That's what fans will do. I was laughing, but I don't think Sarah was that amused.

Leicester were definitely not pants on the pitch. After losing to United and Liverpool, we beat Derby, Manchester City and Middlesbrough and drew with Newcastle. The 1–0 win at City was doubly special for me, because I scored the only goal – and I still have the scar on my finger where my old friend Jeff Whitley stood on it. His studs sliced open my ring finger, and the doctor had to stitch it up in sky-blue thread! It was fantastic to play against Jeff, though. It would have been even better if Jim had been in the team. Jeff and I went out in Manchester afterwards. We relived those Wrexham school days when I copied my exams from Jim and the three of us had dreamed of becoming footballers. We'd made the dream come true.

I scored again four games later as we made Rio Ferdinand look a very ordinary player on his £18-million debut for Leeds. We would enjoy some real battles in the future, me and Rio. I nearly lost my balls the next time I hit the back of the net! We were drawing 1–1 with West Ham when I beat Shaka Hislop for the winner. As normal, I reacted instinctively. I raced up the crowd and just launched myself into the air and at a sea of arms. I don't know what I'd have done if they hadn't caught me. I was lying on top of the supporters, and they were grabbing my willy and my nuts. I couldn't get out!

The Christmas party was another fancy-dress do that year. The theme was '70s night, and Darren and I turned up as Batman and Robin. We looked at everyone in their flowery shirts, flared trousers and Afro hairstyles and realised we might have got the wrong end of the stick! I used to drive Darren mad with a habit I've had since childhood. When I have an argument with someone, and I don't like what I'm hearing, I just stick my fingers in my ears and shout very loudly, 'Can't hear you. Can't hear you. Can't hear you.' Or, even more annoyingly, I yell, 'Na na na na na na na,' and shake my head at the same time. I have been known to do it to the odd journalist too!

Sometimes it is hard to pinpoint the moment things change. It can be either the start of everything going right or the start of everything going wrong. At Leicester that season, the FA Cup quarter-final against Wycombe was the beginning of the end, only we didn't realise it at the time. The signs might have been there already. We were thrashed 6–1 by Arsenal at Highbury on Boxing Day and lost to Bradford, Ipswich and Southampton. The only bright point of January was a goalless draw when the Gunners came to our place – and the start of a great FA Cup run.

The year began well for Robbie Savage. I was voted third top football babe! To be honest, I was a little disappointed not to win it. Kirsty Gallacher and Louise Redknapp finished ahead of me, and I looked better than either of those two! I love stuff like that. I sat next to Miss World once. We were judging a Miss Wales competition, and she was getting quite interested, so I had to tell her I was married. She was only human. Of course she fancied me. She had a pulse, didn't she?

My position as the coolest guy in the squad did come under threat in January when Roberto Mancini arrived. Peter had a connection to him through Sven Goran Eriksson, and Robbie wanted to sample life in England. I love my clothes, but so did he. He came in, hair blowing in the wind, and looked like something out of an advert. I'd watched him play. He was at the end of his career, so he wouldn't have the impact he did at Sampdoria, but to play with him was unbelievable. We roomed a couple of times, and I took him out for meals. When he took over as

Manchester City boss, he even mentioned me in his press conference!

Robbie made his debut in the scoreless draw at Arsenal, which will stick in my memory for my stupidity in winding up Gerry Taggart. 'Fuck off,' were my exact words after we traded insults. 'Oops,' was my next thought as Taggs gave me a look that suggested this conversation still had some way to run when we left the pitch.

He clipped me round the ear and said, 'I'll see you at half-time.' Taggs was seriously hard and seemed to be in the mood to let his fists do the talking. I did what anyone in my place would have done and said sorry – and made sure I was nowhere near him walking down the tunnel!

Having signed my Puma deal that season, I finally plucked up the courage to wear a pair of silver boots for the first time. They finished up in the bin! Soaking one of them in blood for ninety minutes is not recommended. It was the fourth round of the FA Cup and a trip to my favourite club, Aston Villa. By favourite, I mean that we never thought we were going to lose to Villa, and at Leicester and Birmingham I never did. As usual, our Midlands rivals did the team talk for us. John Gregory wasn't very happy about the standard of food at the training ground, and when he complained chairman Doug Ellis replied, 'I bet they're eating beans on toast over at Leicester.'

The papers had a ball. 'Villa put the wind up Foxes' and 'Leicester meanz business': all the usual knockabout stuff but great for headlines. A year earlier, Gregory had labelled us boring before we beat them in the semi-final of the League Cup, and now Ellis was criticising what we ate. Result: 2–1 to Leicester. I played the game after spending the previous night at Leicester Royal Infirmary's A & E department having a huge piece of cut glass removed from my foot. As soon as the Cup tie started, the wound burst open and blood began seeping into the boot. I poured blood out of it afterwards! So how had I cut myself? I blame Sarah, of course. She wasn't there, and that was half the problem.

We were living in a fantastic converted barn in a place called Hungerton by then. My new contract had resulted in a house move. I loved that barn. It cost us £505,000, and we spent £170,000 on it. Tuffy's father-in-law put in a swimming pool, and we had a golf tee with a green. I wish I had that house today. We sold it for £1.2 million when I was at Birmingham, one of the few occasions when I made money on a house sale! Like most old barns, it had a flagstone floor. So if you dropped a glass, it shattered into a thousand pieces.

Sarah was away for the weekend, and I broke a glass. I didn't have a clue where the dustpan and brush were kept to clear away the mess, and I was in the habit of walking round the house barefoot. There was a sharp pain, and I looked down to see a splinter of glass embedded in my foot. I phoned the physio and headed straight to the hospital. They gave me a local anaesthetic to prise out the glass, and I couldn't even put my foot down. The manager was informed, and I don't think he was too happy, but I told him I could play, even though my foot was squelching in blood by the end.

We then beat Bristol City 3–0 to set us up for the quarter-final against Wycombe. We were a Premier League side against a Second Division club. They didn't stand a chance, everyone said. We were going to stroll it. Wycombe didn't even have enough players. They'd signed a striker through the Internet. No one had ever heard of Roy Essandoh. Well, Roy effing Essandoh became one of the greatest FA Cup stories in history as he scored the winner that helped dump us 2–1 out of the competition. The unknown cyberman had his 15 minutes of fame at our expense. I wonder what he is doing now? Wycombe signed him on a two-week contract!

There was still no excuse for what happened, though. They scored first through Paul McCarthy, and Muzzy equalised in the second half. I had a running battle with Steve Brown, who should have been sent off when he went through me. He was booked, and then Steve Bennett did show him the red card when he took his shirt off to celebrate Essandoh's winner.

I shouldn't have been playing that day. I had a 50 per cent tear on my cartilage. On the Friday in training I had landed on my knee and heard a crack. I couldn't straighten it. I panicked and went to see one of the physios. He looked at my knee. 'You'll be all right,' he said.

'Something's gone,' I told him. My knee was swelling up by this time. The physio tested my knee, and I couldn't feel any pain, so he said I was fit to play. Just before kick-off, I knelt down and it locked again. 'I can't play,' I said.

'You'll be fine,' I was told. I came off injured five minutes into the second half. I've always been a quick healer, and I was back after four games, which was amazing.

Even in the treatment room, you could feel the atmosphere change at the training ground. Losing to Wycombe was the start of the rot. Dress it up any way you want, but the quality of the players was not the same. Peter was everybody's mate, so he didn't always seem like the gaffer. We reacted really badly to the Wycombe defeat. We lost eight in a row and luckily beat Tottenham, or we'd have recorded nine successive defeats and been the worst Premier League side in history. At one point that season, we had been top. We finished 13th.

There was still time for some excitement in the never-dull world of Robbie Savage, though. We played Derby, who loved to hate me at the best of times. I nearly scored the goal of the season with a bicycle kick that missed the post by a gnat's whisker. If it had gone in, it would still be shown today. Deon Burton was sent off for butting me, and Jim Smith accused me of making a meal of things. Me and Villa, me and Manchester United, me and Derby: there were clubs where things always seemed to happen.

As the season drew to a close, there was a lot of speculation about my future again. Real Betis were supposed to be interested, and I told my agent I wanted to go to Spain. I would have loved to have played abroad. I could see that the Leicester players were not good enough; the team spirit was not good enough. Next season would be all about being selfish.

The summer of 2001 saw the arrival of Ian Walker, Dennis Wise and Jamie Scowcroft, another £7 million gone just like that. We went away again in pre-season, and Peter tried his hardest to keep us happy and bubbling. Matt Jones gave us our biggest laugh. Matty played for Wales too and had joined us from Leeds. Peter rang me up and asked me about him, and I said, 'Buy him.' Injury ended his career early. I saw him on TV later, and he was saying good things about John Toshack at Wales. I thought he owed me and felt betrayed, but now I'm a TV pundit myself I realise that you have to say it how you think it is, even if it does upset mates sometimes. Once, when we were in Magaluf, we were playing a game called 'Names of . . . '. Someone picked a theme – say, dogs – and everyone had to think of a breed of dog in turn. So, we chose famous houses.

'Buckingham Palace.'

'Chatsworth.'

'Detached,' said Matt. It was hilarious.

The start of the season was no laughing matter at all. We picked up where we had left off. As I've said, the board panicked when they threw money at Peter and at players. They panicked again when they sacked Peter just eight games into that season. He was the first Premier League boss to be shown the door, and I was gutted for him. I think he should have been given more time.

It was a disastrous start, though. We were thrashed 5–0 by Bolton at home, and then Arsenal beat us 4–0. Dennis Wise and Patrick Vieira were sent off that day. It was almost a relief to head off on Wales duty, except that I ended up giving Mark Aizlewood a mouthful after he criticised us for losing to Norway. Back at Leicester, I was finding myself at the centre of more controversy. We played Ipswich and Derby, and I was accused of getting Matteo Sereni sent off.

Not guilty! Sereni got the ball, and he barged me out of the way. George Burley was ranting and raving at me, and I told him to, er, get lost. He called me a cheating bastard. I think Sereni won the appeal against his red card, but it wasn't my fault he was sent off in the first place. The game at Derby, which we won 3–2, was even more heated, if that's possible. I ran into the box, and Danny Higginbotham brought me down. It was a penalty. I jumped up, but Craig Burley – George's nephew – came over and was giving it the big one. I don't really remember Craig playing that much. He chased me down to the corner flag to grab me around the throat. It was because I was Robbie Savage. 'Wait until you get in the tunnel,' Burley warned.

Taggs and Elliott said they would go in first. I was watching the tunnel sway from side to side! I think the police went in to sort it out. As I climbed onto the bus, the fans were spitting and shouting. I was sitting there giving them V-signs. Colin Todd was assistant manager of Derby at the time, and he was getting involved in the shouting and yelling too. I know now that he was one of the best players ever to play for County, and his son, Andy, is one of my best friends. But, at the time, I was thinking, 'Who is this guy?' As we drove away in the coach, Peter Taylor's daughter rang him and was singing 'There's only one Robbie Savage' down the phone.

The following match, we played Middlesbrough at home, and when Matt Jones scored he faked a dive as a celebration. Wisey and I lifted up our shirts, and underneath we were wearing T-shirts with merit marks for diving. The results were crap, but our spirit was still intact at that stage, and we all believed we would turn the corner. Instead, the end came at Charlton in September. We lost 2–0, and Junior Lewis was sent off. Peter was distraught. He'd spent all that money on players, and we felt it was too soon for him to go.

A few of the senior players met the chairman and asked him to give Peter another chance. I think he could have turned it round. Peter can look back at his career with pride, and I enjoyed working for him. He perhaps didn't spend his money wisely, but his man-management was great. The hangover from losing to Wycombe never went away, and he paid the price for it. We went straight into an international break, and Dave Bassett was appointed, with Micky Adams his deputy. I wasn't happy with the choice, and I was very disappointed with Bassett as a manager. Leicester were in a downward spiral, and I still don't know why Micky didn't get the job straight away.

12

FLUSHED DOWN THE PAN

In my final season at Leicester, I regularly downed a bottle of wine in my hotel room on a Friday night before a game. Either that or I'd get bollixed with the Thursday Night Gang instead. Believe it or not, I was knocking back the booze because I thought it would be unlucky if I didn't. Footballers are well known for having crazy superstitions, but going out and pouring alcohol down your throat is not one you hear about too often. It was even more surprising in my case, because I have only ever been an occasional drinker; I'd much rather have a cup of tea!

Looking back, I don't know how I managed it. Apart from the damage it was doing to my body, I was also breaking club rules. We weren't allowed to drink for 48 hours before a game, so the decision to go out for dinner with friends every Thursday night would have been fine if I'd stuck to water. I drank wine like water instead. Sneaking a bottle into my overnight bag was even worse. What was I doing?

I was playing out of my skin, that's what I was doing, but Leicester, a club I loved, was falling apart all around me. We had three managers in one season – Peter Taylor, Dave Bassett and Micky Adams – on the way to relegation. I had a well-publicised feud with Dennis Wise and took the most expensive dump in history, and it was at Leicester that I started my impressive collection of yellow cards. Up until then, I'd never even been suspended. It's amazing to think that now. Everything that could go wrong went wrong that season, apart from my performances on the pitch. And I was winning man of the match every week, because . . .

I convinced myself it was because of the alcohol. But it had to be lots of alcohol, and it had to be before a game. The Thursday Night Gang started as a regular meal out with our friends Tuffy and his wife, Nicky, and another couple, Danny and Claire Gallacher. We'd go to San Carlo in Leicester and enjoy our Italian. One Thursday, I thought, 'So what, I'll have a glass of wine.'

One glass became a lot more glasses. The six of us would regularly go through eight bottles of wine. We didn't need to book a table. We just turned up, and it was waiting for us. It got to the stage where every Thursday night I was bollixed. I couldn't do it now! Tuffy used to struggle to make it into work the next morning, and he couldn't believe I could get up and train, but I was fine. Sometimes, we'd get a bit lairy. I remember pouring vodka into Claire's eye once. An American woman came into the restaurant and reported me to the club and said I was pissed. I'm not sure that I was on that occasion. The funny thing was that I was playing out of my skin. So I thought, 'Well, I'm not going to change.'

It got to the stage where I was drinking on a Friday night. I'd travel to away games with a secret bottle of wine in my overnight bag. The Thursday Night Gang didn't stop until I left Leicester. I was breaking the rules for a crazy superstition. This wasn't about drinking. It was about me thinking that if I didn't drink I would play badly. How stupid can you be?

It was a stupid season from beginning to end. As usual, it started with a training camp in Spain, which is where I met Dennis Wise properly for the first time. I'd played against him a few times. I loved playing against him. He was a smaller version of me! When I tried to nail him, he just used to laugh at me. I learned a few tricks from him too. He was underrated as a player, and he was a great captain. We took to each other straight away. We were so friendly that I met his agent, Eric Hall, and finished up on *Blankety Blank*!

'Lily Savage meets Lily Savage' was how it was billed. I wish now I'd never got involved. It was really cheesy. What on earth was I thinking? I should have said no. I never set out to do anything like that, and from the first moment I regretted it. They say that all press is good press, but I'm not too sure with that one. But it did show how matey I was with Wisey.

By Christmas, Wisey and I weren't talking. It really blew up on a night out at Undecided nightclub in Leicester. We had cancelled the secret Santa, which is where you pull one name out of a hat and buy a present for that player anonymously. Suddenly, Wisey was up on the stage and on the mic. 'I've bought Sav something after all,' he announced. It was a vibrator. Covering it was a mini Leicester strip with 'Sav 8' on it and a wig. 'To the only prick in a Leicester shirt.'

The lads were lapping it up, but I thought it was out of order. Below the belt. Wise was Bassett's good friend and favourite, but I wasn't going to take that from him. I looked round and spotted dessert: chocolate fudge cake. I spread the chocolate all over my face as though it was poo. 'That's what you look like when you come out of the manager's office,' I said.

We didn't speak at all. I told Bassett I wanted to leave. The papers got hold of the story, and we had to say it had all been a bit of banter. It wasn't, although a lot of the lads found it funny. We trained together, and we played together, but we weren't talking. The next and last conversation was about four months later. Wisey came into the canteen and sat down. I was eating a Jaffa cake. 'Who's going to give me a Jaffa cake?' he asked. Not me. I ignored him. We never spoke again, and we haven't spoken since. Do I hate Dennis Wise? No. I actually got on with him. I thought he was a lovely bloke, and he had a beautiful wife and lovely kid. I regret it happened. If there is no harmony in the dressing-room, it makes life hard. The guy is a legend for what he has done in football, and it was a shame it ended the way it did.

As I've said, I wasn't happy with the appointment of Bassett at all. Micky came in from Brighton, where he'd been doing very well, and I'm sure he thought he would be in charge of team affairs. Instead he had to answer to 'Harry', as Dave was known, and there weren't many signs that Bassett would stop us from going down. Morale got worse and worse. I think Micky began to lose his drive, as he was undermined. Bassett's first game was a 2–0 defeat at Chelsea, and his first match at home was against Liverpool.

We were thumped 4–1, and I added the name of Phil Thompson to my never-ending list of wind-up victims. Thompson was in caretaker charge of Liverpool while Gérard Houllier was recovering from surgery.

I smashed somebody across the touchline. Phil was really angry and was yelling at me, so I brought my hand up to my face and gestured: Big Nose. I know. There's me with the biggest nose in football pointing out to a legend like Phil Thompson that his hooter might be a bit on the large side! Phil wasn't too happy, and Bassett told me to go and apologise. I walked up to Phil and said, 'Sorry, I didn't mean to do that.'

Of course I did! As usual, my bust-up with Phil came back to haunt me. A few years later, I was a Sky pundit when Blackburn were playing Liverpool. By that time, everyone knew about my rift with John Toshack. I looked at the two chairs. One had the initials 'RS' on it, and the other had 'JT'. Great. Simply great. I was going to be a Sky guest with the man who had effectively ended my Wales career. I was still thinking about Toshack when the door opened and in walked Phil Thompson. 'I believe I'm known as Big Nose,' he said.

Here we go again. Richard Keys and Phil Thompson started trying to take the mickey out of me. I've done a lot of television and radio since then, and I hope that people realise I'm more than just a cheeky chappie. But that day they thought they could undermine me. 'Remind me what Phil has won,' Keys said.

I know. Five titles, three European Cups and on and on. Fair play. 'Yes, Richard,' I replied. 'But did Phil ever earn £25,000 a week?' Everyone laughed, and from then on it was much easier. So many people look at me and don't see beyond the hair, the teeth, the fake tan, the model wife, the Merc, the big house . . . I'm being tongue-in-cheek, but it's a fact that I am stereotyped by my looks and image. I would challenge anyone when it comes to knowledge of football. I watch every game I can, and I am even doing my coaching badges. I wouldn't have played for so many years at the top level without taking football seriously. It just so happens I do like having a laugh too!

There wasn't a whole lot of laughing going on at Leicester. We beat Sunderland 1–0 at home in November and saw Villa on the fixture list in December and breathed a sigh of relief! Thank God for that jinx we had over them. Ade Akinbiyi and Jamie Scowcroft scored the goals in a 2–0 win at Villa Park on 1 December. Our next Premier League victory was against Blackburn at the end of March, 17 games later. Told you it was bad.

On my birthday in October, Sarah gave me a lovely jumper and jeans. I made the mistake of wearing them to training. I have a feeling that Wisey was behind it, but when I went to change out of my kit one arm had been cut off the jumper and the legs of the jeans were in ribbons. I knew Sarah would be upset, so I bought replacements. I didn't find that funny, but I couldn't help but laugh a couple of days later when my Porsche had a puncture on the M1. I stood there wondering what to do next, and this lorry driver pulled onto the hard shoulder, got out of his cab and came walking towards me. 'Result,' I thought.

The driver thrust this piece of paper at me and muttered, 'Can you sign that, please?'

'Sure,' I replied, thinking a tyre change for an autograph was a pretty decent swap.

'Thanks.' The guy walked back to his cab with his signed piece of paper, climbed in and drove off! As I stood there, all these Derby fans were driving by, giving me V-signs and hooting their horns.

Leicester's problems were far worse than a flat tyre. Bassett wasn't impressing me much either. He didn't seem to know how to handle me. Bolton just after Christmas was a classic example. The match finished 2–2, but that doesn't begin to tell the story. Paul Warhurst and Dean Holdsworth were sent off by Mike Riley – both for tackles on me. The home fans were baying for blood. The board went up after 23 minutes. Twenty-three bloody minutes. I looked round and thought, 'That's me. I'm being subbed.'

What was Bassett playing at? If the manager had known me then he would have realised I wouldn't have got myself sent off. I had never even been suspended before that season, although I did manage to collect 15 yellow cards to finish as the most booked player in the Premier League. He didn't think I could handle it. I was distraught. 'What the hell are you doing, Bassett?' I thought. 'Serves you right if we lose.' Muzzy Izzet replaced me – and was sent off for two bookings.

The games were flashing by with no sign that we were close to stopping the rot. It was a relief to head off to the Millennium Stadium in March for a friendly against mighty Argentina. Further proof that my wine-drinking was working! I was voted man of the match, and I nailed a certain Juan Verón in the opening minutes.

Back in Leicester, we carried on losing. I also had a taste of what it would be like to run a football club! When I first moved into the area and made friends with Tuffy, some of his friends turned nasty. There were snide remarks, and Tuffy felt he couldn't stay with his Sunday League club. So we set one up ourselves. It was called Midshire Old Boys. I was chairman and forked out £500 in pitch fees, and he was manager. I really enjoyed it and would watch on a Sunday morning.

Some people were suggesting that Leicester were performing like a Sunday side too. By April, we were relegated, and Micky finally took over as manager. His first match was a testimonial against Martin O'Neill's Celtic, which brought home to all of us how dramatically things had changed since Martin's departure.

I don't think Micky was too happy at being kept waiting for the job. In one day, we went from holiday camp to boot camp. We were so unfit. He started by introducing double sessions straight away. We were going down as the fittest relegated team in the country. All we did was run. And run. And then we did some more running. We might have been one of the worst teams in Premier League history, but we were fit and I had some decent performances. Micky should have been given the opportunity from the start, and we might have had a chance.

You could have a bit of banter with Micky, but neither of us saw the funny side when he told me I was being fined two weeks' wages for using the referee's toilet without permission before a game. Poogate. Jobbiegate. Take your pick. For seven days straight I was headline news – because I'd had the cheek to nip into Graham Poll's room in an emergency dash to the loo.

I don't like Graham Poll. He thinks he is pretty special, and I'm not quite sure why, because all he will be remembered for is making the biggest reffing cock-up in history: three yellow cards in a World Cup. Josip Simunic of Croatia discovered Poll couldn't count when he was booked three times in the Germany 2006 game against Australia. One, two, three . . . *oops*. He was a laughing stock. I think he wanted to be a footballer, so the next best thing was to be a referee. He would give his five-minute interviews and want to be seen, to be noticed. Now he does newspaper columns, a referee who can't add up. One and one yellow card is two. Equals one red. Not difficult to remember.

There have been times when I would have loved to knock out a referee – luckily, only in my dreams and never on the pitch! Having said that, there are good refs. I like Paul Durkin and Dermot Gallagher, although how Dermot missed the tackle that broke my leg when I was with Blackburn, I will never know. One testimonial I played in, Peter Jones was the ref. What a great guy. There was a lot of laughing and joking in the game, and I actually tried to rugby tackle him. It was the greatest feeling ever. Refs these days have power. They have agents, and they think they are personalities. I wish they'd go away, especially Graham Poll. We had history, and he didn't like me. I think he was jealous of the attention I got. At Bolton once, Jay-Jay Okocha kicked the ball out of play, and the main stand stood baying. Even they laughed when he booked me.

I've read Graham Poll's book. I went out to buy it to see what he would say about Jobbiegate. He's had his say, and now I'm having my say. He came to Blackburn the day after a game for some treatment, and I was there. 'How are you?' I said.

'I just hate being in the limelight,' he complained.

'Why do you do press conferences if you hate the limelight? You're always being interviewed.'

No answer. I started talking about the toilet thing, and he said, 'I will be doing a book some day. My book will sell more than yours.'

This is what happened in April 2002 when Aston Villa came to Filbert Street. It had to be Villa, didn't it? The match ended in a 2–2 draw and will probably be remembered by the fans for George Boateng trying to throw Paul Dickov's boot out of the ground in the dying seconds. But it was what happened before the game that concerned me. I was on antibiotics, because of a cut on my leg that wouldn't heal. The medicine gave me the runs. I'd been up all night, and I needed to go again. It was ten minutes before kick-off, and the bell was about to go to signal the teams onto the pitch. I was desperate for the toilet. Both cubicles in the changing-room were occupied. I had the option of shitting myself there and then or running for another toilet. By this time, I was losing the battle to keep everything in, if you know what I mean.

There was no loo in the physio's room, and the opposition dressing-room was out of bounds. What about the ref's room? I often watched reserve games, and as you walked through reception the door to the ref's room would be open for anyone to use the toilet, so I knew there was one in there. I raced into the ref's room. 'I've got to use the toilet,' I shouted as I headed into the cubicle.

Poll was sitting there with his two linesmen. I'd left the door slightly open, and I could see him from where I was sitting. The assessor came in. Poll glanced over to me and turned to the assessor. 'Guess who's in there.' He pointed towards the toilet.

'Haven't got a clue,' said the assessor.

Everyone was laughing. I came charging out of the toilet, because the bell had gone. I went up to the assessor and pretended to wipe my hands down his blazer. He laughed, and I admit I hugged him then. And, no, I hadn't washed my hands, because I was in such a rush. During the game, Poll was laughing and joking about the whole thing. He didn't seem angry or bothered at all about what happened. That night, it was the player of the year dinner, and Micky pulled me to one side. 'What have you done?' he asked.

'What?'

'Graham Poll has made a complaint that you went into his room without permission and used his toilet. We're fining you two weeks' wages.'

'You are joking. You can't do that, Micky.'

The national newspapers broke the story. One of them called it Jobbiegate, and Mum and Dad were able to read that I didn't wash my hands. Next, I had a call from the FA saying that I was being charged with improper conduct. I'd used a toilet in an emergency. This was nothing to do with football. I hadn't elbowed anyone or been accused of breaking someone's leg or spitting. I went for a poo. And there was no choice in the matter. What upset me was the way Leicester immediately said they would fine me, even though they didn't have a clue whether I was guilty or not. I'm sure Micky had nothing to do with it. I appealed, and, in the end, they never received a penny from me.

The FA was still to be £10,000 better off, unfortunately. I'd moved to Birmingham by the time the case came up, and Steve Bruce came with me to the disciplinary tribunal. It was a bit like *Dad's Army*. Poll sat there and looked smug. He came out with a load of old bollocks, but he was their star ref and I knew I would get done. They fined me ten grand. Ten grand to use the toilet. It was unbelievable.

Leicester were flushed down the pan too. Just two years earlier, we'd won the Worthington Cup and been an established and respected Premier League club. The group was tight and hungry for success rather than money. By the time I left, Leicester had signed players on big wages who didn't care about the team or the city. There were Bentleys and Ferraris in the car park. The club had changed, and it hadn't changed for the better. It was heartbreaking.

I knew I would be leaving. I was a high earner, and the club had told me that they would sell me. Leicester fans say that I wanted to go, but that's not true. I was an asset to the club, and they could get money for me. I went, and it meant that Muzzy could stay – and he was on huge wages, much higher than me. There was a lot of speculation about my eventual destination. I joined up with Wales for a friendly against Germany and was staying at the Vale of Glamorgan Hotel. I saw Mark Bowen, who was Brucie's number two at Birmingham and Sparky's coach with Wales. 'If you go up, I'll sign for Birmingham,' I joked to Taff, as Bowen was known.

Birmingham were promoted, and they came in for me. The first offer was £1 million and was rejected. In the end, I think Birmingham paid £1.7 million, with the deal going up to £2.5 million based on appearances. I thought it was an absolute bargain.

But before I could start to think about a new club, there was a far more important fixture to fulfil: my wedding! The bride wore white, and the groom wore cream, courtesy of Chris Scotney, who provided my suit. Sarah looked amazing that day – and I wasn't far behind her! I was all in cream: cream suit, cream shoes, cream everything. I felt like the cat who'd got the cream too when I looked at my gorgeous new wife. My brother, Jonathan, and my mate Tuffy were joint best man. The three of us turned to watch Sarah coming up the aisle with her father. There were tears in my eyes. I was marrying such a beautiful woman, and I couldn't believe my luck. I knew from the first moment I saw her that I would be with her for the rest of my life.

There was press there, but we're not talking *Hello* or *OK*. More like the *Birmingham Mail*, because I'd just moved to Birmingham! The marriage took place at St Peter's Church in Heswall on what had to be the hottest day of the year. A vintage Rolls-Royce from the 1920s transported us from the church to Soughton Hall. It was a beautiful car but *so* slow. It took us about half an hour to get to the reception, and all our guests were flying past. Jonathan borrowed the Ferrari and overtook us too.

A week earlier, Sarah and I had been guests at the wedding of Darren and Kellie Eadie. Now, seven days later, I was also a married man, and Mr and Mrs Eadie were there to share it with us. Darren and I had arranged a joint stag do. It was a trip to Magaluf for a whole load of friends and family. The first day, two or three of us were walking along the beach and I was wearing a Rolex watch that was worth about £40,000. This group of Spaniards started following, and we were ready to leg it when we realised Darren and his mates were just behind the Spaniards. It all went off. There was a huge fight, about ten of us each side, with chairs being thrown, the lot. The Spaniards came looking for us at the hotel, but we didn't realise they were there. I went outside with Darren's brother, Colin, and saw them hanging around. I was getting really worried, because there were only two of us, so Colin and I acted as if we were an item and pretended to kiss each other! It worked.

Playing in front of thousands of fans, some who hate my guts, has never bothered me. I like appearing on TV, and I'm comfortable on the radio, but standing up in front of a room full of people at my wedding was one of the most nerve-wracking moments of my life. Sarah wanted everything to be just right, and I think it was. The honeymoon was perfect too. We flew to Dubai. I'm not a great believer in upgrading, but we went business class – it *was* our honeymoon, after all. I spent the seven-hour flight staring at the screen, because I was so petrified. I hate flying.

We stayed at the seven-star Burj Al Arab hotel. What a place. The hotel is in the sea, so the views are incredible. The suite was stunning. The bathrooms were gold-plated, and we had our own butler! The idea was to call him up via the TV so he could run your bath or polish your shoes. Coming from Wrexham, I didn't feel very comfortable with a butler, and Sarah wasn't too familiar with butlers in Heswall either. I could just imagine my mum saying, 'Robert, who do you think you are?'

So our butler had an easy time, because Sarah and I were too embarrassed to ring the bell. All we did was sunbathe for two weeks. Well, not quite all! It was our honeymoon. We went out for dinner together at night and had the most fantastic time. The place was so big we'd go by golf buggy to the restaurants. I think Sarah was quite relieved it worked out so romantically. I'd spent our first Valentine's Day evening watching curling on the TV. There she was, ready for a night of passion, and I announced, 'I'm just staying up for a bit. I must watch this ladies' rubber.'

It was the closest Sarah came to a rubber all night! My wife has had to put up with a hell of a lot from me. I'm not easy to live with, surprising though that may sound! The day she became Mrs Savage was the happiest of my life. That summer flew past. I was joining a new club, starting on a new adventure and Sarah was by my side. Brilliant!

13

BIG NOSE TO BLUENOSE

Ask David Sullivan to name his two favourite Birmingham players and one of them would probably be me. Christophe Dugarry and me. The French World Cup winner had such an impact that he came second in the player of the year awards. The winner? Have a guess! I am not claiming I single-handedly kept Birmingham in the Premier League in the 2002–03 season, but I did play a major, major part. Bluenoses don't like me any more, because of the way I left, and I do regret the way it happened. But that first season I was the main man. Fact.

There were doubts when I arrived. Not from me. I have always moved for the right reasons and not for money, which a lot of people find hard to believe. But Birmingham fans weren't exactly jumping up and down at my arrival. I had a reputation as a nuisance, a big mouth, maybe a liability. The doubts and fears were summed up by a local radio commentator in the city called Tom Ross. I respect him greatly now and regard him as a friend. He's also a great radio presenter. The only problem is no one can find his station – it's next to Radio Luxembourg! Tom was Mr Bluenose, the man who interviewed all the Birmingham players. 'What are you signing that wanker for? He'll cause nothing but problems,' Tom warned Steve Bruce, my hero, the man who had just bought me.

'I don't like you, and I think you'll be a waste of space,' Tom said to me when he eventually met me.

'Fine,' I replied. 'I'm going to change your opinion of me.'

We laugh about it now, but I did change his opinion of me. Birmingham were back in the top flight after sixteen years, and what they needed was players who could keep them there: honest, hard-working and, in my case, desperate not to have two relegations in a row on my record. I signed a three-year contract worth approximately £17,000 a week basic and £400,000 up front in image rights. It worked out at about £20,000 a week. When I was at Manchester United, I had wanted to buy Brucie's Golf. When I joined Birmingham, I had a Ferrari, and Brucie took one look at it and said, 'You haven't changed then, son.'

Not when it came to cars. After my modest start at United and Crewe, I went through cars like you wouldn't believe. At Leicester, I had three Porsches, a red, a blue and a yellow Ferrari, three Mercs and a BMW. The blue Ferrari came to a sad end – cousin Matt blew the valves on it. He asked to take it for a run and put his foot down – in first gear. He'd driven about 80 yards from the house when smoke started to billow from the engine. I had just agreed to sell it, and when the guy came to collect it he asked, 'What have you done to the car?'

'It was fine when I last drove it,' I replied, totally honestly.

I arrived at Birmingham with my yellow Ferrari then had a yellow Lamborghini, two Bentleys, four Range Rovers and an Aston Martin. At Blackburn, I bought a Hummer, another Range Rover, another Lambo, a white Ferrari and a Merc 320. Then there were three more Mercs, a white Lambo soft top and a white Lambo hard top at Derby. What an unbelievable waste of money! I suppose cars are my addiction. When you earn £20,000 a week, writing off £15,000 on a car is nothing. My opinion has changed now.

I don't know what the other lads thought about my yellow Ferrari when I arrived at Birmingham. I was actually quite nervous when I met them for the first time. Hors – Geoff Horsfield – was there. The last time I'd seen him I'd invited him to come and do my patio! Paul Devlin was my roomie, and he made me feel really welcome. Dev and I used to have these wrestling matches that lasted until someone submitted. He's 5 ft 2 in. tall! I know he's not, but that's what I used to say to him. Dev would let me get him first. I had to pin him down. Before one Liverpool game, we were in our hotel room trying to bring each other down, and he got me in a death choke. That was his special move.

The banter was fantastic. It was similar to Leicester at the beginning. There were serious players, like Kenny Cunningham, but we had our jokers too. Keeper Ian Bennett looked like something out of *Planet of the Apes*. Stan Lazaridis was 'Skippy' because he was from Australia. He was all head and shoulders; he didn't have a neck at all.

Nico Vaesen was the other keeper, and we had a fight one day. He couldn't get the ball over the halfway line. His kicking was really awful. 'Nico, try to get the ball over the halfway line,' I yelled at him. He didn't like it. He was 6 ft 4 in. tall. He came over and grabbed me by the throat, so I punched him and butted him, cutting his lip. The gaffer called us in, but I knew I was all right. I was the star player, and nothing was going to happen to me.

Clinton Morrison was a really deep character, and I think he needed to be loved. He was a bigmouth, like me. I got on well with him – apart from once. I had a new mobile phone that he liked, and I said I could get him one. I paid for it, and a few weeks went by without any sight of him paying me. He walked past me one day, and I asked him, quite aggressively, when he was intending to cough up. We were in the canteen, and I ended up diving on him. We were wrestling on this collapsible table, and David Dunn split us up. He thought it was hysterical. I was great friends with Clinton before that, and I was great friends with him afterwards. But I outmuscled him that day – and I never got the money.

So here I was at Birmingham, new club, new start and ready to make a big impression. Unfortunately, I arrived with a hangover: a two-game ban that meant I spent the opening day of the season with the Sky commentary team as we lost 2–0 at Arsenal. I missed the 1–0 defeat at home to Blackburn too. Looking at my disciplinary record over the years, it's amazing to think that I didn't really start picking up bookings until my last year at Leicester. I was given 15 yellow cards and regularly hit that total from then on.

I was booked 91 times in the Premier League, and I'd love to have retired as the most-booked player, but Lee Bowyer and Kevin Davies have overtaken me. I do hold the record, with Sparky, for most yellow cards in a season, so that's something. At Crewe, I had been nicey-nicey, and it took a while for the aggression to come out at Leicester. I was slightly built, but the one thing I didn't have was fear. I'm petrified of flying, and I am a hypochondriac, but I am a freak of nature when it comes to my body and pain. Even when I broke my leg at Blackburn, I was still trying to stand up. I've got skinny little legs, but they can withstand a lot.

What Birmingham needed was to see those skinny little legs in action. I made my debut at Everton, but the first time all the Bluenoses saw me was against Leeds at the end of August. We won 2–1, thanks to Dev and Damien Johnson, and I was man of the match. I was commuting from Leicester, and everyone idolised me: Brian in the car park, Rita in the manager's office, the fans, everyone. People had underrated me before, but now they were recognising what I could do. I was getting compliments about how good I was, but I hadn't changed.

Just a couple of months after a start I could not have imagined, my world came crashing in again. 'Mum's had a stroke.' The sentence wouldn't sink in. I mean, your mother's your mother. She was in hospital back home in Wrexham. I've always hated the fact she smoked, and I hated those cigarettes even more that day. I went straight to Brucie and told him. He was fantastic.

'Go,' he said. 'Don't worry.'

By coincidence, we were staying near Liverpool before the game, so it was a quick drive back to Wrexham. I raced into the hospital, found Mum and gave her the biggest hug in the world. She was affected all down the left side. Her mouth drooped, and she could not move her arm properly. Dad rushed home from abroad, and Jonathan was there too. I went back to Pine Close that night to keep Dad company. And the next day I played. Clinton grabbed a great double to rescue a draw, and I did well. Afterwards, in the dressing-room, Brucie said, 'Well done, Sav. You did great.'

People say that football is a matter of life and death, but football is irrelevant at times like that. I felt so helpless knowing Mum was in hospital. She made a good recovery, but even though she has had a second chance she still smokes. You can't believe it, can you?

Aston Villa. The team I loved to beat. The first Second City derby for years was always going to be a hell of an occasion. This was a match between the princes and the paupers. Villa were the all-stars, and we were the working-class grafters. I wasn't really aware of the hatred between the two sets of supporters until I joined Birmingham.

All I can say is thank you to Olof Mellberg. I really didn't like him, but he did us a massive favour in the run-up to the game by saying he hadn't heard of any of us because we'd just been promoted. Er, Olof, I'm the guy who made Villa's life a misery at Leicester – and played the last five years in the Premier League. Brucie told us to remember those words, and we did. Mellberg was hopeless that night too. I'd been a real jinx to Villa during my years at Leicester, but this was a different situation. It was a battle. That was the only way to describe it. I still don't know what the police were doing playing it at night. St Andrew's was electric. Bluenoses were going mad, and the Villa fans were making a noise too. It has to go down as one of the best atmospheres I have ever played in. And we won 3–0.

The first goal was going to be crucial. Aliou Cissé and I bossed the game, and Clinton scored the opener. I looked around me, and there were fights breaking out everywhere. The second goal will go down in the history books as one of the most bizarre goals ever. Mellberg took a throw-in, and the ball rolled under Peter Enckelman's foot and straight into the net. I still don't know if Enckelman touched it or not, but his reaction suggested that he had done. The goal was given anyway. Then a fan raced onto the pitch and slapped Pete across the face.

The tackles were flying in, and they had a goal disallowed by David Elleray, much to the disgust of Graham Taylor. Hors made sure near the end when he robbed Alpay. The Bluenoses were singing, 'We love you Robbie, because you've got blond hair.' I won't tell you what the Villa fans were singing!

I was Sky's man of the match. It was an incredible night, and it gives me goose-pimples just to think about it again. I was still undefeated against Villa, and the Birmingham supporters fell in love with me. I epitomised what they wanted. I may not have had the best technical ability in the world, but I would give it a go. I was honest and hard-working, and they could relate to that. When they went to work, they could imagine they were like me: a trier and a fighter. Cheers, Olof.

Our next derby match was against West Brom, which was quite tasty too. We had Olivier Tébily sent off near the end and took the lead through a Darren Moore own goal five minutes from time – and Jason Roberts still had time to equalise. I took an elbow from Sean Gregan, and a certain referee 'accidentally' caught me in the face. Only Graham

Poll will know whether it was deliberate or not.

The autumn of 2002 was also important from a Wales point of view. We started our 2004 European Championship qualifiers with a 2–0 win over Finland and then beat Italy at the Millennium Stadium. It was an unbelievable result. Simon Davies and Craig Bellamy scored the goals, and it was as if nothing could go wrong. It was really hard playing for club and country sometimes. For some reason, Birmingham didn't like it. You would have thought there wouldn't be a club v. country issue, with it being Sparky and Brucie. They were good mates from the Manchester United days, so they should have found it easy to talk, but Brucie wasn't happy about Mark Bowen, who was his number two, going to assist Sparky with Wales. Taff turned up for one match and wasn't allowed to do anything. It was all pretty unnecessary.

Wales had a match against Azerbaijan in the November, and it got to the stage where David Sullivan threatened to take FIFA to court if I couldn't play for Birmingham against Fulham on the Sunday. It was a seven-hour flight to Baku, and Sparky wanted us all to report *before* the Sunday fixtures. There were other players involved too – Giggsy was one. In the end, FIFA refused to back Wales and I played against Fulham, picking up my fifth booking, along with a very convenient groin injury. Birmingham didn't want me going anywhere. You could see their point. The players they paid went away and got injured, and they were left to pick up the bill. It was well known that, with winnable games, players would fake injuries. I genuinely can't recall if I was injured or not, but I played in the next League game at Sunderland. The physio told me I was injured, and you don't argue with a physio. Luckily, Wales beat the Azeri 2–0.

Sullivan and his co-owner, David Gold, didn't really impact on me that much. When I was at the point of leaving, Sullivan asked me to see him at his house. I didn't go, and I wish that I had now. He wasn't shy about criticising players, tactics and even the manager, but his heart was in the right place, even if his message was tough to take. Gold would turn up at our Wast Hills base in his Bentley. He also had a plane and once landed at the training ground – and crashed it into a bank. The lads thought it was hilarious once we knew he wasn't injured. Karren Brady was managing director, and I had very little to do with her, thankfully. She visited the training ground occasionally.

The two Davids wouldn't have had much to complain about during the first third of the season, but we went on a disastrous run at the end of November. We beat Fulham, but it was our only win in 12 games. The alarm bells must have been ringing in Brucie's office. It was the end of December when we went to Old Trafford. Diego Forlan and Becks scored the goals, and that was the game when I asked Fergie for Becks's shirt – and he said no. I still feel degraded.

New Year was round the corner, but we needed some help and Brucie didn't have to be told. His January recruitment was spot on, especially Dugarry. Stephen Clemence, Jamie Clapham and Matthew Upson also joined what had become a relegation fight. Clapham was a nicey-nicey player from Ipswich. Upson was a great signing, but you only had to look at Dugarry to see that aura. It was like Robbie Mancini at Leicester. I always tried to be friendly to new players, especially the ones who came from abroad. I knew that if I ever ended up abroad I would want help from someone.

Dugarry was one of the best players I've ever played with, and the impact he made on Birmingham was second only to mine. He was also a real one-off. Christophe was a complete law unto himself. He broke the rules and got away with it. Neil McDiarmid was our physio at Birmingham, and he hated players sitting on the low cupboards against the walls of his room. Christophe would saunter in, sit on the cupboards and drive Neil mad. 'I've won the World Cup,' was Dugarry's answer to everything.

'I don't care,' Neil would reply. 'No one sits on my cupboards, not even a World Cup winner.'

Christophe was truly immense and slightly better than me. Only slightly. I went out to dinner with him and his father once. He didn't say much, but I think he appreciated what I was trying to do. This story is typical Christophe: we had to do a run the following pre-season in a certain time, and Dugarry set off at a jog. He never changed pace. We all finished in 11 minutes, and he sauntered round in 25 minutes. Honest to God, he never broke a sweat. We were giving him some stick, and he shrugged those super-cool French shoulders. 'I am a footballer; give me the football. I've won the World Cup.' That was all he said: 'I've won the World Cup.' But he was Dugarry, and we all loved him.

There are two reasons why Birmingham stayed up that season: Christophe and me. Dugarry, Clemence and Clapham all made their debuts at home to Arsenal in January – and we lost 4–0! There was a power cut that delayed the game for 25 minutes. They were dark days all round. We lost to Manchester United, Leeds and Arsenal, drew with Blackburn and then suffered more defeats – against Bolton, United again and Chelsea. Upson made his debut against Bolton. It was my first trip back since that infamous clash when I'd been hauled off early following the red cards to Dean Holdsworth and Paul Warhurst. It wasn't a triumphant return. Ian Bennett had a total nightmare, and we lost 4–2. I was screaming at him. He threw two in, and the pressure was beginning to mount.

There was one bright spot. I was going to be a dad. When Sarah broke the news to me, I couldn't believe it. I wanted a little boy, but we decided not to have a scan and to keep it a surprise. My life was pretty perfect. I felt invincible. The end of February was the turning point to the season too. We won seven out of nine games in the Premier League and, just for good measure, made it nine without defeat for Wales in a 2–2 friendly against Bosnia.

Beating Liverpool gave us the kick-start we needed. We won 2–1, and I was man of the match. I also displayed my amazing ability to embarrass myself. We were in the tunnel waiting to run onto the pitch, and I was having a bit of a laugh with my old Crewe mate Danny Murphy. As I started to run, I tripped coming out of the tunnel! Murph was killing himself laughing.

After Liverpool: Villa again. Three points guaranteed. Unbelievably, given the scenes in the first derby, this was *another* night kick-off. Both sets of fans behaved diabolically too. It was so emotionally charged. We went there buoyant from the win against Liverpool. Skippy headed in Jeff Kenna's cross at the back post, and Hors made sure. That doesn't begin to tell the story, though. Dublin was sent off for headbutting me, Joey Gudjonsson went for a two-footed tackle on Upson, and a couple of fans ran onto the pitch – and one approached me. Peter Enckelman in the Villa goal couldn't handle it. The second goal was the keeper's ball, but Peter hesitated and Hors tapped it into an empty net. People went mad up in the sponsors' box. I was wondering whether I'd get out of there alive. Mark Halsey was the ref that night, and I bet he's never forgotten it.

I'm not quite sure why Dion has it in for me. I played up front with him at Manchester United, and we were fine then. It is widely known now that he doesn't like me at all. Maybe he holds a grudge because I am more popular than him in his own town of Leicester. We've had similar careers: broken necks, broken legs. He was a decent player, though not a world beater, and the same could be said for me. I respected what he did. I'm very pleased I saw the tackle coming that day. It was a red-card offence by itself. 'Fucking wanker!' I yelled at him. He walked over and butted me.

'Prick,' was his response.

Look at the footage. I didn't do anything wrong. Dublin's tackle was appalling, and he butted me. Not the other way round. Dublin had a bad disciplinary record. He was sent off quite a few times. Everybody has a dirty tackle in them. What really annoyed me was that afterwards everyone presumed Dublin had lost it because I'd made a racist comment. He wouldn't have done it otherwise, would he? I am grateful that Dublin came out straight away to knock that one on the head, but it saddens me that he holds a grudge. If he met me and still thought I was a wanker, fair enough.

Brucie did the right thing and took me off. Coins, lighters, everything was being thrown at me. I thought I was going to be hit and knocked out. We were in the dressing-room for an hour, and we couldn't get out. It was incredible. I was glad I'd told my family to stay away. Heard of us now, Mellberg? We climbed onto the team coach, and the fans were throwing coins at the bus and hurling insults. My middle finger was up to the fans.

'Don't do anything stupid,' had been Brucie's instruction as we left the changing-room. And we were giving them the finger! We drove back to the training ground, and dozens of fans were waiting for us. They were shouting and cheering because we'd done something amazing: we'd done the double over Aston Villa. Villa were the bigger club historically, but we'd beaten them twice. Unbelievable. Villa lost the plot that night. In Birmingham, 50 per cent of the fans love you and want to buy you a drink and 50 per cent hate you and want to kill you. The city centre was a no-go area for weeks after that game. It was one of those fixtures where you thought someone could get killed. I received death threats afterwards.

April was a huge month. We knew that if we could beat Sunderland we would be virtually safe. But I was suspended. I was so nervous that I decided not to watch the match. I went out with the dogs instead. Tai had arrived to join Naz by then. Another boxer. We were living in the country, and Naz looked so sad we thought she needed company. We went to a place near Birmingham to get Tai. This lady brought him out, put him down and he fell over. 'You'll do,' I thought. They say dogs are like their owners, and Tai is definitely like me. Especially the bad breath! If I were a dog, I would be Tai. While I was walking the dogs, Bryan Hughes and Christophe scored the goals in our 2–0 win. We had one foot in the Premier League.

Christophe was on fire as we reeled off four straight wins. He scored five goals in four matches as we made sure of staying up. As I've said, Christophe had such an impact that year that he finished behind me as club player of the year. I won the Midlands Football Writers' Association player of the year too. It's funny how I'm hated by the London-based journalists but the guys who saw me at Leicester and watched that season at Birmingham thought I was worth voting for. I joined a roll of honour that included Paul McGrath, Mark Bosnich, Stan Collymore, Dwight Yorke and Paul Merson. Not bad for a Savage!

But the proudest moment of that season was undoubtedly the arrival of Charlie William Henry Savage, born at Leicester General on 2 May 2003, weighing in at 7 lb 1 oz. Sarah was due to be induced just before our match at Newcastle. Brucie was brilliant. He told me to get up to Tyneside if I felt I could play. Charlie was the wrong way round and getting stressed, so it had to be a Caesarian. I went into the operating theatre with my mask and gloves, and I could see they were panicking. There was only a faint heartbeat inside the mother. Sarah was as brave as hell. They cut her open, and it was amazing as the doctor pulled out this blue baby, not crying. He cut the cord, and Charlie caught his first breath. It was like a miracle. I looked down on the screaming face of my son, and I promised myself that I would try to be as good a father to Charlie as Dad had been to me. Dad has always been there for me. I was always going to be there for Charlie.

Sarah had been in labour for 17 hours, and I'd been up all night. I arrived home at about four in the morning, and Dad drove me to Newcastle so I could have some sleep in the car. I managed a quick kip. I might have been in dreamland after becoming a father, but I had a complete nightmare on the pitch! Not that I cared. What an amazing year: marriage, a move to Birmingham, where I was idolised, staying up, beating Villa, beating Villa again, beating Italy. And to cap it all, I was now a father.

14

TO RUSSIA WITH HEARTBREAK

I have probably watched every adult movie ever made. There's not a lot else to do on Wales duty! Eat, train, watch dodgy X-rated DVDs. Repeat as necessary. I've seen some unbelievable things. It was the only way to while away a little time when intense boredom set in. Lads would knock on each other's doors. 'Have you seen this one?'

'No. What's it like?'

'Unbelievable.'

'Oh, all right then. I'll have a look.'

As a kid, all I thought about was pulling on the red shirt of my country. Playing for the Land Of My Fathers. Even now, I can almost hear the national anthem being sung at full volume by 75,000 passionate Welsh men and women at the Millennium Stadium. I would stand there, close my eyes and think of Taid. I hope Taid looked down at me with pride.

I loved playing for Wales, even though we hadn't qualified for a major finals since 1958. How close we were to the 2004 European Championships, though. How very close. One goal in the second leg of the play-off against Russia. Heartbreaking. It didn't happen, but when you look at how far Wales have fallen since then, you realise that it was a special time to be a Red Dragon. When Bobby Gould quit halfway through that double-header with Italy and Denmark in 1999, the FAW put Mark Hughes and Neville Southall in joint temporary charge, but that was never going to work. By the time we celebrated the opening of the Millennium Stadium with a friendly against Finland, Sparky was our new national coach. A sell-out crowd turned up to see us lose 2–1. It was March 2000, and the match was all the more memorable because Ryan Giggs played a friendly for the first time.

That summed up Sparky. We went from being a pub team to an international team, because he demanded the best hotels, the best food and private chartered planes. He also had that special something when it came to dealing with people like Alex Ferguson. It was widely accepted that Giggsy wasn't available for friendlies, but Sparky changed all that. The Welsh FA have always been concerned with money, but Sparky had his own ideas. When he took over, he fought some battles and won them. He persuaded the FAW to fork out for table tennis and pool tables. He nailed the Vale of Glamorgan as the place we stayed. Yes, it cost them a lot of money, but we were playing to full houses. We'd have the second-biggest attendance in Europe – remember, England didn't have Wembley then.

There was always a social side to playing for Wales. We'd rush down to Cardiff on a Saturday for a night on the town. Everyone would go out, and it was a very important part of international fixtures. We felt like film stars in the Sparky days. It was the only time I can remember when the football team was as popular as the rugby team in Wales. Big-hitters like Brazil, Argentina and Germany played at our brand new stadium. The whole country wanted to watch us.

Saturday night was fun time, and we would usually have free rein on the Sunday too. My roomie would be Paul Jones or John Hartson. John liked the room on the corner, so he could sneak home to see his family in Swansea. He borrowed my Ferrari once to go to his parents' house. When he got back, there was a mark on the car. Harts thought he might have scraped it on a gate post! Luckily, I was able to have it T-Cutted out. Harts has always been very family orientated, and we'd go with him to see his mum and dad and his mates. The Halfway Inn, Swansea, was one of our favourite haunts. He had a mate called Colin, whom we called 'Gammon Head' because his ears looked like a piece of gammon on each side. We could relax there; people left us alone.

Harts loved me as a roomie. He was out one night, and I heard him come back around 3 a.m. I pretended to be asleep, because if he thought you were awake he'd do something like dive on you or switch on the telly or something. So I kept my eyes closed while he ordered a tray of sandwiches. Not a plate but a whole bloody tray. There was a knock on the door. Room service. Sandwiches, cans of pop and crisps. It was like being in a room with the Cookie Monster! *Glug, glug, glug, crunch, crunch.* He ate so noisily – and he cleared that tray of sandwiches. I couldn't pretend to be asleep any longer. 'What are you doing?' I asked him.

'I often have a snack at this time in the morning, Sav.' He said it so seriously as he looked over to me. I started laughing, and so did he. We were in fits. We bounced off each other. He'd keep telling me to stop talking to the press so much!

Craig Bellamy was the best at table tennis, but I was one of the stars of the pool table. Kit Symons and Andy Melville – Bessie – were like the grumpy old men from *The Muppet Show*. They had a really dry sense of humour. Mark Crossley, known as 'Norm', could do great impressions. Chris 'Cookie' Coleman was a massive inspiration. He was a fantastic player, and it was a tragedy that his career ended through injuries from a car crash. Mark Delaney didn't get involved with the nights out that much, and I think that hindered him a little. He was a very good player, but he wouldn't go out for a pint – he'd stay in his room. They were all characters. I don't think Wales have ever had another group of players like that.

It took a while for Sparky's revolution to translate into results on the pitch – which gave pundits like John Toshack plenty of ammunition. We could feel the difference, but the 2002 World Cup qualifying campaign wasn't going well as we lost in Belarus, at home to Poland and at home to Norway. We showed promise with draws in Poland and Ukraine, but Toshack and Mark Aizlewood still had a go.

Before the start of the 2004 Euros, we had three home friendlies. We drew 1–1 against Argentina, 0–0 against the Czech Republic and beat the Germans 1–0. Rob Earnshaw scored the only goal, and Cookie came on as a 90th-minute sub for an emotional farewell, after announcing his retirement through injury. In the summer of 2002, I joined Birmingham, and it is no coincidence that one of my best seasons in a club shirt was also one of my best periods in an international shirt.

The European Championship qualifiers started in Finland with a 2–0 win. John Hartson and Simon Davies scored the goals. For some reason, Mark

Bowen – Taff – was not allowed to join up by Birmingham. Harts and I went for a night out in Helsinki, and we walked into this bar. It was packed with Wales fans. At one point, Big John was doing cartwheels on top of the bar and the fans were singing, 'There's only one Robbie Savage.'

Next on the fixture list was Italy. Smooth, cool Italy. I've got Gennaro Gattuso's shirt from that day, and there isn't a speck of dirt on it. The hard man came on as sub and was subbed 20 minutes later. He didn't have time to get his shirt dirty! Read this line-up: Buffon, Panucci, Zauri, Pirlo, Nesta, Cannavaro, Tommasi, Di Biagio, Del Piero, Montella, Ambrosini. Well, we beat them 2–1. Simon Davies and Craig Bellamy scored the goals, but stand up and take a bow also Paul Jones, Mark Delaney, Gary Speed, Mark Pembridge, Andy Melville, Danny Gabbidon, John Hartson, Ryan Giggs . . . and me.

Poor Sparky didn't stand a chance. The minute the whistle blew, I raced over and jumped on him. The Millennium Stadium was an explosion of noise and colour, apart from some very depressed-looking Italians. Italy, full of super-cool superstars, were leaving Wales with nothing. And I had just seen off one of the hard men of football. What a feeling, what an unbelievable feeling. That was the best ride to a hotel I've experienced. Fans were lying down in the road, and it took us three hours to get through Cardiff. Two Euro 2004 qualifiers played and two Euro 2004 qualifiers won.

Sparky had transformed the Wales set-up when he arrived, and now he was getting his reward. He brought in nutritionist Tony Quaglia – one of my great mates – so the food was spot on. Everything was spot on. Especially the results! Wales had won their first two qualifiers, and the next fixture was the long trip to Azerbaijan. That was the game when I pulled out injured after days of wrangling between club and country over the four-day rule. Luckily, Speedo and Harts did the business for us, and the 100 per cent record stayed intact.

We had a friendly against Bosnia in February 2002, a 2–2 draw, which was the warm-up to the home qualifier against Azerbaijan. We beat them 4–0, but I lasted only 20 minutes. 'Go and make your mark in the first few minutes. The ref won't do anything.' That's what Sparky used to say to me. I did it to Juan Verón in the Argentina game, I did it to Ze Roberto of Brazil, and I did it to this guy in the Azerbaijan side. You knew if you clobbered someone early you'd probably get away with it. My mindset was that I was going out to smash them. The whole team knew what was coming, and nine times out of ten I got away with it. Against Azerbaijan, I ended up being taken to hospital, because I hurt myself too! Bellers, Speedo, Harts and Giggsy scored the goals in front of 72,000 people, and the whole country was on a roll.

Toshack was a big critic even then. Leighton James was another. They had agendas, even though we were doing well, and Sparky was criticised for the way we played. Gary Speed was one of the best players I have ever seen. He and Giggsy were modern-day professionals, but they were getting stick. We were being hammered even though we were winning. Sparky was my hero growing up and one of the best players to pull on a Wales shirt, and I didn't like it.

There was nothing wrong in the camp. It was a case of full speed ahead, especially when Giggsy and I got an offer we couldn't refuse: to jump into the back of a police car! Giggsy and I have always got on very well. He could relax with me, and I could always make him laugh. Quags, our nutritionist, asked if anyone fancied a ride in a cop car, as one of his pals was a policeman. Giggsy and I were well into cars, so we accepted the offer. We jumped in and went screaming down the M4 from Cardiff to Swansea at 155 mph. It was four in the afternoon, so quite busy, and we whizzed past everyone, sirens blaring. Giggsy, about the best player the Premier League's ever seen, racing down the motorway! I turned to him and said, 'Can you imagine Fergie ringing you now and you saying, "I'm in the back of a police car with Robbie Savage, and we're going 150 mph"?'

Wales were top of the group, with four wins out of four, when we flew to Belgrade in August 2003. I wasn't myself the day we lost 1–0 to Serbia, and I know why: for the first and last time in my career, I went out onto the pitch determined not to be booked. The next fixture was Italy in Milan, and I was desperate not to be suspended. But I am what I am, and by trying to change my game I didn't give Wales what they needed. Eddie Niedzwiecki, Sparky's right-hand man with Wales and then Blackburn, came up to me afterwards to ask what was wrong. That's how obvious it was.

September 2003 and Wales were off to the San Siro, hoping to do the double over Italy. I have a shirt from that game too. Like Gattuso's shirt, it doesn't have a speck of dirt on it – but for different reasons. In Cardiff, I saw off Gattuso so quickly he didn't have time to muddy his shirt. In Milan, I claimed Alessandro Nesta's shirt, and the classy defender never broke sweat! I had looked forward to this trip so much, playing at the San Siro, and the game was shown live on the BBC. But we let ourselves down that day.

Travelling to Italy, we were full of confidence and determined to bounce back from the defeat in Serbia. It was one of those trips when Sarah came too. Can't imagine what attracted her to the fashion capital of Milan! She flew over with Dad and a friend. The San Siro is a beautiful, daunting, mesmerising place. It was also incredibly hostile. The Wales supporters, including my family, were put underneath the Italy fans, who threw bottles of wee at them. It was disgusting. They were getting drenched in a shower of pee. At half-time, it was 0–0 and Giggsy hit the post. Could we pull it off? No. Pippo Inzaghi scored a fabulous hat-trick, and we were totally outplayed. I was also booked, which meant I would miss the Finland game a few days later.

We flew home still convinced we could top the group. We'd won in Helsinki, so there was no reason we couldn't beat the Finns in Cardiff. I stayed with the squad, even though I wouldn't be playing. Sparky gave us free time on the Saturday night and the Sunday. 'Can we go out?' asked Gary Speed.

'You can go out if you want,' replied Sparky. 'I know you will make the right decision.' The right decision, clearly, was to stay in. Sparky was being very clever. We all loved and respected him so much that's what we did – the families came round to the hotel instead. Killing time was always a problem. You can see why people don't want to be called up for international football if they're not going to play. Sleep, eat, train, adult movies. It wasn't all glamour! I liked carpet bowls too. Dai Williams, one of the kit men, brought them in, and a few of us would play in one of the banqueting suites at the Vale. I've played carpet bowls all over the world. I introduced it at Blackburn too when I moved there. It was just something to keep you occupied.

Finland left Wales with a point after a 1–1 draw in a match where Jason Koumas was sent off. I think Jason will look back at his career and wonder what could have been. He had so much talent, so much ability, and he could have played for one of the really big clubs if he'd done things differently. He used to pull out of squads left, right and centre – and for strange reasons. Not beating Finland meant the final qualifying game of the group was absolutely vital. And I was injured! I hurt my Achilles playing for Birmingham and missed three or four League games just as Wales were due to play Serbia. We lost 3–2, which meant a play-off to qualify for the Euro 2004 finals in Portugal.

Russia were drawn out of the hat. Moscow in November. This game was massive. There was no expense spared. We flew by private jet to Moscow, and we stayed at the Kempinski Hotel near the Kremlin. I don't think the FAW were too happy. They would have worried about the cost. We did the usual things when we arrived – walked round Red Square, bought Russian hats – but we were not there as tourists. We were there to make history. And coming away with a 0–0 draw from Moscow put us within touching distance of qualifying. I'd like to say the whole country was behind us, but there were still some negative voices. I couldn't believe it.

Four days after the first leg, we played the Russians in Cardiff. They had tried every trick in the book to make sure Giggsy wasn't playing. They wanted him banned for a challenge in the Moscow game and took the case to UEFA. They didn't fancy the thought of one of the best players in the world being on the field. We didn't know it at the time, but one of their squad had failed a drugs test, so there might have been other players on performance-enhancing drugs in that match. What a cheek.

Giggsy played, but Russia beat us 1–0, and that was possibly the worst I've ever felt after a game. The lads felt so sorry for Sparky. He walked into the dressing-room, and he was so humble. He thanked us for what we'd done. It made us feel even worse. All the families were waiting for us, but it wasn't like Leicester after the League Cup final. There was no noise, no party, no beer. We threw it away. We'd made a perfect four-out-of-four start, and then we'd underperformed.

I wonder what the Welsh FA thought? I always felt that some of the councillors regarded the trips as a chance for a jolly. I annoyed some of them one day when I asked them whether they cared if Wales ever qualified for a major finals. Maybe that's being a bit harsh, but I suspect they weren't that sad when Sparky went to Blackburn and they could trim the budget again.

Looking back now, the irony is I would have missed the European Championships anyway with a broken neck.

15

PAIN IN THE NECK

I played football for a month with a broken neck – and spent an afternoon on a bucking bronco machine. I was a nudge away from death. Even now, I wake up in a cold sweat at night thinking how close I came to being paralysed or worse, remembering how the physio manipulated my neck every day because no one realised. He'd turn my head until my neck clicked then turn it the other way. No wonder I still get panic attacks. There is a four-inch scar at the front of my neck where the neurosurgeon inserted a section of bone from my hip. Instead of spending the summer of 2004 on holiday, I was flat on my back in intensive care.

It happened at Charlton on 17 April, just as our brilliant season was petering out. With eight games to go, we were in sixth place in the Premier League. We lost three and drew five and still finished tenth. But I was more concerned with my own health by then. Some people say I've always been a pain in the neck! But maybe I should have been a bit more of a pest and insisted on a scan a little earlier. I fell on my head in the 1–1 draw against Charlton and felt this electric current through my arms. It was a horrible feeling. I went to see the doc and the physio.

I didn't go for a scan and just had my neck manipulated every day. But I had pain in my arms, and it got to the stage where I couldn't sit comfortably. I also had pain in my nerve endings, a bit like when a tooth needs filling and you drink something very hot or cold. This is where I have to thank my lucky stars. We had an end-of-season friendly at Cardiff, and in the warm-up we were playing keep-ball. I went to collect a ball from Damien Johnson, bent down and slid to the ground. I couldn't feel my body from the neck down. The feeling came back in my legs, but it was like having no muscles. They were floppy. I recovered then went to play in the first half.

Afterwards, I insisted on a scan. Neurosurgeon Andre Jackowski told me I had a broken neck. It was an impaled disc C5 in my neck. The disc was inserted 60 per cent into the spinal cord. 'It's serious,' he said.

No kidding. He told me that another knock could have killed me. He didn't know what to say when I told him that I had spent an afternoon on one of those bucking bronco machines, which we'd hired for Charlie's first birthday party! Officially, it was diagnosed as an inverted disc – but it was still a broken neck. 'Go home, and don't do anything,' he warned. 'Try not to move.' Don't go on a bucking bronco machine then, Doc?

The following Monday, I was booked in for the operation. They took bone from the hip, and the neurosurgeon promised I would be playing again in two months. I was in intensive care, and eight weeks later I was heading the ball again because of my determination. But one more impact and I could have been a goner.

I could also have been a goner from St Andrew's at the start of that season. Everton came in for me. John Benson was director of football, and he knew about it. I think the clubs even agreed a fee. It got so close that I shook hands with my teammates and said goodbye after a 1–1 draw at Newcastle. There was a hilarious moment in the game when ref Matt Messias accidentally whacked me and knocked me over. It was a bit like Ric Flair versus Randy Savage in the wrestling. Messias's cards dropped out of his pocket, and Alan Shearer picked up a red card and waved it at the ref. Messias had caught me with a forearm smash, and Shearer was killing himself laughing.

I left the ground with Gary Speed because we were heading to Cardiff on Wales duty. The phone rang. It was Steve Bruce, and he was raging. He shouted, 'If you think I'm letting you go, you're mistaken. I'll stick you in the reserves for the rest of your time here.'

I did want to go, but not because I was unhappy at Birmingham. I'd just been player of the season, and the Bluenoses loved me, but Everton were a great club. I am someone who has hogged the limelight, but I have never played for a massive club. When Brucie stopped shouting, I realised I wasn't going anywhere. I suppose I could have sulked, but I decided to get my head down and help Birmingham instead.

Our second season in the Premier League was very different from the relegation fight of the first. Brucie brought in Mikael Forssell on loan from Chelsea, and what a fantastic player he was. The team saw straight away that he was a great lad and a great goal scorer, one of the best strikers I've played with. Mikael scored nineteen goals that season and was one of the main reasons we finished tenth. If you gave him the ball, he'd stick it in the net. He won player of the year that season – just pipping me. Brucie also turned Christophe Dugarry's move into a permanent one and forked out £5.5 million for David Dunn from Blackburn.

Dunny and I clashed when he first arrived, although we became good friends. He had his eye on my number eight shirt for a start! He also fancied taking penalties, but I was designated penalty-taker. All the lads were taking the mick out of me, but I was the big fish and I wanted to take the penalties. We had a bit of a disagreement in a pre-season game, and Brucie stepped in and told me it was my job. The first Premier League match was Tottenham at home. We won 1–0, and the scorer was David Dunn from the penalty spot.

I was brought down in the area to win the penalty. I picked myself up, collected the ball and a thought flashed through my mind. *Let Dunny take the pen to prove there isn't a problem between us.* I handed the ball over, and my teammate duly converted. Afterwards, I stopped for the press guys, thinking quite naturally that my act of generosity was about to be praised.

'Why the fuck didn't you take the pen, Sav?' was how Dave Armitage from the *Daily Star* put it. *What?* 'I had a bet on you as first scorer. I checked with Brucie that you were the designated penalty-taker, and, at 14–1, I thought you were a good shout for a tenner. You've cost me, Sav!'

Apparently, when I went tumbling to the ground the whole press box cheered, as everyone knew about the bet. And when I handed the ball over to Dunny, Dave was on his feet, yelling, 'No. Fucking hell, Sav. Take it yourself!'

By September, the job was mine. We beat Leeds 2–0 at Elland Road thanks to my penalty and a late goal from Mikael. Dunny had stepped up to take it originally and seen his effort saved by Paul Robinson. Luckily, the ref ordered it to be taken again. 'I'm having this,' I thought. I grabbed the ball, put it on the spot and buried it in the bottom corner in the pouring rain. Dunny was the first to jump over me in celebration.

We had an amazing start to that season. The only match we lost out of the first ten was at Manchester United, which I missed with an Achilles problem. At one stage, we were fourth. I was pleased for Brucie. All the lads loved the gaffer. Sometimes, before training, we'd make two circles and have a kickabout. He'd say, 'Premier League winners here. FA Cup winners here.'

'Internationals over here,' was always my comeback.

Brucie has to be one of the best defenders in England not to have played for his country. He also loved a game similar to Simon Says. If he said, 'Do this,' we had to copy him. If he said, 'Do that,' we didn't. He would love catching people out, and then we'd be made to do press-ups or something like that.

Work was fun, with plenty of banter, but as a new father I felt it was time I bought a more serious car. I decided that it wasn't practical to have a Lambo or Ferrari and thought a four-door saloon would be much more sensible. So I bought a Bentley. The chairman, David Gold, had one complete with chauffeur, so I thought I'd get one too, only without the chauffeur. The most memorable thing about it is that I lost about £70,000 on it when I sold it three weeks later! The stick from the other players was amazing. On the first day with the new car, we were driving up to north Wales to see the family and I was speeding. This copper pulled me over, and the look of shock on his face was hysterical. I think he expected a 70 year old to be behind the wheel. He let me off. Another car, another waste of money.

The Achilles injury was proving to be a problem. As I mentioned, I missed Old Trafford and was not fit for a 0–0 draw at home to Chelsea. But the next game was Villa – the club I loved to beat – at home. I was struggling, but it was important I played. What a let-down it was, though, after the excitement of the previous year. It was at midday, and there was no atmosphere at all. We drew 0–0 and moved to fourth, behind

Arsenal, United and Chelsea. I limped my way through it, because I knew it was important for me to play, but sat out a couple of matches after that.

My comeback was at Molineux. We drew 1–1 with Wolves, thanks to Mikael again. I had a real ding-dong with Paul Ince, and he was better. He nailed me – I was too slow. Jamie Clapham should have gone in for a tackle but jumped away from it, and it gave Wolves their goal. I went mad in the dressing-room. 'Shithouse!' I yelled.

'Fuck off!' he shouted back.

Brucie backed me up, and Matt Upson said I was out of order. But that tackle had been 60–40 in Jamie's favour. He was a lovely lad but should have been harder and more determined. Kenny Cunningham was our captain, but I think I should have been, because I was inspirational. Kenny was a good thinker and a good talker, and he organised things well, but I would have loved the job. Our Mondeo-driving skipper also wore the worst gear in the world!

That point at Wolves was the only one we picked up in five games as we suffered our first blip of the season. Blackburn thrashed us 4–0 at home, and that's when I realised that Tugay looked like Worzel Gummidge. He went down, and I booted the ball straight at his head. He said something to me in Turkish, which I'm guessing wasn't the most polite message in the world, so I returned the compliment and told him to get lost. When I moved to Rovers, we lived near each other, and we'd travel to training together. I realised he was a lovely man. One day, we were in the car, and his son was sitting in the back. The little lad said something in Turkish, and Tugay laughed: 'My son has just asked me whether you're that horrible man who kicked the ball at my head at Birmingham.'

I'm the first to admit that I fall out with people on the pitch. But when I get to know them off it, I find out they're really great guys. From Lee Hendrie and Danny Mills to Tugay, the list is endless. Paul Dickov and I used to kick lumps out of each other. Wales beat Scotland 4–0 in a friendly that season, and we had a real battle. Then we became friends later. People who don't know me hate me. That's why I get angry when I'm judged by people who have never met me. Meet me first. Then if you still think I'm an idiot, fine.

To my amazement, that was the message from Leicester fans on my first return there. Not quite return, because the Walkers Stadium had replaced Filbert Street. It was one of the first fixtures I'd looked for at the start of the season. Clinton Morrison and Mikael – who else? – scored, and I was man of the match. Matt Elliott and Ian Walker were sent off for Leicester, Micky Adams was ordered to the stand by ref Mike Riley, and I was booed, which was just incredible. I left Leicester because the club wanted to sell me. I did them a favour. I loved Leicester City. I didn't ask to leave.

They read out my name, and there was a chorus of boos. I couldn't believe it. The game started, and I nailed Andy Impey. Then I nailed Muzzy. By this time, the fans really were booing! Matt Elliott went for a header and elbowed one of our players, and I was asking the ref to send him off. I thought the crowd's reaction was so unfair. Two years earlier, I'd acted the same way in a blue Leicester shirt and couldn't do anything wrong. How fickle can fans be? Silly question, really.

The season was moving along quite well, and soon I would be preparing for one of my favourite fixtures: yet another derby date with Villa. I never had a single negative thought in my head when I played Villa. Mellberg stirred things up again as he accused me of getting away with it in the first game. What a bore he was becoming. He definitely had a problem with me. The atmosphere was better than at our place. I loved going into the lion's den, and, to make it even more tasty, Villa were on a run and challenging for Europe. We were crap in the first half, and Darius Vassell and Thomas Hitzlsperger put them two in front. Their fans were singing, and it wasn't looking good. Then Mikael scored.

My old enemy Hendrie was giving it plenty with the banter. He was taken off near the end to waste time, with Villa hanging on to their lead. When Stern John equalised right at the death, I spotted Lee walking down the touchline. He disappeared down the tunnel, and I raced after him. Unfortunately, he'd gone. I ran back onto the pitch, and Brucie was there. It was a great feeling. I'd played Aston Villa *again*, and I was unbeaten against Aston Villa *again*.

I'd always got on brilliantly with Brucie, but we had words after an FA Cup tie at Sunderland. It was the fifth round, and we drew 1–1. The gaffer brought me off, even though I thought I had been playing well. I said to him, 'What's wrong?'

'I'm allowed to take you off. You've been crap.'

'One game in sixty isn't bad,' I replied. I wasn't happy.

Then we lost the replay 2–0 at home. It was another missed opportunity. I've always felt a bit jinxed in the FA Cup. There was the quarter-final against Wycombe with Leicester, and then I missed a semi-final with a broken leg at Blackburn. The League Cup was unbelievable, and I can only imagine what an FA Cup final would be like.

Mellberg, Dublin, Hendrie. Then there was Danny Mills. What a funny guy and a great, great lad. I bet no one would expect me to say that about him. When we played each other, I thought he was a complete wanker. But, like so many of the players I clashed with, he is different when you get to know him. Getting to know him was the last thing on my mind when I smashed into him at St Andrew's, though. We beat Middlesbrough 3–1, and I lost my hairband! I made a goal, scored a fabulous free kick and was man of the match.

I didn't care if I broke my own leg; I was going to get Danny. I launched myself into the tackle, and I missed everything – the ball, him, everything. He grabbed me by the scruff of the neck and lifted me up. It certainly got the crowd going. That was the Robbie Savage effect. Danny had a go at me, and I suggested he should get a blond wig and Armani tattoo. I might have mentioned that with a face like his any wig would look good! Then we both turned up at Derby, and I discovered he was as good as gold.

The end of that season was strange. We won only one of the last eleven games, and I think it was because we knew we were safe and let up a little, although to be tenth was a massive achievement. The final match was at Blackburn, and I was captain. I also had a broken neck!

After a year of commuting from Leicester, Sarah and I decided to move nearer to Birmingham's training ground. Looking back, it was totally the wrong thing to do. But when we saw the farmhouse in Coughton, near Stratford, in Warwickshire, we fell in love with it. There was a cottage in the grounds and some land. It was down a country lane and very isolated. Worse, it was in the middle of nowhere, with no fences, no gates, and footpaths running across the land.

People would come up to the window and peer in when they were out walking on a Sunday. The first day was a nightmare, and it was pretty much downhill after that. Local policeman Paul Usmer knocked on the door. He asked to have a quiet word with me, away from Sarah. 'Robbie, you have just moved into the most burgled house in the Midlands,' he told me.

Great. We'd just paid £1.4 million for a dream home, and I found out we were likely to have unwelcome visitors any time soon. It turned out the previous owners of our house were antiques dealers, and a well-known gang had targeted the house four or five times. 'Have good alarms fitted,' Paul advised.

The first day I was at training, Sarah had a friend there. I told her not to open the door. There was a knock at the window, and this guy asked, 'Is the old lady in?' Sarah told him that she'd moved out, but I'm sure it was the burglars coming to check again. We had all the security you could imagine, but kids would come and sit on my wall. We had these old sash windows, and I looked out one night and saw four guys in balaclavas with spray cans. It turned out they were just kids from Birmingham. We had eggs thrown at the house, and windows were smashed. We kept calling the police. It got to the stage where Sarah was scared to be there on her own and would have a friend to stay.

It was a six-bedroom farmhouse, ten thousand square feet and with two acres of land and a two-bedroom cottage. If we touched the window, the alarm would go off. One night, one of the sensors was faulty. I was away. Sarah rang me screaming, saying that someone was in the house. It was 3 a.m. She was petrified, and so was her friend. The dogs were barking, and the alarm was going off. The police came and said it was a false alarm. It was totally the wrong decision to buy the place. We even had day trips come past the house. At the time, I was doing *Premiership Diaries*, which was part of an eight-episode television series. The house was featured, my old school, things like that. Maybe it was my own fault, but I didn't expect that.

Some of the land was garden. There were pheasants too, and when there was a shoot we would have thousands of pheasants hitting the house. It rained pheasants sometimes. That's how much in the country we were. The lane ran across a ford, which was not good news if you drove a Lambo. When it rained, I would have to do a detour of four or five miles.

Moving house showed that I was serious about Birmingham. And they were serious about me. In my last season, I was given a four-year contract that went up by £1,000 a week every year. Looking back, I shouldn't have signed it. It wasn't right. But I was Mr Birmingham, and Muzzy Izzet had come in on a big deal. We also got something like £2,000 a win, so, on a good week, I was earning £25,000. It was a hell of a lot of money.

Money was the name of the game in the summer of 2004. Brucie decided to go for it. All the donkeys who did the donkey work – like me – were not good enough. Brucie tried to add quality, and he had to do that to move Birmingham to the next level. The players he brought in were fantastic. There was Jesper Gronkjaer, my old pal Emile Heskey, Muzzy and Mario Melchiot. Mario was a nice footballer, and Emile was sensational. Brucie had asked me about him. Muzzy was given a massive contract, but we never saw the best of him because of his injuries.

Darren Anderton also arrived that season. We called him 'Shaggy' after the character in *Scooby-Doo*. What a funny guy. We all went away for a weekend in Bournemouth once – apart from Martin 'Tiny' Taylor, probably because his wife wouldn't let him – and that's where Shaggy lived. We went to his house, complete with swimming pool, snooker room, the works. We drove down in a bus, and he apologised and said, 'I'm sorry, but I've had to book you into a motel. You could have all stayed at mine, but two of you would have had to share a room.' There were about 40 of us!

Then there was Dwight Yorke. Yorkie was so helpful to me when it came time for me to leave Birmingham. He'd gone through a similar situation at Villa and was full of good advice. If you went out with him, you could see how famous he was. Everybody stopped and stared, in restaurants, in nightclubs, everywhere.

Gronkjaer came from Chelsea. After one game, Brucie had a go at him. He yelled, 'You're crap.'

Jesper looked at him and was deadly serious as he asked, 'Steve, was I really that bad?' All the lads were laughing. He never fulfilled his reputation. He was a Chelsea star, and everyone expected him to set the place alight at Birmingham. But his biggest test was to do it at a club where the players were not as good as at Chelsea. He couldn't handle it.

We moved to the next level, but the results on the pitch were poor. We won only one of our first eleven games – against Manchester City – and I missed it because of suspension. We'd moved away from being scrappers. There had been no superstars in the dressing-room, and suddenly we had superstars. The mentality changed. There was also a problem with the different wage structures. You could see people thinking, 'Well, if he's come on such-and-such an amount a year . . .'

I was fortunate, because I was one of the higher earners, but there was a two-tier system. I told the other lads that it was the only way if we wanted to move on. If we'd stood still, we would have gone down.

By this time, I had a reputation for collecting bookings, but I had never been sent off in my career. It almost happened at home to Chelsea in the second game of the 2004–05 season, which we lost 1–0. Barry Knight didn't see it, but I was charged by the FA, found guilty of elbowing Mateja Kezman and given a three-match ban for violent conduct. Kezman came on, grabbed me and I swung. He was so small that I caught him. I've never elbowed anyone in my life, but the FA didn't understand the circumstances. As far as they were concerned, I was Robbie Savage, the guy who pooed in the ref's room. I flicked the ball over Didier Drogba that day. I've never heard a man scream so much when he was tackled. He may be one of the best centre-forwards in the Premier League, but the noise he made was incredible.

We lost Mikael through injury at the start of September, and that was the beginning of the downward spiral. A month on, we were continuing to struggle for results, but I still had time to wind up yet another legend: Graeme Souness. I know. It's a knack. We were playing Newcastle, and I found out later that Dean Saunders – my old Wales teammate Deano – had told all the players, 'Let Sav have it. He's not that good. Pressurise him, and he'll give you the ball.'

That was also the match when Craig Bellamy turned up with blond streaks and new teeth. He smiled at me, and I said, 'Who's turned the floodlights on?' I didn't realise he'd decided not to go for normal sized teeth. He wanted three times bigger. It was like he'd borrowed them from Shergar. They were massive! Anyway, back to the game. Brucie had turned down the Newcastle job, and I'd read that Souness was fifth choice. We equalised late to draw the game 2–2, and they were fuming.

So, as I walked down the tunnel behind Souness, I couldn't resist. I said, 'How could we not beat them?'

Souness stopped, turned round and said, 'You a good player, are you?'

'Yeah, I am. Better than you.' I started to walk a little quicker now, moved past him and sped up even more.

'Better than me? How many trophies did you win?'

'At least I would be first choice for a job I went for, not fifth choice.'

As he came after me, I put my hands over my ears, like I do, and shouted, 'Fifth choice, fifth choice.' And then I ran into the dressing-room as fast as I could. It was total disrespect for a legend of a player. The funny thing is, when we went up to Newcastle he gave me a big hug. He was a marvellous player, and it was just that emotions were running high. I was petrified, though. Brucie said to me afterwards, 'If he'd got you, he would have killed you. That's one too many you've opened your mouth to.'

It was November when the speculation started about my future. Mark Hughes had left Wales to take the job with Blackburn, and the rumours were flying that I would be following him. Brucie was not daft, and he knew that Mark Bowen was a good friend of mine. Taff had left Birmingham suddenly the previous summer, and I still don't know the full circumstances, but it was never the same after he'd gone. Luckily, he wasn't out of work too long. As soon as Sparky got his first job in club management, he offered all his Wales backroom staff the chance to follow him.

Knowing that I was wanted so desperately made me play well. I had my best spell for two or three months, and that's when I signed my new contract. We beat Liverpool 1–0 at Anfield, and I set up the goal for Darren Anderton. As we climbed onto the team bus, Shaggy said, 'Football's not rocket science, you know.' We all fell about, and it stuck.

At the end of the month, we played Blackburn and drew 3–3. I scored and so did Shaggy and Dunny, against his former club. I wanted to put on a good show. Blackburn fans were singing 'Sav's a Rover' and 'We love you, Robbie'. I just knew I was going there.

First, there was the little matter of another meeting with Villa and the player with the big mouth. You've guessed it. Mellberg managed to stir up a hornets' nest when he announced a few days before the game that he didn't like anything to do with Birmingham City and that he would never play for Birmingham City. Why Mellberg felt it necessary to say the things he did, I will never know. But I am very grateful, because he made it so much easier for us. We were approaching derby day on a run of two League wins in sixteen games, not the sort of form to fill you with confidence.

So Mellberg put his foot in it – and I put my finger in it. I poked Mellberg in the eye during that match, and I have to confess that I was delighted when it happened. I was accused of eye-gouging afterwards, but the FA decided not to take any action because they accepted that I didn't go over to Mellberg intending to do it. I planned to grab him round the neck, and that's why I sneaked up behind him in this big ruck. I reached out in the melee of bodies, and my finger went straight into his eye. Once again, I snatched the headlines, but the most important part of the story was that we beat Villa 2–1 – and Dunny was sensational that day. He scored the second after Thomas Sorensen's cock-up allowed Clinton Morrison to score the first.

It was my last Birmingham derby, and I never finished on the losing side. When you include my Leicester record, then I think it would be fair to say I was a bit of a jinx on Villa. Having seen them off, the next match was also a derby, although the rivalry against West Brom was not quite as fierce. Birmingham were on a roll, and so was I. I scored from the spot in the 4–0 thrashing of Albion and grabbed the final goal in the 3–2 win at Fulham. Two goals in three games – amazing!

But then Blackburn made the first official move for me, and my Bluenose days were numbered.

16

YOU'RE LOVED HERE

I looked into Steve Bruce's eyes when I said goodbye, and I saw hurt, anger and betrayal. As I walked through the door, he called after me, 'You're making the wrong decision.' The gaffer did everything he could to keep me at Birmingham, but I lied to him. I sat in his office and told him things about my private life that were not all true. Some of it was: Dad having to finish work because of Pick's disease, Mum's stroke. I sat there and turned on the tears with help from the onion I had in my pocket! I was having a miserable time, that bit was true. There were death threats. Worst of all was the reaction from the supporters who had once adored me.

Sarah and I went to a car show at the NEC in Birmingham. Fans were coming up to us and pleading, 'Please don't leave.' This guy approached. He was a typical yob: Burberry cap, Stone Island jumper, baggy jeans. I was holding Charlie, and he walked up to me and flobbed straight into my face. It was disgusting. Then he just looked at me and said, 'You wanker.'

I stood there and could feel myself boil inside. I just wanted to leather him. Sarah was totally mortified. I couldn't wait to get out of Birmingham and away from the fans who used to love me but who now hated me. My life was on the edge. I was not saying anything publicly, but I got my message across after beating Edwin van der Sar with a fantastic volley at Fulham. The Sky lads wanted me for an interview. I had no idea what to say. The reporter kept asking me about links to Blackburn and Everton. Other clubs were mentioned. Every time he asked, I gave the same reply: 'I'm a Birmingham player. I'm a Birmingham player. I'm a Birmingham player.'

My answers spoke volumes. I wasn't saying that I wanted to stay or anything like that. I was just giving a one-line reply. I went in to see Brucie and told him I wanted to leave. He said no. Then he said, if a bid of £3 million came in, Birmingham would let me go. I just thanked him and left the office. There was no way anyone was going to pay that sort of money, surely. My head was telling me I wanted to leave, but it was not going to be that straightforward.

'You're loved here,' Brucie told me. He was right. I had everything I could ever want at Birmingham, and yet I felt I needed to go. Blackburn had been in touch too. It's not supposed to happen in football, but it happens all the time. They wanted me, and I wanted out.

I stopped shaving, I stopped eating, I let my hair grow even longer. I started seeing a doctor because of the stress. I stopped going on the sunbed. I looked like a tramp. I was glued to Sky Sports News, hoping for good news. Blackburn wanted me, so surely it was just a matter of time? As I sat there, long hair, unshaven, skinny and stressed out, the words leaped out at me from the ticker tape. Blackburn had made a £1.25 million bid. What the hell? The ticker tape came round again. I hadn't imagined it. There was no chance Birmingham would accept an offer like that, so what was going on?

I was pretty messed up. I started to sulk. I wasn't much fun in the dressing-room, because I was thinking only about myself. What I didn't realise was that things were about to get a lot worse. My last game for Birmingham was against Newcastle on 1 January 2005. A new year but definitely not a new start, as far as I was concerned. I didn't try at all. We lost 2–1 at St James's Park. I looked terrible. It was time to take the bull by the horns. I rang Steve Bruce and said, 'I've got to go.'

'You've just signed a new contract,' he replied.

'I still want to go.'

'David Sullivan would like to see you at his house. To talk to you.'

'No. I want to go to Blackburn or Everton.'

By then, I knew Everton had made an enquiry. In fact, at one point I had one Premier League manager on my mobile and another on my landline both saying they wanted me! I'd given Sparky my word, but I would have loved to have gone to Everton. David Moyes kept me hanging on. Brucie was doing everything to make me stay. I think he thought that I would, but after that Newcastle game he knew. I went out that day, and I deliberately played badly. I looked like I couldn't care less, and it was the first and the last time I've done that. I'd been on fire, but I let everyone down: the fans, the other players and Steve Bruce. He knew that I was playing to get away and that he had a problem.

I needed to force the issue. The weight was dropping off me, I was a mess, and the situation was not going to improve. The only alternative was to put in a written transfer request. I pulled a piece of paper out of a drawer and wrote, 'Dear Steve, this is a written transfer request, Sav.' I had it in my hand when I knocked on his door. As soon as he saw me, he knew. I handed over the request, and he got up, opened the door and didn't say anything. I walked out of his office and bumped into Dwight Yorke. 'I've done it now,' I said.

Yorkie was a good mate and very supportive during that time. He'd gone through something similar when he left Aston Villa for Manchester United, and he warned me it could get nasty. He went upstairs to see the gaffer and was down a few minutes later. 'You're in big trouble.'

Great. Just what I wanted to hear. Brucie told me to go home for a couple of days. I phoned a mate at Sky and told him, 'Listen, I'm going to go into the training ground on the lads' day off. I'll be there on my own, training on my own. Film it, and it will look like I've been banned from the first team.' The Sky crew turned up, filmed me doing a very good impression of a lonely professional and there it was on breaking news: Robbie Savage has been made to train on his own. It was out there, in the public domain. The truth was that I only trained with the kids once or twice, and it wasn't a punishment.

Brucie made me play for the reserves. It was the first, and probably the last, pack-out at Solihull Borough, where Birmingham play their reserve fixtures. It was a bit like being a film star, except that as soon as you step onto the red carpet you realise everyone hates you. Fans turned up and started jeering. 'Judas!' they were shouting. 'You've let us down!'

They felt hurt and betrayed, but I kept my head. Another bid came in from Blackburn. Birmingham rejected the £2-million offer, and I was going totally crazy at home. Sarah couldn't live with me, so she went off to her parents. All this time, the message I was receiving was that Blackburn definitely wanted me. They were taking their own sweet time about it. The £2-million bid was increased by another £500,000. Rovers were getting there. Just a bit more. Then I had another call from someone at Ewood Park: 'Sorry, Sav. We can't go any higher.'

I couldn't believe what I was hearing. Birmingham would let me go for £3.1 million, but Blackburn wouldn't pay any more than £2.5 million. I'd been hung out to dry, and I couldn't see how this one was going to end. I'd put my trust in Blackburn, and there was no way back for me with Birmingham.

Blues offered me the world. I could have every Monday off, a chauffeur-driven car, all sorts of things. I said that I wanted to move to Blackburn to be nearer to my sick parents, and one newspaper worked out that St Andrew's to Wrexham was actually closer than Ewood Park to Wrexham. I was upset about the story, because it wasn't true. I lived near Stratford, which was a two-and-a-half-hour journey to Wrexham. Signing for Rovers meant that I could live in Cheshire and be at Blackburn's training ground in an hour and Pine Close in 45 minutes.

Looking back, I should have gone to see David Sullivan and listened to what he had to say. I was at a crossroads in my life and in my career. I thought Sarah was leaving me, and I didn't know what to do. Every time I play against Birmingham, the fans chant, 'There's only one greedy bastard.' They will be amazed to discover that I did not move to Blackburn for more money. I was earning about £21,000 a week at Birmingham, and I'd been promised that Rovers would give me £25,000 a week for three years. I thought that sounded fine.

The only problem was that Birmingham had rejected Blackburn's offer, and Rovers were telling me they had no more money. Something had to give, so I told Blackburn that I would move for the same £21,000 a week, which would release £200,000 a year, or £600,000 for three years, to make up the difference on my transfer fee. Add that to the £2.5 million, and Blackburn could meet the asking price. So I moved for exactly the same money – and it still cost me £70,000, because Blues demanded I return some of my image rights.

I was sitting around day after day waiting. My hair was white, my beard was white. I looked like Robinson Crusoe. Sarah told me to get a grip before she went off to see her parents, but I was struggling. The phone rang, and it was Rita, the manager's secretary, to say that Brucie wanted to see me. 'I'm on my way,' I said. I thought I was on my way out as well.

'The club want £70,000 in image rights,' Brucie told me.

'Are you joking?' I looked in horror at him. I couldn't believe it. Even though I'd signed a new contract, the image rights belonged to the original deal. I knew deep down that when it came to financial matters Birmingham didn't ever take the piss. But after all the problems off the field, there was still one stumbling block to be overcome. Funnily enough, I believe that Steve had a similar problem over his financial arrangements when he left Birmingham for Wigan. I think they made him give some cash back too. That's why I know it wasn't him, but Karren and the board who made him do it.

'I haven't got £70,000,' I told Bruce, and I was speaking the truth. How could I lay my hands on that kind of cash sum without any kind of notice? I was earning about £55,000 a month after tax and £40,000 was going straight into savings and investment schemes. Footballers earn good money, I'm the first to admit it, but we don't have thousands of pounds of cash just swilling around waiting to be withdrawn. I rang Blackburn: 'Help. Birmingham want £70,000 now, or they won't let me go.'

Blackburn sent through a payment straight away, paid the image rights and made sure I would get the move. I looked into Brucie's eyes when it came to say goodbye and thought, 'I've let you down, pal, haven't I?'

His last words to me were, 'You'll regret it. You're making the wrong decision.' In a way, I do regret it. Steve Bruce was sensational to me and is a great guy. I was so happy when we made up. John Benson was the same. I definitely regret the way it happened. But I went on to play for Blackburn in Europe, we had Cup semi-finals and we finished sixth. I didn't appreciate all that I had at Birmingham, and I bitterly regret hurting Steve Bruce. He was a hero to me when I was a kid at Manchester United, so that was not an ending I would have chosen.

But there I was, halfway through a season and playing for another of my heroes in Mark Hughes. When I had my medical at Blackburn, the doc said I had the worst leg strength he'd ever seen – quads, hamstrings and so on. I was just as weedy as when I had started at Manchester United. I still didn't have Mark Hughes's thighs! Because I was Sparky's first major signing, I did not feel part of the clique. On the very first day, I caused great amusement. David Fevre was the physio, and I knew him from Wales. Chris Short was the masseur, and I didn't know him at all. When I asked for a rub, I was told to 'Get Shorty', but the only Shorty I knew was Craig. I was a little surprised, but I went up to Craig and said, 'Excuse me, but please can I have a rub?' Craig Short, Chris's brother and one of my new teammates, was very amused. The other lads were wetting themselves too.

I made my debut at the end of January against Bolton. We lost 1–0, and I was booked after one minute for a tackle. I did it on purpose. I remembered what Sparky used to say when I was on Wales duty. *Make your mark.* I wanted to make my mark for my new club. I was also wearing a number 31 shirt to signify the £3.1 million Birmingham sold me for. It was a bit of a stupid thing to do, but I wanted to make a point.

There were some very good players at Rovers. And some characters. I arrived at training one morning to hear this buzzing. It was coming from the toilet. What on earth was it? *Buzz, buzz, buzz.* For about 15 minutes. Someone was in the toilet doing something. The mind boggled. The noise stopped, and out of the cubicle stepped Lorenzo Amoruso. He had shaved off *every* single body hair – and I mean every single body hair. He came out of the toilet looking like a goddess that day!

To start with, I stayed with my agent, George Urquhart, near Wigan. Throughout my career, I relied on George. He was second to none in dealing with my transfers. I trusted him implicitly, and he introduced me to a financial advisor, David McKee. I trusted McKee too, but I feel let down because I don't believe his recommendations were in my best interests. In football, players are fair game for hangers-on, but you should be able to trust your advisers, who, after all, should know that you rely on their professional advice and judgement. Early in 2010, the press became aware of potential litigation with regard to bad advice, which affected a number of other well-known players as well as me.

Finding somewhere to live with the family was a priority. I rented a lovely place in Wilmslow in Cheshire. What I didn't know, until I'd moved in, was that it was next door to Alex Ferguson! We lived there for six months, and I never spoke to him once. His brother, Martin, came into the house but not Fergie. I thought he might have come round to say hello, and he saw me walking the dogs most mornings. I used to let them out at about six in the morning. I knew he didn't like that very much.

It's funny how things come round in circles. I was living next door to probably the greatest manager there has ever been, the same manager who had told me I wasn't good enough for Manchester United and who had said, 'No,' and shut the door in my face when I asked for David Beckham's shirt. And in six months we never exchanged a word. Maybe I should have made his life more of a misery! I could have sent my Wrexham mates round to knock on his door and ask for autographs.

My house near Stratford was on the market. There was this lady who lived nearby who'd always loved the house, and I told her she could have it for £1.4 million, which is what we'd paid for it. I'd spent around £100,000 on it, but I wrote that off. The lady said she'd have it. Brilliant! Our nightmare was coming to an end. We were away in Abersoch for the weekend, and the lady wanted to have another look at the house. My policeman mate, Paul Usmer, offered to let her in. He showed her the loft and jokingly said, 'This is where the ghost lives.' At exactly that moment, a door slammed. The next day, her solicitor rang to say she wanted £25,000 off the asking price because the house was haunted! Apparently, her daughter had been downstairs when Paul cracked his joke and was really frightened when the door slammed. Not too frightened to live in the house but too frightened to pay the asking price. Talk about Casper the Friendly Ghost! People think footballers are made of money.

Everything was new and exciting at Blackburn. I was full of enthusiasm and ready to do the business for Sparky, Taff and Eddie. In a lot of ways, it was like being on Wales duty, because I knew them all so well. Taff had left Birmingham the previous summer, and that had been a massive blow. No one has ever explained the situation, but it was probably the beginning of the end at Birmingham. It wasn't the same without Taff, that's for sure. Rovers were more intense than Wales. We had to wear heart-rate monitors all the time, and it was deadly serious. Sparky, as a player, had been one of the worst trainers I'd ever seen. Yet now, as a manager, he bollocked you. I loved playing for him, and I think he let me get away with things because of the Wales thing. His wife, Gill, was also incredible when I moved. She would look after Sarah and make sure things were okay. They are a lovely family. We went round to their house several times. Coming from Wrexham probably helped as well.

Starting my new career with three defeats had definitely not been on the agenda. We lost 1–0 to Bolton, 1–0 to Chelsea and 1–0 at Middlesbrough. My first win in a Blackburn shirt was the 3–0 FA Cup fourth-round tie against Colchester. It set us up for a meeting with neighbours Burnley and my first taste of another special derby. I didn't think anything would come close to those Birmingham–Villa matches, but this was fierce stuff too. The changing-rooms were under the away stand, so all the Blackburn supporters were above us. You could hear them chanting and bouncing on the seats, and it was a great adrenaline boost, because there were 5,000 people above you singing, 'There's only one Robbie Savage.' I was praised by Alan Hansen at half-time. He said I was the best player on the pitch.

This fan came running onto the pitch in a white T-shirt – on a freezing cold day. He was also wearing surgical gloves. He approached me, a skinhead with tattoos on his head, and shouted, 'Put 'em up. Put 'em up.' He could have had a knife. The police got him off. What the TV cameras didn't pick up that day was a naked breakdancer doing his bit in front of Sparky. We drew 0–0, which meant a replay back at our place.

Settling into a new club always takes a little time. As a footballer, you hope to be fit enough and good enough to make the team, and the one thing you absolutely dread is getting injured. I ripped my groin against Norwich in mid-February and ended up carrying the injury all season. I had painkilling injections into the groin, but I knew something was wrong. David Fevre said I could play on, but every time I lifted my left foot my right groin would hurt. 'I know there's something wrong with me,' I told David.

'How can you know? You haven't had a scan yet,' he said.

They sent me for a scan, and I spoke to the surgeon, and he said I had to build up my glutes. David was brilliant. He was reading books and trying to find out what was wrong with me. I tried to play through it, but at half-time in the replay against Burnley I couldn't move. I had been told that if I had three or four weeks off I would be okay, but I had come back the same. I had a big argument with Brad Friedel in one five-a-side game. I just knew there was something wrong. Brad yelled, 'When are you going to try a leg?'

And I shouted back, 'Any chance of you saving a few?'

I hadn't earned the respect of my new teammates, and I was only too aware of that. In the summer, I rang Sparky at home and said, 'I need an op.' David Fevre booked me in. They found a piece of grit the size of a one-penny coin rubbing between the tendon and the bone. I got injured so rarely that I knew something was wrong, so I was relieved to have it put right in the summer. Otherwise, I would have been back to square one the following season. I used to go home in tears, because I was the only person who thought I wasn't quite right. They all thought I was kidding with this injury.

So there I was, desperate to make an impression and struggling with an injury. I missed the whole of March and the first couple of League matches in April, which meant my first game back was the FA Cup semi-final against Arsenal. What a match for my return! Unfortunately, we lost 3–0, so there was no fairy-tale Cup final to cap my move to Blackburn. I came on as sub and was well off the pace. I caught Cesc Fàbregas with a high challenge, and Arsene Wenger was moaning afterwards about how physical we were. Andy Todd was also criticised for elbowing Robin van Persie but insisted afterwards that it was accidental.

Sparky took us to Dubai for five days to prepare for the tie. We played tennis, we relaxed and we trained well. When you first go to a club, you have to be a bit quiet, but I couldn't resist winding up Nils-Eric Johansson. I was hammering his teeth, and he said, 'I'm going to nail you in training.'

Quick as a flash, I came back with, 'I don't train with Glyn Hodges.' Glyn was the reserve-team manager, and it made all the lads laugh. I was getting there, slowly.

When I arrived at Blackburn, the first game I looked at was the Birmingham fixture at the end of April. I'd left in such bad circumstances – even though I'd made them a profit and been one of the best players – so I couldn't wait to go back there. A week or so before the match, Sparky called me into his office and dropped a bombshell: 'You're not available for the Birmingham match.'

What? I couldn't believe it. Having been on the receiving end of a shedload of abuse, I wanted to walk back into St Andrew's with my head held high. Now I was being told that I was unavailable for my big return. 'John Williams has a gentleman's agreement with Birmingham,' explained Hughes. 'They were complaining that it would cost £100,000 in extra policing costs and asked, as part of the deal, that you didn't play.'

As soon as I heard the words 'gentleman's agreement' I knew that was that. Blackburn chairman John Williams is a real gentleman, a lovely guy who would never break his word. It had to be an informal arrangement, because Premier League rules wouldn't have allowed it as an official clause in the contract. Loan deals always stop a 'borrowed' player facing his parent club, and it's pretty obvious why. Birmingham not wanting me to play made sense – for them. They were struggling hugely for results, so the scene might have been set for me to send them down. I didn't believe the police-cost excuse for a minute, but my feelings didn't matter one way or the other anyway. This was a boardroom decision taken during negotiations to buy me, so my return to Birmingham wasn't going to happen just yet. I was gutted, though.

There were only two more matches after that. We lost to Fulham, and I missed the first penalty of my career. I prefer to say Edwin van der Sar saved it. And we drew away at Spurs. I had been signed by Blackburn to help them stay up, and I did have a hand in it, even though I was struggling with injury. We finished fifteenth, three places behind Birmingham.

17

MY WAY OR THE HIGHWAY

When I hear the Welsh national anthem, the hairs on the back of my neck stand up. I can't sing the words. I'm ashamed to admit it. Big John Hartson wrote them down for me, but I never learned them. Sorry, mate. But that does not make me feel any less emotional when the fans raise the Millennium Stadium roof by singing 'Hen Wlad Fy Nhadau'. I was amazingly lucky to be part of the Mark Hughes era. The irony is that when I joined Sparky at Blackburn it coincided with the end at Wales. If someone had told me after the play-off against Russia that I would play only six more games for my country, I would have laughed. We'd come so close to qualifying for Euro 2004, and there was great hope for the future. Within 18 months, the heart and soul had been ripped out of the Mark Hughes team. Sparky left, and a number of senior players announced their retirement. Not me. I wanted to play on.

There was no hint of what was round the corner when we gathered for the first time since the play-off against Russia. It was February 2004, and Scotland were the opposition in a friendly fixture. They were awful that day, and we took them to the cleaners. Rob Earnshaw scored a hat-trick, and Gareth Taylor grabbed the other goal in a 4–0 win. Paul Dickov and I kicked lumps out of each other. He became a good friend later, though. Sparky brought me off, and the camera panned in on me when I was sitting in the dugout. There was me on the big screen holding up four fingers and sticking out my tongue, playing to the crowd as usual.

The following month, we went to Budapest, but I'm not sure our 2–1 win over Hungary could be described as a friendly. I have wound up some people in my time. I seem to have an instinct for it! And they don't come much bigger or more famous than legend Lothar Matthäus, who, last time I looked, had played in five World Cups, won it in 1990 and been European and world player of the year. So a bit better than me, then. Matthäus was also coach of Hungary, who lost to goals from Jason Koumas and Rob Earnshaw at the Ferenc Puskas Stadium. Not that anyone will remember the score.

They had a player called Laszlo Bodnar, and he spat at me. Spitting is horrible, and I'm delighted to say that it's never been part of the British mentality. I was furious and at the end so was Matthäus, who came onto the pitch to have a go at me. I thought his head would explode. I stood there thinking, 'I watched you lift the World Cup, and you're having a go at me?' I said afterwards that Matthäus was the most famous person I'd wound up. He probably still is.

We had a third friendly win in August against Latvia, a 2–0 victory in Riga that we thought would set us up nicely for the World Cup qualifying campaign in September. We were in the same group as England and Northern Ireland, which gave the matches an extra edge. The first fixture was in Azerbaijan. Gary Speed scored in a 1–1 draw, and then it was straight back to Cardiff to play Northern Ireland four days later. My first red card. For years, I had been collecting bookings, but I had never been sent off. There had been some close calls. In fact, when I joined up with Wales I was serving a three-game Premier League ban for that incident involving Kezman against Chelsea.

This was the softest sending-off you will ever see. The game started at high tempo, and Michael Hughes scissored me. He could have broken my leg. Then he pushed me over. Damien Johnson, my teammate at Birmingham, sprinted over. The ref waved two red cards – at me and Hughes. Anybody who saw that incident would have confirmed I did nothing wrong. The first thing that hit me as I walked off the pitch was, 'I'm going to miss England.' That brought tears.

I watched the second half from the box. David Healy was also sent off as they finished with nine, and we came back from 2–0 down to draw, thanks to Harts and Earnie. In the lift afterwards, I bumped into Lawrie Sanchez, the Northern Ireland manager. Sanchez had been in charge of Wycombe when they beat Leicester in the quarter-finals of the FA Cup.

He was on his way to the press room to do the post-match interviews. I was still gutted about what had happened. 'How was that a sending off?' I asked him.

'Oh, Robbie Savage, he would never have been at fault, would he?' replied Sanchez. I was a bit surprised.

I told Sparky, 'I didn't touch him.' I took the case to the Court of Arbitration for Sport, and it was thrown out. But it was a wrong that should have been put right. I don't know what came over Hughes that night, and I wasn't impressed with the way Johnson got busy, especially as he was my club teammate. I know that club loyalties go out of the window on international duty, but seeing him getting involved did make me wonder whether this was more than sticking up for his country. I was Mr Birmingham, after all. Only he could know whether there was any resentment there as well.

The England game was at Old Trafford, part of a double-header that brought Poland to Cardiff a few days later. I felt quite sick every time I thought about Northern Ireland and the sending off that should never have been. Instead of being on the pitch, I was in the TV studio. It was horrible being a spectator. I went to the team hotel the night before and watched the build-up, but it was gut-wrenching to see the lads getting ready. I had that sinking feeling. I didn't feel any better in the studio. Alan Hansen, Alan Shearer and Gary Lineker are legends, and I felt intimidated, because Lineker and Shearer were clearly against me. I didn't have any defence. It was a steep learning curve for me. I didn't think I was worthy enough to sit next to them, and I didn't know if my thoughts were valid.

David Beckham scored a great goal and spoke well of me before the match. He cracked a rib that day challenging Ben Thatcher. The Wales team who played were Paul Jones, Simon Davies, Mark Delaney, Danny Gabbidon, Thatcher, Craig Bellamy, Jason Koumas, Mark Pembridge, Gary Speed, Ryan Giggs and John Hartson. By the time the countries met again in Cardiff a year later, I was gone. So were Speedo, Pem, Thatcher, Melville and Delaney. All gone. For a variety of reasons.

I jumped off my pundit sofa to join the lads for the home qualifier against Poland. Everybody knew Sparky was going. On the Monday, at the Vale of Glamorgan Hotel, I had a cup of tea with Mark Bowen. I was close to Taff, because we had been together at Birmingham. I said to him, 'Listen, when Sparky gets his first club job, I want to play for him. Will you buy me?'

Taff told Sparky, and he promised, 'You'll be my first signing when I get a club.' I was hoping he'd get Manchester United or Liverpool. I would talk to him about his career. He once said to me, 'Sav, when you hang up your boots, you want to be remembered, and you will be, by hook or by crook.'

We lost 3–2 to Poland, another disappointing result. It was to be my last game in a Red Dragon shirt. Straight afterwards, I did a hot-headed interview, saying I thought Gary Speed and Brian Flynn would be the perfect people to take over and not John Toshack, because he had a hidden agenda. It was a heated moment, and it proved to me what a fickle world football can be. Speedo came out to say he wasn't interested in being the next Wales manager, but Brian was ringing me and asking for help to get the job. Flynny went on to be part of Toshack's set-up and has done a great job with the Under-21s and kids. But he never called me afterwards to say thanks. As for me, I was left high and dry, nailed by my own comments.

I didn't realise it at the time. Toshack took over and made all the right noises about judging everyone on their merits. He came to watch me play for Birmingham against West Brom. I was magnificent that day and totally overshadowed Jason Koumas, who was in the Baggies side. Toshack and I had a long chat. It makes me sick to think about it now. 'It's a fresh start,' he told me. 'I'll judge you on your performances.'

I believed him. Speedo's retirement from international football meant there was a vacancy for the armband as well. People were putting my name forward as a candidate to be the next skipper. Could I convince Toshack that I was captain material? He named his first squad. It was the reverse friendly against Hungary in February 2005. I was in it. New start. I had just moved to Blackburn, and I was also struggling with a groin injury, but I still turned up because I was desperate to show him my commitment to Wales. We met, and I was struck by the aura that surrounded him.

'Mr Toshack, please can you sign this shirt for me?' I asked. Toshack reached out, took the Wales shirt I had brought and signed it. Next to his name, he put the number one. 'What's that for?' I asked.

'One European Cup.'

Fair play. But then I spoke to Dad, and he told me that Toshack didn't win the European Cup. He certainly didn't play in either the 1977 or 1978 finals with Liverpool. He might have a medal, I suppose. It is a bit like Paul Scholes in 1999. Scholesy missed the third leg of that amazing treble season through suspension and always says that he doesn't count the Champions League medal as he wasn't on the pitch against Bayern Munich. I have never had the opportunity to ask Toshack about it. Toshack loved talking – about how good he was and what he'd won. And he was one hell of a player. He also had a great record as a club manager, but he didn't realise that the game had moved on.

Under Sparky, no expense was spared on Wales duty. There would be about six or seven menu choices. It would be good, healthy stuff, but there would still be a king's feast waiting for us at mealtimes. My mate Quags produced fabulous food. Walking into the dining room at Toshack's first get-together, I stopped in surprise. There was nothing on the table. I looked at Giggsy, and he looked at me. We sat down at this empty table, and it was like being in school: sit up straight, and then you can have dinner. The waitress came in to take our order. Plain chicken, no sauce. Or spaghetti bolognese. Fried bananas or rice and broccoli.

I wanted chicken with gravy, but we weren't allowed. I looked down at this plate of dry chicken, one veg, no gravy, fried bananas – and then I followed the habit of a lifetime and acted out of instinct. Up went the white tablecloth as I pushed back my chair. I dropped down to my hands and knees, and I crawled under the table. The lads were laughing but trying not to let Toshack see, and I started my hunt. 'Where's the veg?' I called out. 'Maybe there are some sauces under here.' I could see Toshack's face, and he wasn't amused.

'Is there a problem?' he almost snarled.

'My chicken's dry, and there's no gravy or sauces.'

'Ah,' he said. 'You should have used your initiative and put the bolognese sauce on your chicken.' I could not believe I was having this conversation.

After dinner, we had a team meeting upstairs, and I told the lads that I had to say something. The lads were urging me on, but when it finally came to it none of them stood up for me. Good old Sav. I'd say what they were all thinking, and they just sat there without uttering a word. I should have seen the writing on the wall then, because it looked like I was the only one who had a problem with the food. Toshack laid it on the line in the meeting. 'It's my way or the highway,' he told us.

A month later, I found myself on the bloody M56! At that point, I didn't have a clue how near I was to the end of that particular road. Sitting there in that meeting, I put up my hand just like you do at school. 'Excuse me, John,' I said. 'Can I say something about the food? The game's moved on since you were a manager, and we have needs. I might have been brought up on beans on toast, but I need vegetables. I need sauces. Quags is one of the best nutritionists around, and we usually have lots of choice. My chicken was dry.' Toshack just stared at me; then he ran his gaze over the other lads. They didn't say a word. And that was the end of me. I said to Giggsy afterwards, 'He's going to bin me.'

'Don't be daft,' Giggsy replied. 'You're one of our best players.'

The next morning, we went training. Toshack came out of the changing-room. He had his shoelaces tied around his ankles, and he probably needed Vaseline for his nipples, the waistband of his tracksuit bottoms was that high. 'We'll do some warm-ups and then some foot-ins,' he announced.

Harts looked at Giggsy. They both looked at me. Harts whispered, 'What are foot-ins?' To this day, I have no idea what they are. The get-together ended early for me, because I had a groin injury and went home. I wasn't impressed by Toshack. You couldn't argue with his record as a club manager at Swansea at all. He was a great player for Liverpool, and he was a great player for Wales. I was a Liverpool fan, and I know what a fantastic partnership Toshack had with Kevin Keegan. I have total respect for what he did at Liverpool. I'm not sure about the European Cup, but he won the UEFA Cup twice – in 1973 and 1976 – and a Super Cup winners' medal in 1977. I didn't get his attitude at all.

I went back to Blackburn and waited for the next Wales squad to be announced. I was so thick. All the talk was about me becoming the new captain. Even Gary Speed had said I would make a great one. I never saw what was coming. And I made it so, so easy for Toshack. I did a Savage and reacted instinctively when the phone rang early one Monday morning. We had a World Cup double-header home and away against Austria. The Hungary get-together hadn't gone well, but I wasn't expecting what came next.

'Hi Robbie, John here.' I am almost cringing as I relive this conversation, because I seriously thought it would finish with me being appointed captain of my country. 'Hi Robbie, John here. I'm just letting you know that I'm going to try something different. I'm not selecting you.'

Try something different? Are you sure? I could feel myself boiling up inside, and I then made a fatal mistake. 'You can stick it up your arse,' I told Toshack. 'I'm retiring now.'

The TV and radio bulletins were full of it. Robbie Savage has retired from international football and will not be part of the Wales squad for the qualifiers against Austria. Except that retiring was the furthest thing from my mind. I had 39 caps to my name, and I always felt I could reach the 50 mark. I loved playing for Wales, pulling on the shirt and feeling the hairs on the back of my neck stand up when I heard the national anthem. Mum and Dad were so proud of me. So was Nan. Playing for Wales was a part of my life – and a very important part at that. My temper had brought it to an unexpected and early end.

What was I doing? At the time, I thought it was something I had to do to save face. Looking back, I realise my stupidity. I cut off my nose to spite my face. I didn't get a load of support from Sparky either. When I mentioned I was thinking of calling it a day, he didn't say anything. From his point of view, it would have been a good idea, because no international fixtures meant I could concentrate completely on Blackburn. But Sparky was also a proud Welshman.

What I needed was someone to tell me not to be so stupid. No one did, and I paid for being an idiot. Toshack named his squad and announced my international retirement. I had made it so easy for him. I don't blame Toshack for the premature end to my international career. I blame myself. If I had kept my mouth shut, and my availability open, then the pressure would have been unbearable on him. I was playing well, I was a Premier League player and he would have had no choice but to pick me. If only I'd announced to the world that I was still available for selection and that playing for Wales was all I wanted. Every time Wales had a match, I put on an act. It was all bravado. Inside, it was killing me. What a fool, what a total fool I'd been. My ego had taken over. I'd just thought, 'Toshack is not leaving me out.'

I wish that Sparky, Taff or Eddie had stopped me. They were happy, because I wouldn't be going away. I'd let all my frustrations out. Toshack didn't need to ring me that morning, but he took the trouble to do so, and I have to remember that. But if I'd stuck with it and tried to get back into the team, then I don't think I would have given Toshack any choice. There would have been a huge clamour for me to be picked. I gave him the easy option, and who can blame him for taking it?

The fallout from our fallout lasted weeks. I had an on-air row with Leighton James, who was one of Toshack's great mates and had an agenda. People think that I heard Leighton James having a go at me on the radio and phoned in, but I was always scheduled to be on the programme. Craig Bellamy's great mate David Bishop, the rugby player, was doing the show, so it was pre-arranged. So there was this guy giving me stick, and I was about to come on air anyway. 'Will you speak to him, Sav?' Bishop asked me.

Of course. So I had a well-documented exchange with Leighton James. He said I wasn't good enough for the squad, which was laughable. I'd done my homework on him before and spoken to my father about him as a player. 'Decent, but you wouldn't want him in the trenches with you,' was Dad's verdict.

So I suggested on the radio that he wasn't the bravest around, and James threw the headphones down, crying, 'It's a set-up. It's a set-up.' I got the better of him on the radio. That's what I'm like. I'm headstrong. Listening back to it now, it's a bit cringeworthy, but that's how I am. He asked me why I hadn't written a letter to John Toshack. What manager in this day and age doesn't have a mobile phone? There was an agenda. I wasn't in the squad because I was such a big personality and I was an influence on people. There was no other reason.

Toshack has gone now. He has been replaced by Gary Speed, who inherits a squad used to playing in front of pitiful crowds. Toshack brought in a whole load of kids and promised to qualify for a major tournament within five years. It didn't happen, and now it is Speedo's turn. I wish him well. He is a mate, and I even forgive him for not calling me out of retirement! I look at players like Gareth Bale, Aaron Ramsey, Jack Collison, and they are exciting talents. I do hope that better times lie ahead for my country.

18

ROVER THE MOON

The 2005–06 season started in the Alps and finished in the peaks of the Premier League. We discovered a head for heights!

'Why did you go to Blackburn?' Birmingham fans still ask me that question. The answer is there in black and white. Sixth in the table, qualified for Europe, last four of the League Cup. May 2006 was party time. And Birmingham went down. It was no coincidence that Robbie Savage left Birmingham to join Blackburn and that one of the clubs was relegated while the other made it to the UEFA Cup. I might not be the most gifted person in the world, but I add something to the team. People say I've been a mediocre Premier League player. I've proved I'm not.

And I'm definitely a better midfielder than Rio Ferdinand. I kicked Rio up the arse in the tunnel and smacked his bum on the pitch that season as we did the League double over Manchester United – only to lose to them in the semi-final of the Carling Cup. Thoughts of United were a million miles away when we all reported back for duty that pre-season, though. I was fit again after my summer op and raring to go. Sparky's contacts from his playing days at Bayern Munich meant a trip to their training camp in the Bavarian Alps, near the Austrian border. It was a lovely situation. After training every day, Sparky made us jump into this icy stream. It must have been minus ten. We had to get up to our waists for three minutes.

My room-mate was Shefki Kuqi, and he was that hard he would just dive in and swim. He was born in Kosovo, so he knew all about a war-torn upbringing. I introduced him to wrestling, like I had done with Dev at Birmingham. It was not such a good idea with this guy. He always let me go first, and he always won. His finishing manoeuvre was the bear hug. I went from the death choke at Birmingham to the bear hug at Blackburn. He came to my house for Christmas one year because he didn't have any family in the UK and was on his own. As much as I loved him, he was not the best trainer in the world in terms of his touch and stuff. His shooting wasn't the best, even though he did it in games. He came in one day with these boots called 'No Miss'. That's what they had on the side. I said they should have been called 'Always Miss'!

Sparky had signed someone who hardly ever missed. Craig Bellamy was the big arrival for £5 million from Newcastle, and I was absolutely delighted. He's a big mate of mine and a fantastic player. You knew that it was almost a case of him passing through, though. I was saying to the physio one day that I'd never thought I'd play for a club like Blackburn, with their history – winning the title, Alan Shearer and so on – and Bellers said, 'I didn't think I'd be playing for a club like Blackburn. I'm doing them a favour by being here.'

He was right. Craig has so much talent. I knew what he was like, and I could handle him. If he spotted a weakness, then you'd had it. People think the two of us would clash, but we are good mates. To get Bellers to Blackburn was a massive coup. You had to wrap him in cotton wool, tell him how good he was, and he would do it for you. He had everything at Blackburn. Sparky knew how to handle him too. Craig scored 17 goals that season, and he was on fire. His game just moved onto another level.

One day, Catherine, one of the secretaries down at the training ground, came out onto the pitch and said, 'Mark, Craig has just been on the phone. He's en route, and could you clear the pitch, please, because his helicopter is about to land?' That was typical Bellers. We all killed ourselves laughing.

Craig ran the show, and not everyone could take it. Morten Gamst Pedersen was the nicest person in the world, but he was really affected by Bellers. Pedersen was great until Craig came, but Craig used to keep on at him. It was funny, but it affected Morten. Craig tried to get the best out of a person, because he wouldn't accept second best. On one occasion, it was half-time at Portsmouth, and they had scored two bad goals. Craig turned to Pedersen and said, 'Oi, have you ever played left-wing in your life before? Any chance of you putting a ball in?'

'Morten, he's got a point,' said Sparky.

Craig was running the show. He said it how it was. He told me, 'Just give it to Tugay.' Worzel Gummidge – Tugay – is the best player I have ever played with. I've been fortunate to perform on the same pitch as Roque Santa Cruz, Dugarry, Mancini, Benni McCarthy, Giggsy. In terms of aura and star quality, it was all about Giggsy. But to play alongside Tugay was unbelievable. We called him the maestro. You could give him the ball in any area, three men around him, and he would do something brilliant. But on the way to training, he'd have four fags in his mouth at the same time. After the match, the first thing he would do is go outside and light up. As a person, as a player and as a friend, what a top guy.

David Bentley arrived on loan from Arsenal. He wanted to be the new Becks and turned out to be a fantastic guy. We called him 'Trigger'. He was a London boy, although I think his family came from Rochdale. He bought a lovely house but had a BMW with body kit hanging off and looked like a boy racer. I got him properly one day. He was desperate to be in the England squad, and there was one due to be announced. So I phoned him and, in my best fake Swedish accent, said, 'Hello, it's Sven here. You are in the England squad.'

'Thanks, Sven, I can't wait,' he replied.

'You must add some pace to your game, David.'

'Yes, Sven. Of course, Sven.'

I was pissing myself. He came racing out to us and announced, 'I'm in the England squad. Sven's just rung me.' Then he spotted me in bits, looked at the other lads, who were all laughing, and realised he had been fooled. He still had the last laugh, though, because later that day he was called up to the England squad.

Bents also thought he was invisible, that no one would recognise him as a high-profile Premier League and England player. We went out in Manchester once and finished up in this nightclub. The fire alarms went off, the sprinklers came on and two or three thousand students were milling around outside with plenty of drink inside them. So David, a

Blackburn player, climbed onto the roof of a taxi and started to sing, 'There's only one David Bentley.' In Manchester! Unbelievably, all the drunk students sang along with him.

It was a dressing-room with lots of laughs. Mickey Gray's banter was as good as mine, and we would tag-team on people. It was hilarious. We did a number on one of the physios. Paul Kelly lived in Urmston, near the sewage works, and we would call him 'Stinky' and tease him about his clothes smelling after they were hung on the line. We'd take it in turns. Mickey was also in charge of organising the Christmas do. It was fancy dress that year, and I was Scooby-Doo. It was a memorable night, although Superman disgraced himself by falling asleep on a park bench. No, I'm not saying who it was!

We didn't have the best start to the season: one win in the first six games. I was also beaten by Aston Villa for the first time. We lost 1–0, and the Villa fans chanted, 'Where's your Robbie gone? He's gone to see his mum.' I thought they would give me a rousing round of applause for leaving Birmingham, but they still hammered me.

A trip to Old Trafford at the end of September should have been daunting after our average start, but we weren't scared of anybody. We didn't sit off United, and Pedersen scored both goals in a 2–1 victory. To go back to Old Trafford any time was a sweet feeling, but to go back there and win and prove Fergie wrong again made it even more satisfying.

The two fixtures I'd ringed in the calendar were both Birmingham, home and away. I'd been robbed of my chance to play against my old club the previous season, so I couldn't wait. Blues came to Ewood Park at the end of October, and it was live on Sky. I was nervous, the occasion got to me and I didn't play well. But I still knew what was going to happen. Over the tannoy, five minutes from time, came the announcement, 'And the man of the match is . . . Robbie Savage!' I could have had the worst game in the world, and I still would have won. The Sky commentator expressed a little surprise at the choice.

My form wasn't great, but I didn't need anyone to tell me that either. I'd been okay in fits and starts, but I was playing really rubbish when we travelled to Charlton for the fourth round of the League Cup at the end of November. It was a nightmare. I look back now and see it as a turning point, but I didn't spot it at the time. We were 2–0 down, and Sparky took me off. Rovers, minus me, went on to win 3–2. David Bentley scored a late winner after goals from Shefki and David Thompson. We were in the quarter-finals, but no thanks to me. Knowing that Sparky couldn't change the team after that, I went to see him in his office. 'I know I'm not playing well. What can I do?' I asked him.

'All I want you to do is what I bought you for. Stop trying to be something you aren't.' He told me he was going to drop me for the next game against Everton.

'Please don't leave me out.' I was almost begging.

'It will do you the world of good,' was his reply.

'Right, gaffer, I'll tell you now that this will be the last time you ever leave me out. I'll make sure of that.' I looked him in the eye when I said it, and I wasn't being nasty or sarcastic. It was a fact. I wasn't going to let it happen to me again. We lost to Everton, and next game – West Ham at home – I was back in. I hit the bar twice with free kicks, won man of the match and we beat the Hammers 3–2. I looked at Sparky and said, 'I told you.' From then on, I was outstanding. It's funny how little things can sometimes trigger you off. I was Sparky's massive signing, so it must have been a hard decision to leave me out, but he was not afraid to make it. He felt it was the right one, and he didn't care whether you were a player he'd just bought for £3.1 million or if you were someone who had come through the ranks.

In December, we beat Wigan 3–0 in a completely unmemorable match but one that would prove to be significant for me. Paul Jewell was manager of Wigan, and I discovered later that he used my Prozone stats as an example to his players. I found out by accident. I bumped into Wigan's Prozone guy in a bar, and he told me that the stats were the best there had ever been in the Premier League in terms of sprints and high intensity. At 3–0 up, I was still doing it. Jewell was so impressed he went on to buy me when he was at Derby.

The team hit consistent form around Christmas-time, which was just as well, because we faced the prospect of playing Manchester United three times in three weeks. We were paired with United in the semi-final of the League Cup, and then they had to come to Ewood Park in the League. And I got into a bit of bother with Rio Ferdinand. The thing with Rio is that he's a nice guy. He's a world-class player – for me the best centre-half in England – and we live near each other. I went out in London one night with a few mates, and we couldn't get into this place. Rio was sitting at the bar, saw us and said to the bouncer, 'They're with me.' We were allowed in.

That night was the last thing on our minds in the second leg of our semi. The first leg had ended 1–1, even though we were the better team. We were going to Old Trafford as underdogs. Ruud van Nistelrooy scored quickly; then Steven Reid equalised before Louis Saha grabbed the winner in the second half. Brad Friedel saved a penalty. I tackled van Nistelrooy in the corner, and he went down and kneed me in the head as we fell. I thought he'd done it on purpose. As I jumped up, I pushed him, and we called each other names. The whistle went for half-time, and Ferdinand sprinted 50 yards, nudged me and called me something. I can't recall the exact words, but they weren't complimentary! 'I'm not having that,' I thought, as I chased up the tunnel after him and booted him up the backside. Not hard, but I kicked him.

Out of nowhere, all these security men appeared. They pinned me against the tunnel, which I thought was a bit unfair, and Ferdinand hit me. Not hard, but he hit me. Then I was punched in the back of the head by someone. Not hard. All the lads saw what was happening and raced into the tunnel. There was a lot of shouting and yelling, and I was being held by this huge security guard. He finally released me, and I escaped to the dressing-room. 'What happened?' asked Sparky.

'Well, gaffer,' I replied. 'Rio's nudged me, I've kicked him up the arse, and he's hit me. Then the security man's held me and someone's punched me in the back of the head.'

On the way back out, I told Andy Todd what happened. Toddy wasn't playing, so he stood waiting for the United players to come through. He's a great mate and hard as nails. He went up to Rio and said, 'Two against one? That's not very fair.' I don't think Rio said anything. He knew that Toddy was sticking up for me, just like the player who had punched me in the back of the head was sticking up for Rio. It was one of those things in the tunnel, and I'd been the main target again. The most disappointing thing was losing the game.

PS to Rio: you might be the best centre-half in England, but I'm a better midfielder than you! I proved it too, about a week after the Cup game when United came to our place in the League. The scoreline provides a clue to what happened. We won 4–3 thanks to David Bentley's hat-trick and a goal by Lucas Neill. At 4–1 up, we were cruising. I was having a good game against Ferdinand. That's my turf, Rio. Then Ruud van Nistelrooy came on and scored twice, and we were hanging on for the win.

In the last few minutes, Rio came flying in with a high challenge and hardly touched me. I hit the deck and screamed out like I'd been shot. Didier Drogba would have been proud of the noise I made. Yellow card for Rio, to go with the one he'd already collected. Ferdinand was sent off, and I was stretchered off and back to the dressing-room – where I started jumping around at the final whistle! I came out afterwards wearing this big surgical boot, even though there was nothing wrong with me.

February marked a hot streak for Bellers – and another trip to Dubai for us. Sparky liked to reward us and took us twice. There are only five cloudy days a year there, and on both trips there was no sun. No good for my tan whatsoever! We beat Sunderland 2–0 before the trip, with Craig scoring both of them. He would go on to net eight in eight, which effectively launched us into Europe.

The first match after the break was Arsenal at home. It was a muddy pitch. Arsenal didn't fancy it. They hated playing against us, because we used to smash them all over the park. They could play their fancy football if you let them. We used to kick lumps out of them – but fairly. Pedersen scored the only goal to give us the win. I ran past Jens Lehmann at the end and roared at him. He sprayed a bottle of water in my face. That was a satisfying result.

Tottenham away next. It was up there as game of the season. I record every match that is shown on Sky. I play them back and see how I can improve. We were 2–0 down to a Robbie Keane double then pulled it back to 2–2, and Martin Tyler was saying, 'Blackburn are going to score again in a minute.' Instead, Mido got the winner for Spurs. It was a fantastic match. Even though we lost, we were full of confidence and would be defeated only twice more all season.

On a personal note, I was about to learn how it felt to be sent off for the first time in club football. I'd already been dismissed – completely unfairly – playing for Wales against Northern Ireland. Now it was Chris Foy's turn to have his name up in lights. We were entertaining Middlesbrough and beat them 3–2, thanks to two from Craig and one from Morten. Bellers was sensational that day, otherwise a lot more would have been written about Foy's terrible decision. How on earth it was a sending off, I will never know. I might have got away with a few in the past, but . . .

The first tackle on George Boateng wasn't worth a yellow card. Foy still booked me, because that was the agenda he had. I was told once that referees were instructed to book me in the first half, and I'd calm down. I would love to know whether that was true. Just after half-time, I was in the middle of the park, five yards away from Boateng, who smashed the ball as hard as he could at me. I tried to cover my face, the ball hit me on the arm and the ref blew the whistle and sent me off. I looked in disbelief. I didn't even bother to argue. It was a joke red card. I was sent off because I was Robbie Savage. 'That's what you want,' I thought to myself. 'When you write your book, you can say you were the first Premier League referee to send off Robbie Savage.'

I scored only one goal that season. I scored only one League goal for Blackburn during my time there. To think I had been trying to make it as a centre-forward at Manchester United! Me being me, the goal could come only at one place: St Andrew's. I don't know who writes my script, but this was an amazing first return to Birmingham. It would have been a proper fairy tale had Mikael Forssell not scored a late winner, which meant we lost 2–1.

There was so much hype in the build-up. Afterwards, chairman David Gold accused me of not shaking his hand. What a load of nonsense. I was warming up on one side of the pitch, and he sent a steward across the pitch to say, 'David Gold is over there, and he wants to say hello.'

'I'm sorry,' I replied. 'I'm warming up, and I can't go over to shake Mr Gold's hand.'

I wasn't refusing at all, but I couldn't do it at that moment. I became some kind of bad guy who'd snubbed David Gold. I felt a bit let down. Of course I would shake his hand, and I have done so since. When I came out of the tunnel, I was right beside the Blackburn fans. They were going berserk. Because Blackburn is only a small-town club, the following of fans is not that great. There was only a handful of those fans, but they were making a right noise. They were singing, 'We've got Robbie Savage.'

'Greedy bastard,' came the reply from the baying Birmingham supporters.

They absolutely hammered me. There were some friendly faces that day, though. A few women kissed me and said I'd been great for Blues. Scoring was the last thing I thought I would do. We were aiming for Europe, and Birmingham were near the relegation zone, and I would have loved to have scored the goal that sent them down – because of the hassle I'd had.

They scored through Nicky Butt, and then the ball dropped to me on the edge of the area. What I was doing there, I don't know. I sidefooted it in, and something took over me. I ran round like a mad man. I looked up at the directors' box and pointed to my shirt. It was aimed at the two Davids, Sullivan and Gold. 'Hey, this is what you're missing.'

It was a great feeling to ram the words down the fans' throats. Those supporters should have given me a standing ovation for what I did for that football club, on and off the field. They should have. They should have thought, 'He was magnificent for us. He's made the club a big profit.' I gave them three great years, and they should have bowed to me really. But they didn't, so I thought, 'Right, I'm going to celebrate this goal.'

What people didn't see was me giving Mikael a low five and saying, 'Good goal, mate,' when he scored. It was no coincidence that Birmingham got relegated when I wasn't there. Was the reaction wrong? No. I was absolutely delighted to score. I was gutted for the likes of Steve Bruce, John Benson, Rita – the manager's secretary – and Brian in the car park when they went down. But for the fans who gave me so much stick, for Karren Brady, people like that, I was delighted they went down. You do things on the spur of the moment, and that's how I reacted that day. I still can't believe I scored!

My reactions were very different a few days later when we were hit by lightning as we flew back from a 2–0 win at Charlton. Fear of flying, hypochondria and obsessive compulsive disorder: I blame my mother for all of them. If she has a headache, it's a brain tumour, and I'm the same.

And I am particularly petrified of flying. It was at Blackburn when it really kicked in. We were in a 30-seater and about to land when the captain came on over the tannoy: 'Just to warn you, there's a huge storm ahead for the final descent.'

I was petrified. On one side of the plane, you could see blue skies, and on the other side it was just a big mass of black clouds. There was a bang like a bomb. I saw this blue light. The cockpit door flew open, and one side of the plane had no power. One of the lads wet himself, he was so frightened. When we landed, everyone cheered and clapped. They told us afterwards there was a hole in the rudder because the lightning hadn't conducted.

Since then, I have been responsible for getting a senior pilot fired. He invited me into the cockpit on a private flight back from Europe with Blackburn, because he knew I was frightened. For him to have been sacked for that was ludicrous. They said I was a terrorist threat: me, with my big white shiny teeth. He was so nice too. He'd flown in the war on bombing missions, and he lost his job because of me. I hate flying.

I was fine when it came to flying up the table. We beat Chelsea 1–0, and I still believe I scored the goal to send us into Europe. Steven Reid is officially down for it, and said he touched it, but I'm not sure about that. My in-swinging free kicks had become a bit of a trademark. The ball was going in, and Reidy, who's got no hair really, claimed it glanced off his head. It was mine, Reidy! What an amazing season. Sparky had saved us from relegation the year before and taken us to sixth in the table. We beat Manchester United twice, saw off Arsenal, beat Chelsea. Our bonus was something like £30,000.

I was also very settled off the pitch. After six months as Fergie's neighbours, Sarah and I found our dream house. There is a corner of Cheshire that should be called Footballers' Triangle. Players from Manchester United, Manchester City, Blackburn – most of the north-west clubs – live there, and it is a beautiful part of the country. I could be at my parents' in 45 minutes and Blackburn's state-of-the-art Brockhall training ground in about the same time. Sarah spotted the house first. When I saw the brochure, I thought it looked like a big greenhouse with scaffolding around it. 'Is it finished? I asked Sarah.

In actual fact, I loved it. It was a beautiful, modern house and helped us forget our Stratford nightmare. There was only one problem: it was white on the outside, white on the inside, and I have OCD. We also live in a country where it rains. A lot. So it meant my house was always going green on the outside, and it did my head in. When the lads came to jet wash my car, I'd ask them to jet wash the house too! Young kids, two dogs: all Sarah and I ever argue about is the cleanliness of our house. I'm petrified of people visiting in case they leave a mess, even though I'm proud of showing it off.

The house cost £2 million. I said to Mum, 'You'll love it when you see it.' She walked through the front door and burst into tears. Then she started cleaning it. Only joking, but it is another thing I inherited from my Mum. She goes off like a bottle of pop, and so do I. She hates things being a mess, and so do I. She's a hypochondriac, and so am I. She has been known to pick up dusters and cleaning stuff on her visits. I don't do that.

Luckily, she wasn't there the day it nearly caught fire. The house is all glass with plenty of wood too, so it would have gone up in seconds. My cousin Matt saved the day. It was about seven in the morning, and Sarah asked me if I could smell smoke. It was a bit like when a fly or moth hits a light and sizzles, that kind of smell. Matt was staying with us, and his room was downstairs. Suddenly, Matt was racing up the stairs, yelling, 'Smoke!' The smoke alarms didn't go off.

Next to his room was the cinema room, and there was smoke coming from it. All the electrics were in there, on a wooden board in a cupboard. Matt and I ran down the stairs and opened the door of the cupboard. Flames were shooting out. I panicked. Water. That's what was needed. On an electrical circuit? Luckily, Matt realised and ran for the fire extinguishers we had in the house. We let one off and were choking at the fumes. Now I know how those guests felt in La Manga all those years ago with Leicester. We had to replace the circuit board, and I was known as 'Fireman Sav' after that. It didn't put us off loving the house, though.

Everything had fallen into place perfectly. I was an important part of a top-six team and looking forward to a season in Europe. And Birmingham were back in the Championship.

19

LEARNING TO WALK AGAIN

Beetroot can turn your pee red. When it happened to me, I thought I was passing blood. Seriously. Something had to be dreadfully wrong. It was only a matter of time. 'Quick, Doc. There's blood in my wee.'

'Have you eaten beetroot?'

'No. Of course not.'

'Are you sure?'

'Yeah, I'm sure. Well, I did have the one slice.'

See what I mean about being a hypochondriac? Because I am so lucky in my life, I always think something will go wrong. I have to ask four or five doctors for their opinion on everything, and I blame Mum. I was kicked in the thigh once, and a lump came up in my groin. The doc said it was bruising, but I didn't believe him. 'This is it,' I thought. 'I've got cancer.' Eventually, I badgered the doctor at Blackburn to arrange a scan. It was all clear. Yet the day I suffered a horrific compound fracture to my leg I tried to stand up and walk on it! There was a horrendous crunching sound. The physio pulled my sock down. There was blood everywhere, and the bone was sticking out of my leg. My season of promise was over, ended by a career-threatening injury at Watford.

It had been going so well up until then too. I was given a new contract that went up in stages from £24,000 to £26,000 a week, plus a £100,000 signing-on fee. New players arrived to replace the likes of Craig Bellamy, who joined Liverpool. Bye-bye to Bellers, but hello to Jason Roberts, Benni McCarthy, André Ooijer and Shabani Nonda. I went to Craig's wedding that summer and sat next to Craig's agent, who was telling me that Bellers had always been a Liverpool fan. I was gutted to see him go, but some of the lads would have been pleased, especially Morten!

Nonda came from Congo and couldn't speak much English. His most memorable moment came when we played in Kraków in the UEFA Cup. Sparky had a go at him at half-time, and Shabani put up his hands and said, 'Gaffer, I just want to be loved.'

André Ooijer was a Barry Chuckle lookalike, except Barry Chuckle was probably quicker! Andre and I went through our rehab together, because he broke his leg the week before I broke mine. Steven Reid had a long-term injury during that time too, so the three of us would sweat it out in the gym together. We didn't start the season too well, losing to Portsmouth and Chelsea and drawing against Everton. In the 0–0 draw at Sheffield United in September, Brad Friedel saved two penalties. Brad was the best keeper I ever played with. He'd give you ten points a season. He was a lovely guy, a real gentleman and one of my wife's favourite players.

We were all looking forward to Europe, our reward for finishing sixth. To reach the group stages of the UEFA Cup, we had to beat Salzburg over two legs. There was a familiar face in charge of the Austrian club: Lothar Matthäus, whom I had managed to wind up so successfully when he had been Hungary coach and I had still been playing for Wales. We drew 2–2 on the artificial pitch at the Red Bull Stadium. It was my best game for Blackburn. I scored a great free kick, bent it into the top corner. Before the home leg, I saw an interview with Matthäus in which he was saying it could be a hard game because Blackburn had some exceptional players – like Robbie Savage. Matthäus saying I was exceptional? It was unbelievable to hear one of the best players in the world compliment me like that. I was thinking, 'Right. I'm on fire here.'

We beat Salzburg 2–0. David Bentley scored a great volley, and we went through. Our League form started to turn too. We beat Manchester City, Middlesbrough and Wigan and drew with Liverpool, then headed off to Poland on another European adventure. Kraków was a very daunting place to go, but Savage scored: a trademark header! I celebrated in style. It was the day after my birthday. All the lads grabbed me, pulled down my shorts and soaked me. It was their idea of a birthday present.

Injuries are the biggest blight on any footballer's career. Until I broke my leg, I'd been reasonably lucky through my career. The broken neck was the worst before that. I was always very confident of avoiding muscle pulls, though. If you haven't got any muscles, you can't tear them! I wasn't quick enough to pull them either. But in a 1–0 defeat at home to Bolton I did my thigh. *Bang*. Gone. I have always had great powers of recovery and was back and raring to go for the UEFA Cup fixture against Basle. Unbelievably, I did my thigh again. I just stopped, turned and it went in exactly the same place. I was subbed after 38 minutes, and the lads went on to win 3–0.

I missed a few games after that, and the season was becoming very stop–start for me. I played against Feyenoord and should have scored in the goalless draw. Morten was hit by a pint of beer thrown out of the crowd. We beat Nancy 1–0 too. This was why I had joined Blackburn. Having shaken off the thigh injury, I was coming back into form – and so was the team. Worzel Gummidge – Tugay – made it a memorable Boxing Day. We beat Liverpool, and Tugay produced one of the best stepovers you will ever see on Steven Gerrard. He put in Pedersen, who crossed for McCarthy. One–nil to Rovers. A great feeling.

Then it was Middlesbrough at home. The game should have been called off. The Ewood Park pitch was thick, thick mud. I was sensational and put the ball in for Benni, who headed the winner. I'd had my best game for Blackburn on AstroTurf, and I had my second-best game on mud. Afterwards, Benni joked, 'Why can't you play on grass like you play on artificial pitches and mud?'

Blackburn played Derby a few years later, and Benni said, tongue-in-cheek, that I was the worst technical player he'd ever seen. When he saw the headlines, he rang and apologised, but I knew what he had meant. Benni called me 'Stinky', because I once took my suit jacket off and was sweating under my arms. To me he was 'Benni No-calves', because he didn't have any!

We went straight from the Middlesbrough game to a Manchester hotel to prepare for Wigan on New Year's Day. I was probably asleep when 2007 arrived! We beat Wigan at the JJB, and I was fantastic. I was at the peak of my Blackburn career. I was the player Sparky had bought for £3.1 million. I wanted to be the best player in training, I wanted to be the best player in games and I had an aura. I couldn't do anything wrong. In fact, it got to the stage where the other lads used to call Sparky my dad and take the mick out of me: 'Ask your dad what we're doing.' I loved it all. The highlight was Sparky pulling me into his office before we played Manchester City. 'I want you to be my captain,' he said.

What an honour. What a turnaround. I went from arguing, not performing and not earning the respect of the lads to being offered the armband. Ryan Nelsen was our club captain, but he'd been injured for all of the season. He tore his hamstring off the bone and had even played with it. He eventually had to have it pinned back to his arse. He was a great leader, a nice guy and a really tough New Zealander. In his absence, Lucas Neill skippered the side, but he joined West Ham in the January. Now I was being asked to be the new leader. My hero had named me captain, and we were still in Europe and still in the FA Cup.

We beat City 3–0, and André Ooijer broke his leg. I went over to him and looked down. He was in so much pain he was screaming. I hugged him and said, 'Don't worry. You'll be all right.' It took the shine off. André was from Holland. He found it hard in his first six or seven games in the country, and I hammered him for that. 'You were hopeless,' I'd tell him. But he turned it around and became a key figure – then broke his leg.

I phoned my missus after the game, and she said, 'Oh, you won 3–0, and you were captain.'

'But André broke his leg,' I replied. I sat on the team bus thinking about him. I felt distraught for him. I couldn't go through that: the pain, the shock, the long road to recovery. No. I couldn't go through that. I imagined how he felt. Three days later, I knew exactly.

Every minute of that trip to Watford is imprinted in my memory. It is like having the DVD in your head ready to play at any moment. We didn't start the game that well. Alhassan Bangura tried to elbow me. Right. Next chance I got, I was going to nail him. The ball dropped between us, and I went in fair and square. I was about to give it everything but sidefooted it, so my leg was open. Imagine sidefooting as hard as possible and following through. He came as well, and he did the cowardly thing. Straight-legged, studs up, over the ball. I kicked, and his leg was there. I was at full power, and he caught me, studs up. I've seen the photos, and he wasn't even looking. Dermot Gallagher, a referee I respect and admire, was right there. I will never know to this day how Dermot missed that. He never even booked him.

'That's not right,' I thought as I went down. It was similar to when I broke my neck, but instead of pins and needles down my arm I had pins and needles down my shin. 'It's a nerve. I've jolted a nerve,' I thought. I've seen the pictures since, and the shock on my face was clear. I was a deathly white colour, despite the fake tan. I looked across at Sparky and said, 'I've broken my leg.'

'No, you'll be fine.' It was the physio.

'Hang on,' I said. 'It's come back a bit. I think I'm okay.' I stood up and put my foot on the grass. The grinding noise was horrendous.

The physio pulled down my sock, saw blood everywhere and the bone jutting out, and shook his head: 'It's broken, Sav.'

As I was stretchered off, I could not help but think about André the week before. Why me? Why now? The biggest thought in my head, banging away along with my throbbing broken leg, was 'Am I ever going to play again?'

I'd seen Luc Nilis, Roberto di Matteo, David Busst. When you follow football, you know that a compound fracture is 50–50. The Watford fans were laughing and cheering. I was in shock in the medical room. Their doc grabbed my ankle and my shin halfway down, moved them, and the whole leg moved. 'Yes, it's broken.'

I knew that! I burst into tears and phoned Mum. I was crying my eyes out. Doc Batty, the Blackburn club doctor, was tremendous. So was physio Dave Fevre. They loved me even though I was a nuisance. I did wind them up. We flew back to Lancashire, and I was at the back of the plane. The lads didn't know what to say to me. Reidy came up to me, and he said, 'How are you?' I started crying and didn't stop for the whole of the 45-minute flight. There was an ambulance on the tarmac. I wasn't in that much pain, funnily enough. David Fevre had said to me before we boarded the plane, 'I can't believe how good you are being about this.'

'Don't worry, Dave. I'll be back in five months.'

By the time we took off, my emotions had got the better of me. I was going to miss Europe. I was going to miss the FA Cup. Would I ever play again? We went to the BUPA hospital in Whalley Range, where a surgeon called John Hodgkinson saved my career. He is one of my idols now. He showed me the X-rays. It was one of the worst breaks you could get. It was a compound break, fragmented, coming out of the skin. Six months later, John admitted that it had been 50–50 in terms of playing again.

'I'm warning you now that when you wake up in the morning it will be the worst pain you have ever had,' John told me.

'It can't be any worse than I'm feeling now.'

'Trust me,' he said. 'You will be in pain.'

They put a nail into my leg. I woke up the next morning, and the pain was indescribable. I went home that night, and I was on all the painkillers you can think of. I was throwing up on the way home in the car. I slept downstairs for a week. My leg was in a right mess. It was like a car accident. Absolutely horrendous. The club were great, sending me flowers, and Doc Batty was great, phoning the family. I just lay there and cried for a week. I couldn't believe it had happened to me. Sarah was pregnant with our second son, Freddie. This time, we knew it was going to be another little boy. She was three or four months pregnant, so the last thing she wanted was someone moping about the house being sick. It was like having another baby there. I couldn't cope. I didn't eat. Why me?

I couldn't even imagine myself walking. You have to learn to do it all over again. David Fevre was laughing at me, because I couldn't even manage that. As soon as I took my first step, I thought, 'I'm never going to play football again.' But I was determined to get right. I was in the gym every single day. The encouragement of everyone around me was incredible. André and Reidy were going through it too, with bad injuries. Reidy did his knee ligaments.

We went to Marbella that summer for a week, and we paid for a physio to come out there with us. Every morning, we were on the sand. Before that, we were in early at Brockhall and home late. We swam and had the most rigorous routine you could imagine. I actually looked all right, for once! There was some muscle in my legs, chest and arms. Tony Strudwick, who is at Manchester United, and Simon Bitcom, who is at Manchester City, rehabilitated me. It was Simon we took away on holiday with us. They gave me motivation, and without them I would have packed it in.

I still needed to see a psychologist, Steve Peters, because I was so down and depressed. I thought I was never going to play again, that I would never be Robbie Savage again. This could be it. Doc Batty told me that other players had visited Steve, and he said, 'I think you should see him.'

I couldn't cope, and I'm not afraid to admit it. I was mentally distraught. I went along, and Steve gave me a great hour. My biggest worry was that I wouldn't get back into the team and that I wouldn't be the same. 'You will,' he promised. It did me the world of good to speak to him.

After the first month, I had an appointment with the surgeon. The big fear was that if you didn't get any growth in the bone it could calcify. 'This is unbelievable,' he said. 'It's filling in well already.'

John Hodgkinson is prim and proper with grey hair. I jumped on him, scuffed his hair and called him Johnny! 'I'll be back for the FA Cup semi-final,' I announced.

'I wouldn't start planning that. You've still got a long road ahead.'

It was a long road, but I stayed on it and kept working hard. The first time I went out to kick the ball, I felt the leg was going to snap again. I had to build up confidence. I would like to thank everyone for that. Catherine and Julie were the two girls who worked at Brockhall. I burst into tears in front of them once, and they were so supportive. I had pins in my leg, and one of the pins was on my nerve. I couldn't even put my foot down properly, and emotion took over. I've had the pins out since, but the nails stayed. It still hurts. Every day of my life, I will have a pain in my shin somewhere. I deal with it by recalling how I felt when I broke it and how I thought I'd never play again. 'You're daft as a brush,' the surgeon said. 'But you're one of the most determined, nicest people I've ever met. That injury would have finished a lot of people.'

I was such a nuisance to Doc Batty at the club that it got to the point where he'd see my number come up on his phone and not answer. While I was injured, we went out of Europe to Bayer Leverkusen in the third round, but the boys had a great Cup run to the semi-final. Part of me wanted them to win, but part of me hoped they wouldn't, because I was on the outside looking in. It was a horrible feeling. They were out training, and I was in the gym. When you're injured, you are not part of it. The manager doesn't want to know. You're no use.

I was in the Sky studio for the semi against Chelsea at Old Trafford. I sat there, and half of me was thinking, 'Please don't win.' Imagine the lads going to Wembley. I should have been there, leading them. At 1–1, the ball fell to Morten at the back stick and he missed the header. Half of me was yelling, 'Just put it in.' The other half wasn't. It wasn't very nice of me. These were my teammates, my friends, and the Blackburn fans deserved a trip to Wembley.

'You hope we lose, don't you?' It was David Dunn.

'No, I don't.'

'Yes, you do.'

He was half joking, but he was half right. Michael Ballack scored in extra time, and Chelsea won. When I saw the lads in the dressing-room afterwards, I had to take a long hard look at myself. I saw the dejection of Sparky, of John Williams. They had shown so much faith in me. It was me, me, me, and I didn't like myself very much. I was only considering one person: Robbie Savage. I carried on working hard on my rehab. The summer was a slog, but I also became a father for the second time.

Freddie Jack Savage was born on 17 July 2007. Jack was the name of Sarah's granddad. Freddie weighed 8 lb 1 oz. Sarah had had an epidural and a caesarean for Charlie, but she had only gas and air for Freddie. It was funny, because she used up the gas in the first ten minutes. She was telling me in no uncertain terms how she was feeling. Her language was disgusting! Freddie was born at Macclesfield Hospital, and Charlie had a baby brother. I was such a proud father. My two little boys, my little angels.

When they are older, I hope they will be proud of the way I came back from my broken leg. Fittingly, it was in a pre-season friendly at Wrexham. The fans were wonderful with me – what a change of attitude – and it was very emotional for Mum and Dad, who were there too. The pain was still horrendous. I had special shin pads made, because the callus on my leg was huge. It was like having a tennis ball on your shin. We won 2–0. Benni McCarthy knew I was from Wrexham and knew how much it meant for me to come back in that game, and he let me take a penalty.

Once again, Sparky was busy in the summer. Stephen Warnock arrived from Liverpool. He'd had two broken legs so knew what I'd gone through. We also brought in 'Gorgeous'. Roque Santa Cruz moved from Bayern Munich and in his first training session blew everybody away. He was up against Chrissy Samba, who'd started to make a reputation for himself, and Roque made Chris look like a schoolboy, he was that big, that strong, that quick. We couldn't believe we had him. What a signing he was and a wonderful guy, probably the best-looking guy I've seen and a massive player. It was me who nicknamed him Gorgeous.

My first Premier League match was at Middlesbrough. We won 2–0 thanks to Roque and Matt Derbyshire. David Dunn and I also proved we could play alongside each other. For some reason, it was always said at Birmingham that we couldn't. I don't know why. He liked to get on the ball and drive forward, and I was the one who scrapped and gave the ball to Dunny. In the first five minutes, I made an unbelievable challenge. Boro had an open goal, and I managed to sprint back and tackle. I celebrated like I'd scored. I was back. It was a great start for us, and there were no ill effects from my leg.

Then we played Manchester City at home. Benni dropped a ball short to me. I saw Richard Dunne galloping towards the ball, and I knew he wouldn't stop. 'I've got to go for this,' I thought.

Richard made a wonderful tackle. He took my leg too, and I thought I'd broken it again. The pain was the same. I couldn't walk, so I was stretchered off, straight into the ambulance and to hospital for an X-ray. All clear. Thank God. Richard Dunne didn't try to do me at all: it was a fair, firm tackle. I was straight back for the next match, which was a 0–0 draw at Chelsea. I made a last-ditch challenge on Michael Essien, and Taff came up to me after the game and said, 'That's the Robbie Savage I know. You haven't given Essien a kick all afternoon.'

He was right, but I was in total agony. I lay on the bed in tears at how my leg was feeling. I said I would be able to play against Greek side Larissa in the UEFA Cup, but I wasn't fit. I did myself no favours. It was a nightmare, and we lost 2–0. By the time we met them in the second leg, Sparky could see I was struggling and pulled me out. I went on as late sub, and we beat them 2–1 but still went out 3–2 on aggregate. I was going through a really dark time, but there was one patch of light: I made up with Steve Bruce.

Birmingham were due at Ewood Park, and in the run-up to the game I did a lot of thinking. Going through those months with a broken leg had made me realise a few things. I told myself a few home truths. Brucie, my hero when I was growing up at Manchester United, had given me a fantastic opportunity at Birmingham, and it had not ended well. So, before the 2–1 win, I made a beeline for him, gave him a big hug and apologised to him. It was something I was glad to do. He deserved it. 'I was wrong,' I said to him.

'Listen, Sav, people do things for a reason,' he replied. 'There are no hard feelings. You were wonderful for me.'

I looked him in the eye and thought to myself, 'I've shit on you, really.'

When I look back over my career, I can nearly always point to a match or an incident as the reason for what happened next. The beginning of the end at Blackburn came in a 2–1 win at Tottenham late in October. I went to tackle Robbie Keane just before half-time, and my foot stuck in the grass. I thought I'd done my cruciate ligament. My knee went under me. I looked at Robbie, and he looked at me. The expression on my face must have scared him, because he signalled straight away to the physio. I went off at half-time, and my knee was like a balloon. The docs opened me up, and I'd only ripped off a bit of cartilage and muscle. It was going to be fine. First my leg, now the knee. I was getting older. Things were conspiring against me. I had only 18 months left on my contract.

I was out for the whole of November with the knee and made my return as half-time sub against West Ham in December, a match we lost 0–1. I was back in training, but I was on the bench for three or four games. Sparky was playing Aaron Mokoena in the middle of the park. We called him 'the Axe', because of his tackles. But Aaron wasn't playing well. We were beaten 4–0 at home by Villa, and I was sub. I couldn't understand Sparky's thinking. Nothing against Aaron, but I thought I should have been playing. I went to see Sparky. 'Why aren't you changing it, gaffer?' I asked.

'I'm just looking after you.'

'I'm fit. I've been fit two or three weeks, but I'm sub.'

Sunderland and Derby were both after me. I knew it, although nothing official had been said. That's how football works. I was joking around the training ground, telling the lads that I was in demand. I wasn't happy about being sub, but I trained as hard as I always did. I was still a massive influence in the training room. The lads loved me. I was the biggest joker, but there was somebody at Blackburn who had it in for me. I didn't know who it was, but someone didn't like me. I'd be in the treatment room saying, jokingly, 'Oh, don't worry. I'll be playing for Sunderland next week.'

Then, when we travelled to Derby at the end of December, I was not even on the bench. Sparky stood in front of the lads and said, 'I just want people who want to play for me.'

I was furious. I stormed away from the dressing-room and did something I shouldn't have done. I knew that Paul Jewell wanted me, and I was convinced that someone at Blackburn was putting down poison. Without thinking, I walked straight into Jewell's office. He was there with his assistant Stan Ternent and coach Mark Seagraves, and I announced, 'Can you believe it? I'm not even on the bench.'

In effect, I gave away the team to an opposition manager. My only defence was that he would have found out in about five minutes anyway. On the Monday morning, I went to see Sparky and asked, 'Why did you leave me out of the squad?'

'I heard that you were going round the training ground saying you don't want to be at Blackburn any longer.'

'Sparky, I know you better than anybody in football, and I would have come to tell you if that was the case. I was doing it tongue-in-cheek.' I could feel myself filling up as we spoke. My emotions were getting the better of me. 'Sparky, I respect you too much to do that. Someone here has got it in for me, and they're spreading stories.'

He accepted it, but I didn't get back into the team. I was training with the reserves – not as a punishment but because I wasn't part of the first team. I kept my head down, but I was worried about what was happening. Eventually, I went to see Sparky again. 'I want to go,' I told him. 'I can't do any more for you. I'm not getting in the team as regularly as I would like. I'm not a big influence any more. Can I go, please? I will never put a transfer request in, but let me get one last decent contract somewhere else. Sparky, this is the hardest thing I've ever done. You're my idol, and I'm asking to go.'

'I want you to stay, Sav,' he said. 'You'll be involved – but not every game.'

I felt like I was in danger of finding myself in the knacker's yard, what with my leg and then my knee. I didn't want Sparky to see me like that. I wanted to walk out with my head held high. We'd stayed up that first season and qualified for Europe, and he had given me the armband. I didn't want him watching me, thinking, 'You've gone, Sav.' I would rather someone else said that to me, someone who didn't mean as much. If I couldn't be much use to Blackburn, then maybe I could do a job somewhere else. Sitting on the bench and fading into the background wasn't my scene. I wanted to be a presence in the dressing-room and a presence on the pitch. I explained it all to Sparky.

'OK, Sav. You can go.'

20

RAM TO THE SLAUGHTER

'**Y**ou'll have an easy life at Derby.'

They were Mark Bowen's last words to me at Blackburn. If I'd known what was waiting round the corner, I would have run a mile in the opposite direction – probably to Sunderland! Taff couldn't have been more wrong. The day I signed for the Rams, I stepped into a living nightmare, even if I didn't realise it straight away. On the face of it, I'd made a fantastic move. I definitely couldn't believe the contract: two and a half years at £23,000 a week. No escape clause for relegation, but no pay cut for relegation either. My future was secure until the age of 35. What a result – even though it was a drop from what I was earning at Rovers.

In the end, it was an easy choice between Sunderland and Derby. Roy Keane couldn't make our meeting. And when I met Paul Jewell, we got on like a house on fire. Blackburn chairman John Williams was brilliant when it came to letting me go. I told him I didn't want to leave with a penny, and John very generously priced me at £1.5 million to help speed my departure. Both clubs met the valuation, and I was given permission to speak to them.

Sunderland were offering an 18-month deal, and the Stadium of Light was a long way from home. Those were the downsides. But they were a huge club, and Keane was a legend of a player. Jewell wanted to tie me down for longer, and I could commute to Derby from Cheshire, but they were cast adrift at the bottom of the Premier League. The pros and cons were flashing through my mind. I was due to see Keane first, at a hotel in Hale. I was just about to leave home when Keane's agent rang: 'Roy can't make it.'

That swung the decision. The next day, I met Jewell. He loved me as a player, and he struck me as my kind of manager. I thought he was great. Even though I knew Derby were going down, I was signing for a manager who believed in me and who wanted me to help with coming back up. When I went to say my goodbyes at Blackburn, I was full of optimism and hope. I hugged Sparky and thanked him. I think it hurt that I was leaving because I was loved there. I don't think John Williams or Sparky would have done that for any other player. It was solely because it was me. They repaid me for what I'd done for them.

My medical at Derby took half an hour. I couldn't believe how short it was for a 33 year old who'd just come back from a broken leg. Jewell and I sat down properly for the first time, and it struck me straight away that I was going to get on with this guy. He was laughing and joking and very complimentary towards me, and I thought this was the start of a wonderful relationship. On the first Friday, he pulled me into his office and made me captain. We were due to play against Wigan.

I have never been so nervous before a debut. This was Derby, remember. During my time at Leicester, I'd had more than my share of bust-ups with our main East Midlands rivals. When Jim Smith was in charge at Pride Park, he had accused me of always starting riots. All week, I'd been reading in the papers and on the Internet about the reception the Derby fans were planning, and I didn't see anything about a red carpet! I was scared. All I could think of was the number of times I had managed to rile the Rams while wearing a Leicester shirt. To make matters worse, I wasn't too sure about my reception in the dressing-room either. Matt Oakley had been captain, but Jewell sold him to Leicester as I came in. I knew Matt was a good lad, a mate to the players, and I felt a bit bad.

There were people like Darren Moore and Marc Edworthy, who'd been there a lot longer than me. But I was coming in as captain. It just showed what faith Jewell had in me, and I was very honoured. And, despite the scare stories in the week, the crowd gave me a fabulous reception. I didn't play well. I hadn't played for ages at Blackburn, and I was knackered. The occasion got to me. We lost 1–0, and that was a sign of things to come. I didn't realise how bad things were at Derby. I'd looked at the League table and thought, 'It can't be that bad.'

But Andy Todd, my old mate from Blackburn, was there, and he'd warned me. It was bad. So that was the first game, and the first week of training was pretty grim too. Confidence was that low after going so many matches without a win. The lads couldn't string three or four passes together, and I was thinking, 'Oh God almighty.' But I thought I could be a big influence and help turn it round.

The gaffer was so complimentary to me. He pulled me into his office and told me I was a good player. He wanted a big personality. My first act was to start a lookalike board. We'd done it at Blackburn, and it had worked a treat. Someone pinned up a photo of an Afghan hound. That was supposed to be me! Darren Moore was Kimbo Slice, the wrestler, and David Jones was Wallace from Wallace and Gromit. And Jewell? I thought he was the spitting image of a famous cartoon character, so up went that picture.

Jewell loved it. Or at least he appeared to love it, and I felt we were creating some spirit in the squad. But the next picture of him didn't go down too well. It was another cartoon character, but he took exception and came charging in to have a go at me. I'd overstepped the mark. You could almost see the pressure building on Jewell. In that transfer window, he brought in Lauren Robert, Hossam Ghaly, Danny Mills and me – all good players. Danny and I had clashed during my Birmingham days. That's probably an understatement! There was a great picture of Danny shaking me warmly by the throat when I was at Birmingham and he was at Middlesbrough.

I know I've said this before, but it's true. When people who hated me got to know me, they realised I wasn't that bad! Geoff Horsfield, Lee Hendrie, Paul Dickov, Danny. The first day I walked in at Derby, I was a bit apprehensive about meeting Danny. I took one look at the picture stuck onto my locker and realised everything would be fine. It was the one of Danny grabbing me. On it, he'd written, 'Dear Sav, love you always, Danny.'

Everything was fine. He was a really nice guy, and we got on well. It was just a shame that he had an unfortunate injury that ended his time at Derby. The new arrivals, including me, couldn't help. Jewell could have signed Steven Gerrard and Patrick Vieira, and it wouldn't have made a difference. It was that bad a team, that low. Game to game, it got worse and worse – and worse. We were getting battered. We crashed 6–0 to Villa, we were thumped 6–1 at Chelsea and Arsenal beat us 6–2. The results were dreadful. I was getting to the stage where I was going to matches thinking that I didn't want the ball. I hated football. I couldn't run any more, even in training. I lost all my enthusiasm for the game.

It was soul-destroying, because we knew that we were going to lose. No matter what the manager said, deep down you knew. Players hid because the crowd would start to have a go at them, me included. You didn't want to do anything that might go wrong and attract even more stick. It was horrible. Paul Scharner of Wigan was quoted as saying, 'If Derby beat us, then we deserve to go down.' When I was at Leicester or Birmingham or Blackburn, no one would have dared say that about one of my teams. But Derby? You knew he was right. Jewell pulled me into his office after seven matches.

'Listen,' he said. 'Why have I brought you here? I'll tell you why: because you're a good player. But I'm going to leave you out against Sunderland, because I don't think you're doing yourself justice. Come back with a bang.'

I didn't have a problem with it. I came back in the 6–1 thrashing at Chelsea. The next game was Manchester United at home, and it turned out to be the only highlight of the season. I had one of my best games in a Derby shirt, even though we lost to a Cristiano Ronaldo special. The fans even chanted my name for a split second. That night, the chairman texted me: 'Sav, you were wonderful.'

My mate Andy Todd came on when we played against United. The ball went down the line, and Toddy could have headed it out, but he tried to let it run out for a corner. Toddy was robbed at the back stick, and Ronaldo scored. Up until then, I hadn't said a dicky bird, because I was playing poorly. But after a decent match against United I felt I had the right to say something. 'You should have got rid of it,' I said to Toddy.

I went on and on and on. Toddy chucked his bottle of water at the wall and started to come towards me. I looked at his eyes, and they'd gone. As he reached me, he somehow stopped himself. In the shower afterwards, I apologised. And he said, 'If that had been anyone else, I would have ripped his head off.'

It was my fault. I'd had one good game and thought I could rule the world again, but it wasn't like that. I always seem to pick on the big 'uns. I did it to Darren Moore, and he was a great professional too. In the Arsenal game, I fed Mooro, who tried to pass it. The ball came off his heel and went straight to Robin van Persie, who scored. At half-time, the gaffer had a right go at me and said, 'You need to know your players. Don't pass the ball to Mooro.'

Hang on a minute. This was a fellow professional. Surely I should be able to pass the ball to him? After the game, I was feeling down on myself and talking to friends in the bar. I was blaming myself for that goal, and they were telling me it wasn't my fault. 'It's because I've passed the ball to Mooro and the gaffer said I shouldn't have done it,' I said. 'I blame myself, but Mooro should be able to handle the ball.' Mooro was great at heading and tackling, but he would be the first to admit that, like me, he was not the best on the ball. That was all I said.

The next match was at Blackburn, which we lost 3–1. I had a go at Mooro. He stood up in the dressing-room and turned round so I had this 6 ft 5 in. centre-half staring at me. He just pointed a finger at me and said, 'I'll see you on Monday.' I was dead scared. I wondered what I'd done, but he wouldn't say anything more to me. On the Monday, he pulled me to one side. 'You're lucky,' he said. 'You're so lucky that I haven't lost my temper with you.'

'Why, what have I done?'

'You were heard in the players' bar saying that I was rubbish and that I can't pass the ball.'

'You're wrong, Mooro,' I said. 'I blame myself for passing it to you, but I feel, as a professional player, you should be able to handle the ball.'

That was how stories got blown out of all proportion. If it had been anyone else, both Toddy and Mooro would have knocked that person out, but they knew me. I'm not a nasty person. I haven't got a nasty bone in my body. I just have a big mouth. Anyway, there was no point hitting me, because they both could have killed me with one punch!

The United game was the only flicker of light in a dark period. I was subbed after 63 minutes at Middlesbrough. Jewell could have taken anybody off, but he chose his captain. Another signal that things weren't going well. I was as bad as everyone else on the pitch, but I was wearing the armband. I've always been insecure and a worrier, so I thought there was something up. I asked Jewell's assistants, 'Have I done anything wrong?'

The answer was no. But as a group there was no team spirit, no togetherness. It was every man for himself. Players were playing to get away at the end of the season, but I knew I was at Derby for two and a half years. I didn't have an escape clause, but, then again, the way I was playing no one would have taken me anyway. And I wouldn't have earned anything like what I was being paid by Derby. I was stuck. Training got even worse. One morning, we had the traditional yellow jersey to be worn by the worst player in training. I was given it, and I wasn't the worst. I snapped and said, 'This is a disgrace.' I stormed off with the lads laughing, but it really got to me. We couldn't wait for the season to finish, and I was thinking to myself, 'What have I done?'

I was playing Premier League football, but it was embarrassing. *Match of the Day* would come on, and I didn't dare watch. I didn't watch *Soccer Sunday*. I didn't read any newspapers. The fans were giving me stick. Every time my name was read out, they booed. Jewell stuck with me. To hear your name jeered when it is read out is the lowest of the low. People were saying that my legs had gone, and I honestly thought they had. I was going home thinking, 'Paul Jewell's bought me, given me a two-and-a-half-year contract and I'm letting him down. I'm letting down the club and the chairman, Adam Pearson.'

There was somebody in the dressing-room who had it in for me. There are always moles at clubs, and this one went to the papers and told them I had a white Mercedes with black wheels. I picked up the paper to read that I'd spent £169,000 on a car while Derby were bottom of the League. I've always loved my cars. This wasn't a case of splashing out for the first time. I wasn't rubbing it in. There were stories circulating that Paul Jewell said to me at half-time at Reading, 'What are the showers like, Sav? Because you're going in them.'

He didn't say it. Someone made it up. He brought me off that day, and, again, it could have been anyone. I was a shadow of myself. I was in my shell, I was nervous and the will to play football was ebbing away from me. I was badly affected by everything. I'd been accused of doing things for show. I picked up a little girl and her father at the bus stop. I was on my own in the car and spotted the Derby scarves so stopped to offer them a lift. They couldn't believe it. It wasn't done for effect. I gave a couple of thousand to charity, because I wasn't earning my wages. That wasn't for show. Derby were paying me all this money, and I wasn't doing anything for it. My teammates didn't like me because of the flash image of cars and nice clothes, and on the pitch I wasn't even worth £1,000 a week. I didn't think I could be any lower, but it was going to get even worse. My mind flashed back to the conversation I'd had with Taff before I left Blackburn. Mark Bowen's final words: 'You'll have an easy life!'

I started to take it out on Sarah and the kids. I was shouting at them all. Football is my life, after my family. But this was beginning to ruin everything. It was getting to the stage where I was picking on my missus at home, yelling at the kids. I was snappy. I needed a holiday.

Having lost a fortune on cars, I should have thought twice about buying a boat! Now that is a sure-fire way to chuck money away. It was like throwing notes down a black hole. But, in the summer of 2008, my fifty-foot twin-engined yacht came to the rescue as the four of us enjoyed a fabulous family holiday away from it all on the *Elementary Sarah*, named after my missus. She – the boat not the missus – cost me £500,000, and I sold her for £330,000, so I wasted a fair few quid! I'd always wanted a boat. My passion has been cars, but I loved that boat. With cars, there is a price ceiling. With boats, you can spend millions.

Before I bought it, I did two weekend courses at Abersoch. The first course meant I was allowed to steer a thirty-footer, and the second one let me take charge of a seventy-footer. My cousin Matt and a couple of other friends did the first course with me. I was on my own for the second one. We had to go out on a boat with an instructor, moor the boat, turn it, learn how to deal with someone going overboard, how the engine worked, the safety. I enjoyed every minute of it.

A friend found us a mooring in Antibes in the south of France. Tuffy and I drove down so we would have a car there, and Sarah and the kids flew over a couple of days later. We did it in one seventeen-hour stretch, filling up with fuel every hour! It was the longest drive of my life. We took it in turns, three hours here and three hours there. When we were 40 minutes from the boat, we had to stop and sleep. We were shattered. There were times that summer when sailing away and never coming back seemed a wonderful option. We stayed on it for six weeks, and I was Captain Savage. We lived the high life, our small boat moored between these monsters. We had a 150-footer one side and a 75-footer on the other, but I was proud of the *Elementary Sarah*. We might have just gone down as the worst team in history, but I needed a break.

It was one of the best family holidays I've ever had – after one of the worst seasons I've ever had. There were just the four of us on the boat. We'd eat breakfast in the morning, take the boat out, moor up, have lunch and sunbathe. It was wonderful. Sarah was my crew. You can imagine. We'd be mooring the boat in the marina, and all these people would watch. I would be screaming, Freddie would be crying and she had to do the ropes. The arguments we had! But it was so much fun. Cousin Matt was sometimes able to fly down from Germany for the weekend, and I blame him entirely for the day we nearly got lost at sea.

There was room for a six-foot dinghy in what was like a garage space in the boat. You'd press a button, and the door opened. I'd never used the dinghy, which had an outboard motor. Whenever we dropped anchor offshore, a small taxi boat would come to collect us so we could eat at one of the seafront restaurants. Matt thought it would be very James Bond if we went in the dinghy. I sent Sarah and the boys on the official little boat, and Matt and I zoomed to shore separately. When we'd eaten, the beach taxi took Sarah and the boys back while Matt and I jumped back into the little dinghy. We untied the ropes, thinking we'd drift out a little way first. The wind had got up, the water was choppy . . . and we couldn't start the motor. No petrol. 'Fucking goofy idiot,' I swore at Matt.

It had been his idea, after all. We were a mile away from the boat, drifting with no motor on rough seas. I was fuming and tried to ring Sarah so she could get the official little boat to come and find us. And I dropped my phone overboard. I didn't speak to Matt for the rest of the day once the beach taxi had rescued us.

That holiday, I also followed the same fitness regime that I have done every summer since Crewe. Three weeks before starting back at pre-season training, I ran three or four miles every day. In the sand. Sarah will tell you that I did it every single morning to make sure I was fully fit. I liked to report back fitter than most people. I would get up in the morning as the sun came up, have breakfast on the boat and then head for a 45-minute routine on the beach. I would run on the sand, up and down hills. I was determined to go back fitter and stronger than ever, because I honestly thought it was going to be easier at Derby.

I reported back as fit as I could have been. When we went running, there were three groups of eight, according to ability, and I was in the top one. I was coming third or fourth every run. Gary Teale was up there with the fittest. So were Stephen Bywater and Paul Green. My legs couldn't possibly have gone. I've never been one for the short, sharp bursts, but over the long distance I was still up there, even at the age of thirty-four. We went to Holland in pre-season, and Jewell put Dean Leacock in the middle of the park with Paul Green. Dean wasn't a midfielder; he was a centre-half. So I pulled Mark Seagraves, the coach, and said, 'Ziggy, am I going to be part of the gaffer's plans?'

I knew straight away. We were absolutely hammered 3–1 by TOP Oss. The first pre-season friendly is always a bit hit-and-miss. We'd been running our bollocks off; it was one of the hardest pre-seasons I've had in my life. Paul Jewell wanted us to be as fit as we could be, so there would be no excuses, and we were. We were fit to the point of near exhaustion. I sulked in Holland. I thought I wouldn't even be playing in the Championship. On our return, Jewell pulled me into his office and said, 'If you can find anywhere to go, go. People tell me your legs have gone.'

'Well, you're the man who counts,' I thought. 'Do you think my legs have gone?' I didn't know what to do. I had two years left on my Derby deal, but my manager felt he'd made a mistake. He suspected I wasn't the player he thought I was, that I'd gone. And, if I'd been honest, I would have asked myself, 'Why on earth did I sign for this football club?'

We clashed. We couldn't be honest with each other. I was still near the top in the running groups. We played a couple of pre-season games, but I was not involved. What was going on? I came on as sub at Burton for about 20 minutes and did well. Nigel Clough was the manager, but at that point no one knew what was going to transpire and that he would succeed Jewell. I was sub at Oldham, but in the next friendly, at Mansfield, I wasn't involved at all. I was told to train on the morning of the game with the ones who weren't in the squad.

I kept doing everything right. The manager told me to find somewhere else. I was on the phone to my agent, George Urquhart, asking him if he could find somewhere. He said to me, 'Sav, after what happened last season, no one wants to touch you. Everyone says your legs have gone. You can't get near anybody any more. You're not the player you were. The game is all about high energy and high intensity, and no one wants to touch you. Nobody in the Championship, nobody in League One, nobody in League Two.'

The money I'd earned was irrelevant at that point. My life was being ruined. The chairman walked past me in the corridor one day. It wasn't a pre-arranged meeting. We started talking in the corridor, but because of the way the conversation was progressing he suggested we move into his office. He said, 'It's not working out. People are saying your legs have gone. The manager has told you to find somewhere else. Would you be looking to take a settlement?'

'Yes.' I didn't think there was any option. So I worked out some figures and told him, 'If you give me £1.2 million, I will leave and say it hasn't worked out for me.'

It had not got personal by that stage. There was a personality clash between me and Jewell, but we were both grown men. We could move on. I gave the chairman my piece of paper with the sums on it. The next morning, I drove into the Moor Farm training ground. The gaffer was sitting in main reception waiting for me. He frogmarched me to his office. He said, 'You've gone behind my back.'

'What are you talking about?' I asked.

'You've gone to the chairman for a pay-off.'

'It's not like that. We talked, and he asked me for a figure.'

'You should have come to me. You went behind my back.'

I was suspended for the weekend. Sent home. I came back in on the Monday and trained with the kids. Mark Seagraves came to tell me – he was only the messenger. I was training with Brian Burrows and David Lowe. So now I was out in the cold. 'Right, keep your head down, keep strong,' I thought. If I joined the kids and gave it the big one, they'd think, 'Who are you?' So I trained well. I was a model professional. I was recalled to first-team training for a practice match, and I have to confess I didn't give it everything. I'd done everything by the book – everything – but I knew I wasn't fancied, that I was only there to make up the numbers.

I gave it 80 per cent. Why bother? The gaffer wasn't bothered about me. But, by doing that, I gave him the opportunity to dig me out. I'd been doing everything right. The players' union, the PFA, had told me to log everything. I was becoming more and more paranoid. I wouldn't eat or drink at the club. Not even a cup of tea. I was very picky with my food. I was going so crazy that I began imagining things that were straight out of a cheap thriller. What if someone put drugs into my food so it would be easy to sack me? That's how bad it got. Who on earth was going to tamper with my food? No one. I look back now and can't believe that's what I thought. It was insane.

What I should have been more concerned with was the training session I'd messed up. After it, the chairman came through to see me. He pointed me towards his office. I convinced myself this was it. I was about to be sacked. 'What have you done?' he asked.

'Nothing,' I replied, expecting the worst.

'I've had the manager in here absolutely raging. You were slacking.'

I was always honest with the chairman, and I told him that I was trying 80 per cent. Adam Pearson had told me to do everything right, and I had, up until this point. But even my 80 per cent was better than some of those in the team, and that's what I couldn't understand.

'The gaffer doesn't want you anywhere near the ground or training,' he said. 'Can you train at Wrexham, Macclesfield, anywhere? He just doesn't want you at the football club.'

It was incredible. I was shaking. I said, 'Mr Chairman, I have done nothing wrong. If people don't think I'm good enough any more, fair enough, but don't treat me like this. I want to train here.'

'If you want to train here then you have to change with the kids and train with the kids. The gaffer does not want you anywhere near the team, because he thinks you are a bad influence.'

That's what upset me more than anything, because I wasn't a bad influence. I was being punished because I'd cost so much money and everyone thought I was crap. I *was* crap. I was a shadow of myself. Eventually, Adam Pearson asked me to keep away, on full pay. I didn't know whether to stay at home or go to games. It was still pre-season. One Sunday night, the chairman rang: 'Sav, back in tomorrow. It's the team photo.'

They only wanted me in there for the picture. No one spoke to me. I pulled up a chair 50 yards away from everyone else as a joke. I had not changed. I bit my tongue and got on with it. From the outside, I stayed strong. Inside, it was killing me. To my utter amazement, I was asked to train with the first team and was named as sub for the first fixture of the season.

I hadn't had a pre-season. I was lacking match fitness, because I'd hardly played any games. If I went on, I would make a right arse of myself. Przemyslaw Kazmierczak, who was in the team ahead of me, was hopeless. He was 6 ft 4 in. tall, and I was a far better player than him. I could accept Paul Green, because he was a fantastic player. Not a problem. With Kaz, even all the lads were saying I was better than him. Dean Leacock was ahead of me too, and he was a central defender. I was fifth- or sixth-choice central midfielder. Jewell brought in Andrejs Pereplotkins, and he turned up the day before the season and played the first game against Doncaster. I came on as sub, gave away the free kick for the only goal, couldn't move and felt really down.

My head was seriously messed up now. I'd been told I wasn't needed in pre-season. I hadn't been involved, and then I was sub for the first game. The transfer window was shutting in three weeks. If I'd played well then they could have got some money for me. I was in the team for the 1–1 draw at Bristol City and did okay. Then we played Southampton at home against a team full of kids, and they won 1–0, but it could have been 20–0. I was horrendous, absolutely dreadful. I had no confidence; I was getting booed every time I touched the ball. It was my last game under Jewell.

21

YOU'RE A CELEBRITY . . .
GET OUTTA HERE!

Derby wanted me out. Brighton, Beirut, the jungle. They didn't care as long as Robbie Savage cleared off as quickly and quietly as possible. There was one problem. Nobody would have me. No one wanted to touch me with a barge pole. *I'm a Celebrity . . . Get Me Out of Here!* What a joke that was. I realised how far things had fallen when Adam Pearson called me into his office and said, 'Ant and Dec are your mates, aren't they?'

'Well, I know them,' I admitted.

'Why don't you give them a ring and try to get into the jungle?'

'Pardon?'

'You've tried everywhere else, and no one will take you. Give them a call.'

I sat there and looked at him in amazement. I was a professional footballer, earning 23 grand a week at Derby, and the chairman was telling me to get on a reality TV show. What about playing football? The last thing on my mind was a trip into the jungle with Ant and Dec on *I'm a Celebrity . . . Get Me Out of Here!* No bushtucker trials and eating bugs for me, thanks. I politely rejected the chairman's suggestion and went back to training with the kids instead.

Jewell wouldn't tell me why I was training with the kids. He wasn't talking to me at all. I would like to thank him. Seriously. Thank him for making me realise how much football meant to me. He told me once that he'd been made to train on his own when he was a player at Bradford and how horrible it had been. I've never been a manager, so I can't say what I would do in the same circumstances, but it must have been a hard decision for him to do to me what had been done to him. He thought it was best for Derby, even if I couldn't work it out. Like I couldn't work out what I was doing back in the team up until the Southampton game.

I looked like a heap of rubbish, as if I had never kicked a ball in my life. My energy had disappeared along with my enthusiasm. Butterflies were going crazy in my stomach. I was even nervous about driving my car to the ground. The family were under orders from me to stay away. I was costing the club a fortune, and there seemed to be no end to the nightmare. Jewell was slowly starving me of football. I would be in on the days the lads were off. Back with the kids. I wasn't allowed to play in reserve games either. I didn't deserve it. I could have been a bad influence in that dressing-room, but I wasn't. I could have caused havoc, but I didn't. I felt I'd let Paul Jewell down. He showed massive faith in me: paying a lot of money, giving me a big contract and naming me captain on the first day. I'm a decent guy, and I wouldn't have caused trouble; there were other players worse than me in that changing-room.

Looking back, I try to work out where it went wrong. Perhaps Jewell thought I was chipping away at him. Shortly after I arrived, the lads were really down in training. Derby were bottom of the League, and everything was doom and gloom. I pulled aside Jewell's assistant, Stan Ternent, who is old-school. He was a decent guy, and I respected him. 'We need to work a bit harder,' I said. 'Can we do a bit of high-intensity?'

The gaffer called us together and had a go. He knew it was me speaking on behalf of the lads. He made us run our nuts off, and it made the situation even worse. All those things added up to why Jewell decided I was not for him. Coach Mark Seagraves was the messenger, never the gaffer. I tried to speak to Jewell. 'You're training with the kids,' he screamed at me. The conversation was over.

I didn't go and see him again. I wasn't scared. The meeting would have become heated, because I'd have lost my temper, and coming to blows with my manager was not an option. Luckily, I was still on good terms with the chairman. 'Mr Chairman, I'm not a bad influence. I'm not a bad egg,' I told him.

'I'm sorry, Robbie, but my loyalty has to be to the manager.'

I understood that. Mr Pearson had to support his manager, but it wasn't helping my case. I often stayed with my mate Tuffy at Leicester to cut down on my travel time, and he started to worry about me. I was close to self-harming. How stupid. How unbelievably stupid. Suicide never crossed my mind, but going outside and banging my head against a wall certainly did. Or crashing the car. I was in such a bad place I couldn't concentrate on driving. I couldn't concentrate on anything. I started to suffer blinding headaches and had severe chest pains, stomach cramps, diarrhoea. I felt dreadful. I had a brain scan to make sure – don't forget I'm a hypochondriac – but the problems were all because of what was happening to me at Derby. I went to the doctor, and he treated me for stress. I saw him privately. He put me on medication for depression.

At home, I just sat on the sofa and didn't move. My little boys wanted to play football in the garden, and I wasn't even interested in doing that. I didn't wash my hair for days. I was suffering from stress and depression and fighting the feelings I had to self-harm. Only cowards do that, I thought. What a selfish thing to do. But there were times when I didn't know what I was doing, because I was that low. Coming back from a compound fracture of the leg was bad, but this was worse, because there was no light at the end of the tunnel. I was facing the end of my football life, and this was not how I wanted it to end. Not Robbie Savage, legs gone, bad influence, a bad egg. I was embarrassed to go home and face Sarah and the kids.

'Why aren't you playing, Daddy?' Charlie asked me one day. He had a Derby strip and couldn't understand why I was not involved on a Saturday. I didn't think he would ever see his daddy playing again, and I was too ashamed to say so. I would have swapped every single penny I had to finish on a high. Derby could have had every penny back. I was spending Saturdays shopping with Sarah. People came up and asked, 'Have you retired? Who do you play for now?'

One day, I overheard someone saying to a friend, 'Is that Robbie Savage? It can't be.' Well, it was. I was a Saturday shopper instead of a professional footballer, and it was eating me up inside. I didn't know what to do. I didn't know who to turn to. I couldn't speak to Dad. The man who had been my biggest and most loyal supporter as I grew up was not the same man any more. Pick's disease had robbed him of understanding and robbed me of a shoulder to lean on. He would have known what to do before he became ill. How I wanted to open up to him. I couldn't speak to Mum, because she'd have been a bag of nerves and so upset. I felt very alone. I took it out on my wife too, I am ashamed to say. Every time she spoke, I snapped at her, and she even threatened to leave me: 'I love you to bits, but I can't live with you like this.'

Sarah's words were another hammer blow, but I couldn't blame her at all. I was a horrible, horrible person. Somebody was denying me my footballing life. I was used to being high-profile, to being the focal point. Handling rejection is hard when you've been at the top. I understand so much better now when people say they have depression, because I've gone through it too. If Jewell had suddenly decided to put me in the team again, I would have been in no fit state – mentally or physically. I wasn't having the right training, I wasn't eating the right food, I wasn't sleeping. I was all over the place, and if he'd asked me to play, I would have been a wreck. I was even told to stay away from first-team games, because the fans hated me so much that they started to boo when they saw me and that might affect the team. I was cut out of everything.

Why? I still don't know. Was it personal? I don't think it could have been. I haven't been able to put my finger on why I was treated like that. Jewell thought I had a big mouth, and he might have wanted to knock me out, but, deep down, I think he saw me as a decent person. In the first instance, I let him down. But I can't understand the way I was treated after that. We both could have handled the situation better. To train with the kids was the lowest ebb of my career. To be told to do so by one of the manager's coaches was degrading.

Finally, Jewell spoke to me. He asked, 'What do you want to do when you finish? I'll help you if I can.' I said I quite liked media work. By this time, I'd disappeared from the back pages, there were no headlines and no one wanted to know me. That was the scary thing. There were no interviews and, as far as I was aware, no interview requests. I have always got on with journalists – well, not all of them! But when a reporter takes the time to speak to me then I think I have changed a few perceptions. I don't pretend to be something I'm not. I have views and opinions, and I'm not afraid to give them. But no one was asking me anything at Derby. I discovered afterwards I'd been barred from doing interviews. I couldn't speak out either, because that would have given the club the excuse to fine me two weeks' wages.

'If you want to do media or coaching, I'll help you. If you want to take the kids in the afternoon, just say,' Jewell told me. Brilliant! We were getting somewhere. Except that nothing happened. There were other players who were suffering at Derby. Jewell had done it to me – his captain – so he could do it to anybody. My mate Toddy was frozen out, and keeper Roy Carroll was suspended for two weeks after a row in the dressing-room.

The club was falling apart. Results weren't going well at all. Just before Derby played Sheffield United, the word was that Jewell was on the brink of the sack. The manager and I were staying out of each other's way, but he sat me down before that match and we chatted for half an hour. He was not apologising exactly, but he spoke about his time as a player and I felt that it was his way of saying, 'We haven't got on, but when you're a manager you will have to make these decisions.'

I was desperately hoping, wishing, praying that they'd lose. My only chance of playing for Derby again was if Jewell wasn't there. I didn't mind whether he left by mutual consent, his own accord or was sacked. But they won and went on a great run: seven unbeaten. The team appeared to have turned the corner and were going from strength to strength, which was great for them but not much good for me. Jewell came up with an escape route. Micky Adams, my old gaffer at Leicester, was manager of Brighton, and he wanted me on loan. 'Yeah, I'll go to Brighton,' I told Jewell. 'I'll go to Brighton, and I'll prove people wrong.'

Jewell was glad to get rid of me. And I was so, so glad to feel loved again. Micky put his arm round me, and he was great with me. The only reason I went there was because he was manager. He took me out for meals, and we ate with his chairman, Dick Knight, who was a real gentleman too. I will always remember that month with affection and gratitude. The lads were fantastic to me, and Brighton is a cracking club. When I left my hotel, I sent a cheque for about £1,000 to cover all the extras. Brighton sent it back, because I had been such a good ambassador for them. I couldn't say a bad word about them.

Laughter. Jokes. Banter. They have always been a major part of my personality. Winding up people and making them smile off the pitch.

Winding up people and making them snarl on it. If I can crack a joke about something, then I will. My humour has sometimes been misunderstood, but it has never been malicious. At Derby, I'd forgotten how to smile. My self-esteem had disappeared. There was no sign of a swagger. What was there to swagger about? Hopefully, a change of scene would do the trick.

Being wolf-whistled on my first night in Brighton was very welcome. I must have washed my hair. I'd never been wolf-whistled before. Well, not by men. The hotel that Brighton found for me was in the gay area of the town. I'd never seen myself as a gay icon, but I would have taken anything at that moment – not literally! I hadn't been loved by anybody, and I was attracting attention again. I could have a bit more of this, I thought.

My first day pretty much summed up my time at Brighton. The lads trained at the university, and Micky set me up brilliantly. 'What car do you drive?' he asked me innocently.

'A Merc.'

'OK,' said Micky. 'The car park steward at the university is your biggest fan. He's really excited about you signing for us, and he will have a place for you in the car park. Make a bit of a fuss of him, and he'll be so happy.'

The guy was waiting for me. Wig, false teeth, glasses, orange jacket. He guided me to my space. 'Oh, Robbie,' he said. 'I've always been your biggest fan. I've followed your career. I'm so pleased you've signed for Brighton. I can't believe a big star like you has come here.'

He went on a bit and then asked me to sign his autograph book. Not a problem. I went into the dressing-room. The car park attendant followed me inside. Slightly strange, I thought. The wig was removed, the teeth came out, the orange jacket disappeared. It was coach Bob Booker. All the lads were in fits, and I thought, 'This is great.'

It was like a weight off my shoulders. I was there to enjoy my football again. My first visit to the Withdean Stadium was funny too. I turned into the car park at the ground, expecting a parking space. I was in a Merc with a low body. 'Robbie Savage,' I announced to the steward. He looked down at his piece of paper.

'Oh yes, we're full. Can you park on the grass over there?' Over there was a patch of grass on top of a foot-high kerb. I had to drag the bottom of my car over the kerb and park it on the grass.

My first match was against Cheltenham. I came off after 89 minutes with cramp. We were 3–2 up, and I felt I'd made a huge impact. But Cheltenham equalised in the final minute. Then we went to Leeds and were hammered. I also exchanged words with Neil Kilkenny, whom I had played with at Birmingham. To be fair, he had something about him, and he has gone on to do well for Leeds.

At Birmingham, I had tried to bring him down a peg or two. He announced in the canteen one day that he would be playing for the England senior team by the age of twenty-one. That's how cocksure he was. But he couldn't even get into the Birmingham team. I kept him out. He would have a dig at me in training, because presumably he was jealous of me. Here I was, playing against him for Brighton. He took me late and was booked. He also taunted me nastily: 'Oi, old man, your legs have gone!'

I was at Brighton for a month to prove to myself that I could still do it. Derby were paying most of my wages, with Brighton contributing. I soon realised that the lower you go the harder it is. I was twice man of the match down at Brighton. It was the sponsor's choice. That could have been anybody, because what sponsors do on match day is have too much to drink and vote for anybody they like or for the players they want to meet afterwards – because the winner collects his bottle of champagne or whatever from the sponsors' lounge.

Away wasn't quite so great. Just after half-time at Hartlepool, Micky took me off as their fans yelled, 'You've gone.' I threw my sweatband at the ground. *Are you sure?* I couldn't understand why Micky had brought me to the club just to do that. In fact, it was the right decision. I was doing okay, but it had to be either me or his captain, and he couldn't take his captain off, so I was the obvious one. I apologised to Micky afterwards, and he was as good as gold about it.

The lads were all as good as gold too. They were a really genuine bunch, and the welcome they gave me was wonderful. Nicky 'Fozzie' Forster, Glenn 'Muzza' Murray, Tommy Fraser, Adam Virgo, Kevin 'Macca' McLeod. Thanks guys. They used to wind me up about what had gone wrong at Derby and tell me to take Fraser's granddad back with me to sort out everyone. His granddad was Mad Frankie Fraser, the famous East End gangster. Virgs had been at Celtic and was the player who'd earned the most money. When I went there, the lads would say, 'Sav's here now, Virgs.'

At Derby, I was hammered by the papers as a big-time Charlie because I had expensive cars while the club were being relegated. At Brighton, the players were saying, 'Bring your Lambo down so we can have a go in it.'

Macca must have thought I'd played for Real Madrid or something and was made of money. He asked me one day, 'How are you getting home? My mate's got a private jet, so you can fly.'

'I'm only playing for Derby, Macca!'

I did drive the Lambo down, and he took the key and hid it. I couldn't find my beloved car. I was fined left, right and centre and paid them all. I enjoyed my time there. Buddies Café became a regular haunt. We'd go to a nightclub, and at four in the morning we'd head for a fry-up, and Buddies was always packed. One Saturday night, I went out with a couple of the lads. We ended up in Buddies. They had my shirt on the wall, and everyone in the place was singing, 'There's only one Robbie Savage.'

Unfortunately, it was the Saturday before a Tuesday game, and I shouldn't have done it, but I was bored. The other two lads got into trouble, but it was my fault. The lads may have been impressed by me, but one Brighton bouncer wasn't having it. My first night out with them turned into a disaster. We'd been to a few pubs, and then we went to the Arches, down by the seafront. It was blowing a gale, and the queue went on and on. 'Go to the front and get us in,' the lads asked.

So we all jumped the queue. They were about to let us in, but one of the bouncers decided to be busy and said to me, 'Have you got your student card?'

'Are you sure, mate?'

'You can't get in if you haven't got a student card.'

He knew exactly who I was. I told him that we weren't going to cause trouble but that we just wanted to go in for a few drinks. He said no. A few yards down the road, there was another club, so we walked down to that. The bouncer got on his walkie-talkie and told the doorman at the next place not to let us in either. I wouldn't have minded, but the lads told me they'd never had a problem until I arrived!

Training at Brighton really brought me back down to earth. The university facilities were great, but the physio's room was a Portakabin. The first day I walked in, Rooney licked my legs. 'There's a dog here,' I said to Malcolm, the physio.

'Yeah, he's mine,' replied Malcolm. 'This is Rooney.'

'Rooney?'

'He's my dog. He comes to work with me, and he's been here for years.'

You'd have a massage, and he'd lick off all the oil! He was a lovely dog. I was really enjoying myself at Brighton, but the end was around the corner. We played Leicester at home, and we were 2–0 down at half-time. I honestly thought I was the best player on the pitch. The *Leicester Mercury* said so too. But Micky had to make a change, and that change was me. Brighton won 3–2, which meant there was no way Micky could pick me for what would have been my last game of the loan. 'Tell you what we'll do, Sav,' he said. 'I don't want to say I've sent you back early because I can't play you. We'll just say you're injured.'

Micky made it known that I had a calf strain. I didn't, but he wanted to spare me the humiliation of not being picked. I couldn't get into Brighton's team. Even if Micky had said he was playing me, I would have found it hard to go into a winning team. I travelled back to Derby and felt down straight away. Jewell asked me if I wanted to sign for Rushden in the Conference. I could have gone to Wrexham as well. There was a lot of talk about becoming player-manager or player-coach there. Dean Saunders said, 'You don't really want to do that yet.' Deano wanted the job, and Deano got the job.

My options were running out. MK Dons wouldn't touch me. I tried to get back to Leicester. Milan Mandaric fancied it, but Nigel Pearson didn't. Everybody was saying my legs had gone. My agent told me to stick it out and that I might be at Derby longer than the manager. The relationship between George and me was torn apart when I needed him most. In the Brighton times, when I was at my lowest ebb, I felt I couldn't turn to him, because he got that mad with me phoning him 14 times a day. In the end, I didn't want to phone him. I felt that I was a burden to him, and I didn't think I should feel like that. It wasn't about getting me thousands of pounds a week; it was about being there for me. Maybe I expected too much from him.

I would recommend George to anybody. He's an honest guy. He always had my interests at heart, and it was a pleasure dealing with him. But I have moved on. Paul Mace handles my media and sponsorship commitments, Stephen Lownsbrough of niche law firm Blacks Solicitors in Leeds is my legal adviser and Phil Glyn-Smith of HSP Tax is in charge of my tax affairs. I have known them all for years.

So my agent was telling me to sit tight, and Derby were desperately trying to push me out of the door. The chairman asked to see me: 'Sav, are you sure there's no one who will have you?'

'Nobody wants me, Mr Chairman.'

I'd been to Beirut by then. My friend Tony Quaglia was big mates with the guy who managed Al-Ansar. His name was Karim Diab, and his father, Salim, was high up in the Lebanese government. They owned the most successful club in Lebanon. Would I be prepared to have a look? I flew out to Lebanon, to Beirut, one of the most beautiful places in the world. The people were beautiful. The food was great. Karim treated me like a king. Everywhere we went we had two plain-clothes policemen with us. The football was worse than our Conference, but it was an option. I didn't want to go there to play, but I would recommend it as a holiday destination.

Brighton, Beirut – and now I was in the chairman's office telling him that no one wanted me. 'Not even at a grand a week?' he asked.

'No. Nobody. Nobody at all.'

And that's when he made the suggestion about Ant and Dec. I'd like to have a go at *Strictly Come Dancing* or *Dancing on Ice*. But not *I'm a Celebrity . . .* No way. Even though I liked Ant and Dec. I met them in Amsterdam. They were with Robbie Williams in a nightclub, and we ended up at Robbie's concert the next night, having watched David Beckham score against Ecuador in the World Cup first. I was in Holland for a couple of days to have treatment on my leg with a guy called Andrew Radiven. That night, I was in a nightclub. Suddenly, there was a shout: 'Sav!'

I turned round, and Robbie Williams and Jonathan Wilkes were in the VIP area. Ant and Dec were there too. Robbie and Jonathan were creased up with laughter. They'd been playing lookalikes. When they'd seen this guy walking past – long blond hair, fake tan, white teeth – they'd shouted out. Then they realised it was actually me! They called me over, and I joined them in the VIP area. 'What are you doing tomorrow?' asked Robbie.

'Nothing. Just treatment,' I replied.

'Watch the football with me. I'm performing in the Amsterdam Arena tomorrow night, so come and watch the concert too.'

I went to the stadium and into his room beforehand to watch the football. He was so into his football. He was sitting there in his underpants with his staff around him. Ant and Dec were there and Jonathan Wilkes. We all watched the football. I couldn't believe how surreal it all was. Then it was time for the concert. Robbie was about to sing 'She's the One'. Everything went silent, the music died down and Robbie said, 'My special friend is in the audience tonight – Robbie Savage.'

The camera panned onto me, and 75,000 people were watching on the big screen. Andrew Radiven was standing next to me. 'I'd just like to congratulate Robbie and Andrew. They have decided to become a couple,' announced Robbie.

Everyone started singing 'She's the One'. It was unbelievable. Robbie Williams was such a great guy. He invited me to Milton Keynes with Sarah. We went down in a minibus – Sarah, her three friends and me. We met him before the gig. He looked shattered. He was pale, hair all over the place, not very good clothes on.

'Give me five minutes,' he said to the girls. He came back out. He'd done his make-up, done his hair and was wearing a suit. He looked great. He put his arms round the girls and said, 'Now I'm a pop star.' The girls actually melted. Wayne Rooney and Michael Carrick were there – big hitters – and Robbie Williams said, 'I would just like to welcome my friend Robbie and his wife Sarah. They are here in the audience, and I wish them a Happy Anniversary.'

Watching Robbie Williams in concert seemed a long time in the past as I sat in the chairman's office and contemplated teaming up with Ant and Dec. I decided against the jungle and went back to training with the kids instead. Very strangely, I was picked for the reserves at Leeds. 'Okay,' I thought. I was ready to show that Robbie Savage was still alive and kicking. My mate owned a Rolls-Royce Phantom, so I turned up at Leeds for a reserves game in this car. We parked it where the bus was, so everybody – Jewell included – could see it. 'That'll show them,' I thought. 'I may have been forgotten about, but I'm still here.'

People would have looked at me and thought, 'What an idiot.' I didn't care. We lost the game 3–1, and it was my first match since I'd come back from Brighton. I was still nowhere near it, no enthusiasm, lifeless really. Not being involved did mean that I had four days off at Christmas for the first time in my career. I spent it with my kids and my missus, but my heart and soul were still in the football. At five to five every Saturday afternoon, when I came back from shopping or had been out with the kids and switched on the TV or the radio, my belly would be full of butterflies and I would be hoping Derby had lost.

It was horrible to wish that. The players were my teammates and my friends. I accept I was being completely selfish, but the only way I was ever going to get back into that Derby team was by Jewell leaving – either quitting or being sacked. The day it happened, I took a phone call at ten at night: 'Just to mark your card, the gaffer's gone.'

My first reaction was to burst into tears, which slightly surprised my missus, who was sitting next to me. They were tears of joy. Then I opened a bottle of wine and drank it.

I wasn't thinking 'Have I lost it? Have my legs gone? Can I do it?' any more. All I was thinking was that Jewell had gone and maybe, just maybe, there was a way back. Funnily enough, I don't bear any sort of grudge against him. I would love to sit down with him over a glass of wine and discuss exactly what went on and what he really thought. Did he seriously think I was a bad egg? Did he like me? I would like to convince him there is more to me than he thought. And we may meet up in a TV studio one day.

Chris Hutchings took temporary charge, and that morning I went to the training ground. There were eight cars waiting to get past the electric gates at Moor Farm, and all the lads were jumping around and beeping their horns – the ones who had been frozen out. Hutchings was Jewell's man, so I wasn't expecting drastic changes, but I was named sub at Forest Green away in the FA Cup – although I didn't get on. Strangely, it was Manchester United who played a part in what turned out to be the first step on the road back.

'You will come back to haunt me,' Ferguson had said all those years ago. Haunting United was the last thing on my mind. As usual, when a club loses a manager, everything was uncertain and edgy. Hutchings followed Jewell out of the door, which left David Lowe, from the academy, in charge of the team for the Carling Cup semi-final against United. My mate Toddy was picked, and I am sure it was the chairman's decision. He pulled out Darren Powell to bring in Andy. Adam Pearson also invited me into his office: 'Listen, we've got a new manager coming in after the Manchester United game, and one of his questions was, "Have his legs gone?" I told him that he has to make up his own mind.'

I was soon to find out it was Nigel Clough, who was sitting in the stand that night. More immediately, I was named as sub for the visit of mighty Manchester United to Pride Park. We won the first leg 1–0, with Kris Commons the scorer. Andy Todd was magnificent. Like me, he had been out in the cold, but what a return. I was delighted for Toddy, because he'd been through hell as well. Were things about to change?

From my point of view, the match was also important because I came on as sub with ten minutes left and the crowd gave me a decent ovation. It was quite bizarre, because I had done nothing to earn it. I guess it was because we were 1–0 up against Manchester United, and if they'd booed it would have reflected on the team.

Those ten minutes were the first step in my rehabilitation. I had to rebuild my life. I had to regain my confidence and rebuild my relationship with my wife and kids. I had to de-stress myself and start all over again, as if I'd just been released by Manchester United as a teenager. That's how it was. I'd had to learn to walk again after breaking my leg, and now I had to learn how to play football again, because I had gone. *Gone*.

There wasn't an ounce of confidence in me. I was used to walking into the changing-room and people thinking, 'I'd like to have him with me in the trenches.' But I'd been walking into the changing-room and people were thinking, 'It's only Sav.'

I always believed in myself, but I knew I had to start from scratch again and I wasn't sure that I could do that. All the time I was with the kids and the reserves and the first team – apart from that once – I'd trained well. 'Train like that, don't do anything different and you'll be fine.' That's what I was telling myself as I prepared for the arrival of Nigel Clough.

22

LIGHT AT THE END OF THE TUNNEL

Muriel the lollipop lady works in the beautiful Derbyshire village of Brailsford. I would drive through it on my way to training every morning. Whatever the weather, Muriel would be at her post as I came by. As soon as she heard the Lambo or the Merc growling along the road, she would step out to stop me. 'Keep going, Robbie,' she used to say. 'It'll work out in the end.'

I don't know whether she really believed it, but thanks, Muriel, for being there in the bad times. When things started to improve at Derby, Muriel couldn't have been happier for me. It was hard to wave back and chat sometimes when I was dreading the prospect of training on my own or being blanked by Jewell and the coaching staff. But Muriel saw a very different Robbie Savage once Nigel Clough arrived. I rediscovered my smile.

Nigel Clough. The gaffer. I have been so incredibly fortunate to play for some legendary figures: Martin O'Neill, Steve Bruce, Mark Hughes and now Nigel Clough. Not that I knew I would be playing for the gaffer when he arrived at Derby in January 2009. I wasn't convinced I could put on a pair of boots and perform for anyone after what had happened under Jewell. But at least there was a chink of light at the end of the tunnel, where before there had been a big black empty hole.

Nigel took over at Derby between the two League Cup semi-final games against Manchester United. He was in the stand for the first leg and was in charge for the second at Old Trafford. Once again, United would play an important part in my career. Somehow, my life has always been linked to United, and now it's my son who wears the red shirt. Charlie started playing there when he was just five. Every Wednesday he is at The Cliff, where I spent all those years as a boy. I've shown him my digs and told him, 'This is where Daddy lived.'

Back then, I was taking my first step on to what has turned out to be a long and, I believe, successful career. When you see that finishing line in sight, you want your life to go into slow motion so that the dreaded day is delayed a little longer. I feared I'd crossed the finishing line already. If Jewell had stayed at Pride Park, then that would have been it. What a horrible ending. Instead, Nigel Clough arrived. On the first day, he got everyone out in the car park – the fit players, the injured players, everyone. It was freezing cold. He didn't give us an *Any Given Sunday* speech. He told us straight that he would treat us all the same and we had to get on with it. 'You've been used to your warm, cosy comforts,' he told us. 'But you are lucky to be professional footballers. Remember that.'

Nigel came from Burton Albion and arrived with Andy Garner, Martin Taylor and Gary Crosby. I spoke to Andy Garner and told him I wanted a chance. Then I asked him to be honest with me and tell me if my legs had gone. 'The gaffer will be 100 per cent honest with you,' he said.

'That's all I want.'

In training that week, I had some good feedback, and for Nigel's first game I was on the bench against QPR. We were beaten 2–0, but he told me that if I kept showing the form I had in training then he would try to find me a place as soon as possible, which was a massive boost to my confidence. Then we went up to Old Trafford for the second leg, and pictures were taken of the gaffer and me sitting on the bench together. It was very strange. Earlier that day in the hotel, I'd suffered the worst stomach cramps I've ever had, while my roomie, Stephen Bywater, had been sick in the bathroom. We had either come down with a bug or got food poisoning. Neither of us felt in any fit state to play, but we didn't want to say anything and we were both subs. When the gaffer came and sat next to me, I felt myself going red and asked him, 'Do you want me to move?'

'No.'

As the game wore on, he was talking to me and having a laugh and a joke. He talked me through the game, even the United players. It was unbelievable. This guy was already trying to help me, and he hadn't even seen me play yet. As far as he was concerned, I might not have been able to do it any more. Nigel threw me on, and I did extremely well, even though we lost 4–2. At half-time, the gaffer said, 'Get the ball in the right areas; don't complicate things.'

I followed his orders to the letter. And, from that day, I never looked back. The one thing I have found out about the manager is that if you are honest with him, and if you do what he wants you to do, then he will look after you – just like Martin O'Neill. If you don't, he will get rid of you. From that point on, I missed only one match: Sheffield Wednesday away. That was the following season. He rested me, because we had two games in three days. To start with, the fans were still mad at me, even though I was back in the team. I think it's utterly wrong for your own fans to boo you when your name is read out. It happened to Gary Teale and Rob Hulse and to me for a bit. I don't mind them booing at half-time, or after the game, but booing you onto the pitch is wrong.

There was a turning point. There always has been, at every club I have been at, and invariably it's been in a cup match. My Derby turning point came against Nottingham Forest in the FA Cup. We played Forest at home and drew 1–1, but I played well. People were beginning to realise that I might still have something to offer. All I was doing was what the manager had asked me to do. Andy Garner said to me, 'We can't believe you weren't playing.'

The replay was when everything clicked into place properly. The signs weren't great as we were driving down Brian Clough Way to the City Ground, though. Dave, our bus driver, was always under strict instructions to arrive at a match an hour and a quarter before kick-off, and he'd get a bit nervous. If he was likely to be even five minutes early, the gaffer would tell him to stop. It was a 7.45 p.m. kick-off, and Dave took a wrong turning. We didn't get to the ground until 7 p.m. Dave struggled to park the bus, and he was sweating. I sat behind Dave. I would wind him up, clip him on the ear, smack him in the head, pull his hair. He hated it. He was really nervous and panicky as we got off the bus 35 minutes before the start of the game.

We were 2–0 down within a quarter of an hour. But we ended up winning the match 3–2. Someone threw a scarf, so it was the most natural thing in the world to pick it up and wave it. For the first time in my Derby career, I was just me. I didn't think of the consequences. All I thought was that I was going to enjoy this moment. I was not disrespectful to the Forest fans whatsoever. I celebrated in front of my own Derby fans. It has probably gone down in Derby history. If anybody had told me that I would be waving a scarf in front of the Derby fans as they sang my name, I would have thought they were having a laugh. Not that long before, most of them would have liked to have strangled me with that scarf!

Shortly afterwards, we went back in the League and won again. We were magnificent again too. We put together a four- or five-match unbeaten run. I was playing every week and starting to win people over. The gaffer came in and kept us up. It was a difficult job. I know this is a little thing, and the lads will hammer me for it, but, at the end of the season, I won the Ilkeston Supporters' branch player of the year. That trophy probably means more to me than any trophy I've ever had. Winning Birmingham player of the year and Midlands player of the year were fantastic achievements, but this award showed I was starting to win over the fans. It was the hardest job in the world, and I never thought I would do it. The gaffer asked to see me and said, 'You're doing fine. Just be you.'

There was more confidence about me. I was a transformed man. It was like Robbie Savage had gone into his body from ten years previously. If Nigel had not come in, my career would have been finished. I was lucky to find somebody who appreciated it when you gave everything to him. They could have appointed a manager who would have thought I was too much of a character. The other big change in my life was my contact with the media. I felt that Derby were stopping me from doing virtually everything. It was once agreed that I could do *Final Score* with the BBC, but as I was driving down to London the phone rang. It was the press officer, telling me, 'You can't do it now.' No explanation.

Under Jewell, my career had been at a standstill and so had my life. I couldn't play for him, but it seemed as though I couldn't do anything else either. I wanted a career in the media, but it was going nowhere. That all changed once Nigel took over. I linked up with Paul Mace, who had been head of media at Leicester when I was there. He has since formed his own business. We met at a pub near Moor Farm, and he said he could fix me up with some media work. Who could have guessed that by the summer of 2011 I would have contracts from ESPN, BBC Radio 5 Live, *Football Focus* and *Match of the Day 2* after becoming the first player to present iconic phone-in *606*? He certainly kept his word. The ball started rolling with a column in the *Daily Mirror*. They liked me and within a few weeks I was filling a page every week. William Hill gave me a weekly podcast and, slowly but surely, the offers started to come in.

Being me, I was also up for some fun. I joined Twitter. I thought it was what birds did until Macey told me about it. One year on, I'm the king of the banter, exchanging insults with Rio Ferdinand, Chris Moyles and Piers Morgan, just to name three. I had ten thousand followers in the first six weeks and now I'm over the quarter of a million mark. When I started, I wanted to show that footballers are just normal people, so I posted pictures of me in training, receiving treatment or going out to dinner with Robert Mancini.

Some people hammer me, some people love me. Twitter allows me to say what I think. It's the attitude I have when I am a pundit or co-commentator on radio or TV as well. I don't want to be regimented, like 99 per cent of footballers who answer the questions in exactly the same way. I am different. If you're reading this book, you will know that anyway! Whatever I do, I want to be the best, which is why I had suffered so badly during under Jewell.

As the 18-month nightmare under Jewell began to fade away, I regained my bounce, my energy and my sense of humour. I also began to realise just what an appalling person I must have been to live with. How Sarah put up with me during that time I will never know. I'm very grateful that she did. I don't think any other woman would have stuck it out. We celebrated our seventh wedding anniversary in the summer of 2009 – by getting 'married' again. The seven-year itch. It was either remarry or have an affair! I arranged it as a big surprise.

We have a holiday home in Barbados, which I bought when the boat went, and that's where it happened. It was like restarting my life. Tuffy and his wife came over, as well as Sarah's best friend, Fiona, and her partner. It was all planned down to the last detail. The friends were staying at another villa, so she didn't have a clue. I bought her an eternity ring, and the ceremony was on the beach at The Cliff Restaurant, which is one of the finest on Barbados. Sarah was wearing a beautiful cream dress – she'd packed a few for the holiday – while I wore white linen trousers, a white shirt and a black jacket. I was boiling. Our two little angels were there. If I remember one day of my life, then it will be that one. It was to say 'Thanks for being there' to Sarah, and it signified a new start. It also put to bed the option of having an affair!

We spent five weeks in Barbados, and two weeks into the holiday I started running every day. I was doing three miles a day, because I was utterly determined to report back for the final year of my contract as fit as I could be. Stevie Bywater had said to me, as we were leaving for the summer, 'Have a good one, Sav. It could be the last one.'

I decided that if it was going to be my last season then I would go out with a bang and give it everything I had. I went back in great physical shape. My first pre-season under the gaffer was very hard and so enjoyable. We had a track day. I was in the second group, but I was coming top. We'd run 800 metres. I'd be like Steve Cram and wait until the final lap to make my move and beat everyone. All the lads would be cheering. Then we had long jump. After that, it was off to Allestree Park for runs up and down and round the lake. There would be no scientific madness. Get round the lake in five minutes. To that tree and back in 45 seconds. Go. Simple, basic stuff, and the lads had a whale of a time.

Because we were all enjoying it, we didn't mind the hard work. The feeling of waking up the next morning in pain was great. It was old-school, which I loved. Not the modern, typical, wrap up the footballer in cotton wool. If there was dog poo in the park, you had to run through it. The gaffer didn't mollycoddle us. He wanted to test us all the time. My biggest nightmare is swimming. I can't swim at all. I would rather run 10,000 metres than swim. Unfortunately, the gaffer loves it, so we'd make use of the facilities at Repton School.

We would split into teams of three: a good swimmer, a medium swimmer and a pathetic swimmer. I was the pathetic one. Stevie was incredible, and I was in his team. The pool was full length, and I was being asked to do the most horrendous things. We'd already done about 30 lengths of pushing the ball and heading the ball. We weren't allowed to touch the ball with our hands. But there was worse. We dropped a brick in the shallow end, and that was up to your nipples, so you couldn't have a breather. We had to dive down and push the brick the length of the pool. I nearly drowned about eight times. The gaffer didn't care if it took 20 minutes. He was challenging you. Miles Addison was also a hopeless swimmer, and he did it. Nigel was as delighted as everybody else.

The gaffer took us away to Plymouth to play a few games. We held a table-tennis tournament, and Johnny Metgod, who joined us that summer as coach, was the champion. He beat me in the quarter-final and the bus driver in the final, with all the lads watching. I think he won about £300. Everyone was cheering, and you could see the first signs of a team spirit. We'd eat together, and we couldn't leave the table until eight. We had to stay there for an hour. We had to stretch together. It was all about togetherness. Nigel's tests kept coming. He sent us into the sea to see how far we could swim out. First one to step back on shore would be punished. No one would leave the sea. The waves were crashing, and everyone was freezing, but no one would go. In the end, the gaffer said, 'Everybody out.'

Everything was geared towards getting us mentally right as a team. I loved every moment of it. We went to an adventure centre, where we'd team up in threes again and have to help each other cross a stretch of water on a tiny dinghy, or we would have to pick up and put down planks to help us across. It was all about teamwork, problem solving and a physical challenge. The dressing-room was a much happier place. The lads were a great bunch. Nigel got rid of the players who had no interest in playing for Derby, who just wanted to pick up their wage packets. That was the beginning of a new era, and it looked as though I could be a part of it as I came into the last year of my contract.

Nigel brought in players like Jake Buxton from Burton and Shaun Barker from Blackpool. Really good, honest pros. We already had guys like Paul Green, who was my legs man, and my roomie Stevie. He's one of my best friends in football and happily married to Zoe. I discovered that his wife wrote him letters and put them in his bag for him to find on away trips. He would start reading them. That's when I discovered she called him 'my Little Tunky-wunky' and his pet name for her was 'Squiggly-wiggly'.

The final year of my contract. What a depressing thought. Every time I did something that season it would be for the *last time*. Stevie Bywater kept winding me up: 'You've only got eight months left.'

I happened to be sitting with Martin Taylor, one of Nigel's backroom staff, one morning, and we started chatting. Martin, incidentally, is the only person I know who can drink 40 pints and still be standing at the end of it. 'I want to stay round football,' I said. 'I've had a taste of life without it, and it nearly killed me. I'd take two or three grand a week to stay in football.'

Don't get me wrong. I know that two or three grand a week is still a lot of money, but it was a lot less than what I was earning. Martin must have had a word with the gaffer, who must have had a word with the chairman. Mr Pearson asked to see me.

'Would you be prepared to help Derby out? You're the highest-paid player at the club. If you are willing to take a pay cut, we'll give you another 12 months. What would you take?'

'I don't know, Mr Chairman,' I replied. I really didn't know. I was a 35 year old taking home £55,000 to £60,000 a month, and that is a lot of money. I could have just stuck to my contract and finished in the summer, but I felt that I owed something to Derby, to Adam Pearson and, especially, to Nigel Clough. He must have thought I was worth an extra 12 months, or the chairman would never have suggested it. If I took a drop, then the manager might have been able to bring in one or two loan signings. I could really help him.

I agreed to drop £8,000 a week, to £15,000, and I was given an extra year, which took me to the summer of 2011. It was still telephone-number money, but this was it, my last contract as a footballer. The chairman appreciated the gesture and so did the gaffer. As a squad, we also got together and scrapped the bonus system – unless we were promoted to the Premier League. Derby needed every penny, and we were willing to help.

I felt like a new man as the season approached. My *Mirror* column began, to rave reviews, and I was beginning to generate plenty of interest as a media pundit. But, most importantly of all, I was still a professional footballer with a job to do for the gaffer and for Derby County. The first match of the season was billed as the battle between the two 'sons of':

Nigel Clough against Darren Ferguson, who was boss of Peterborough. Paul Green, Stephen Pearson and I played in a middle three, and in the first half we were like Brazil. I was playing with confidence. It was wonderful. We won the game. But even then some of the fans suggested Nigel was only playing that formation because my legs had gone.

Cousin Matt, wherever he is in the world, always reads message boards online. He told me that I was probably the most-hated player Derby had ever had. I think I was voted one of the worst signings in Rams' history. There will always be 5 per cent of fans at Pride Park who hate me, who never wanted to give me a chance. Luckily, I did win over Nigel, who reminds me in so many ways of Martin O'Neill. We went to Malaga for a couple of days, and, like Martin, Nigel didn't come with us. There were no fire extinguishers in sight either! We've also been to Portugal golfing and had a short trip to Amsterdam, which included a friendly. I turned up at East Midlands Airport at three in the morning, pulled my passport out of my pocket and found I'd picked up Sarah's by mistake. The frightening thing was that the check-in lady reckoned a quick shave and a bit of make-up and I could have got away with it.

The season was up and down. We were in a relegation fight for a lot of it, and results were not always great. After one poor performance, I drove through the gates of Moor Farm and saw all the cones set out on the training pitch. 'We're going to be running our bollocks off today,' I thought.

We stood there waiting. The gaffer appeared carrying two big bags full of cricket gear. He even asked the groundsman to mow a wicket. We played cricket, but he was still testing us. If the ball was whacked at you and you ducked, he would go mad. Even in cricket, he wanted to win. I picked my team, made 30 not out and we won. He took us out for a Chinese meal a couple of times. We went go-karting. Nigel would watch who took a chance to overtake. He slowly builds up a picture of you. Every manager has put his arm round me, even though they know what they're going to get from me. I think and I hope that the gaffer has respect for me and what I have tried to do for him. To give me the captain's armband back was the icing on the cake. Nigel made me skipper before we drew at Blackpool in August. I was almost speechless with pride.

In the 2009–10 season, apart from three or four games, I made an impact. Andy Garner, Gary Crosby, all of them treated me with a great deal of respect and valued my opinion. I was on the same wavelength as Nigel and I even went on the radio to defend him. The local station suggested that players didn't think much of him or his coaching staff. I was furious. It was perfectly acceptable to criticise us for our performances, but this was out of order.

If that was a low point, ending Nottingham Forest's 19-game unbeaten run at Pride Park in the January was a definite high. I've experienced all the fury of a Second City derby between Birmingham and Aston Villa, then played for Blackburn against Burnley, but the games against Forest have turned out to be just as action-packed, controversial and full of hate. The clubs have always had a rivalry, but it has become even more spicy with former Rams boss Billy Davies in charge at the City Ground, while everyone knows of Nigel's Forest connection. Forest had done us 3–2 in the August, and revenge was certainly on our minds.

I was worried about that first fixture, and not for the reasons you might think. I'd just had my teeth done! Imagine going to Forest with a gleaming set of pearly-white gnashers. It was probably asking for trouble – but not as much trouble as Nathan Tyson was asking for when he pulled up a corner flag and taunted our fans at the final whistle. Billy Davies said afterwards that it was because I'd waved a scarf the previous season. I did that in front of Derby supporters and had showed Forest complete respect. Tyson could have started a riot with what he did, and Davies didn't help with what he said.

The return was in January, and revenge really was sweet thanks to Rob Hulse's late winner. Davies went into orbit again. We could have won by a far bigger margin. I resisted the temptation to pull out the corner flag and wave it at the Forest fans, though. There was a huge scuffle at the end, and Davies actually accused the gaffer of kneeing him in the back of the leg. Billy really has a problem when it comes to playing Derby.

The 2009–10 season was memorable for many reasons. Amazingly, I was named player of the year. It was a club award, and I was selected by a panel of four: *Derby Telegraph*'s Steve Nicholson, Johnny Metgod, Tom Sloan of the *Burton Mail* and the chairman of the supporters' club. Four expert Derby watchers. What an honour.

The other thing to celebrate was the number of games I played. My legs had gone, according to nearly everyone but Nigel Clough. Well, no-legs Savage was involved in all 46 Championship games. My strike rate over the previous few years had been in the 20s, because of injuries and what had happened under Jewell. I treated every match as if it might be my last. I enjoyed every second of every game. I even attracted a few headlines again. We played against Birmingham in the FA Cup, and every national newspaper turned up for what was just an informal preview press get-together.

I've always got on with the Midlands guys. I've given them plenty to write about, and they've mostly been pretty fair with me. The Cup tie against my old Bluenose mates was bound to attract extra interest. As we chatted, I was trying to make the point about how much football meant to me. I started by saying, 'People don't usually see beyond the hair, the teeth, the tan . . . ' The lads, plus Janine, of course, were loving it. They started to chip in. Soon we'd got to, 'People don't usually see beyond the hair, the teeth, the tan, the big house, the Merc, the wardrobe of Dolce & Gabbana clothes, the houses all over the world. What they don't see when I go home – to the model wife, for a dip in the pool and to look over the golf course – is that I watch Spanish and German football. The lot.'

When I picked up the papers that Saturday morning, that quote was plastered everywhere. It was tongue-in-cheek, a bit of a laugh, and everyone who was there that day saw it that way and presented it that way. But outsiders didn't. I was slaughtered in a Sunday column the next day. I have always been able to laugh at myself. For some reason, there are journalists who like to have a go even if they haven't met me. Meet me first, then hammer me.

The Birmingham fans hammered me. They kept chanting 'There's only one greedy bastard', and my message to Bluenose reporter Colin Tattum afterwards was to wait for my book to come out so that the fans would know I wasn't a greedy bastard at all. Birmingham won, and I had a bit of a to-do with Roger Johnson, who told me he would be drinking champagne that night and asked me what I would be having. I had a pop back. I suggested that when he'd been around a bit longer in the Premier League he would be able to drink Dom Pérignon, like

I'd done. My big mouth has got me into trouble so many times, but I think I've always treated my seniors with respect.

Spaniard Gorka Pintado didn't treat me with respect when we played Swansea at home in February. He lunged in two-footed, and I'm sure he did it on purpose. He was sent off for the tackle, and I'm just glad he didn't break my leg. That game showed once more how far I'd come. My teammates all piled in to help me after the challenge. I was their skipper, and I'd been fouled. If they backed me that day, then I think I repaid them a couple of weeks later when I ended up in goal as we lost 4–1 at Reading. What a boring job that is. You stand there, get colder and colder, and you're not involved at all. And the next day your groin hurts from wellying the ball. I would just like to point out to goalie Stevie Bywater, however, that I made a world-class fingertip save and managed to put off Shane Long when he took a penalty too. He must have been dazzled by the teeth, the hair, the tan and the big nose.

Stevie was struck down with a back spasm, and replacement Saul Deeney was sent off. The gaffer thought I might as well go into goal, as I wasn't getting a kick in midfield. I had some great banter with the Reading fans. They were giving me some stick, and I was giving it back. When I switched my phone on, I had texts bleeping at me non-stop. Craig Bellamy said, 'You've wasted your career,' while Roberto Mancini joked, 'I need a goalkeeper!' Eric Steele, the United goalkeeping coach, thought I was the sixth-best keeper in Wales.

Having been roundly abused by the Birmingham supporters, I wasn't that surprised to find myself on the end of some stick from the Leicester fans too. The Derby supporters gave Steve Howard and Matt Oakley a fantastic reception, but the feeling wasn't mutual. We beat the Foxes 1–0, and I was cheered by the Rams fans and booed by the people who used to think I was a hero. I still don't know why. I loved Leicester and played some of the best football of my career at Filbert Street. All that is forgotten now.

As the season wore on, I began to do more and more media work, but the football always came first. It was great being a media pundit, though. I was sitting in press rooms, rubbing shoulders with guys who have hammered me, as well as the journalists who have treated me fairly. I worked for 5Live at Villa a couple of times and made my mark, much as I did as a player. Actually, the first mark was on me – I was whacked straight on my nose from a cleared ball as I co-commentated with Darren Fletcher. A couple of weeks later, I forgot to put a coat in the car. My mate Tuffy came to the rescue – with a woman's coat borrowed from his missus. It still had the tag on, because it was going back to the shop the next day.

Nigel did not stop me doing all these extras, because he knew that football came first. And with the bonus of another year at Derby, I was going to make every last second of my playing career count.

23

RISING STAR

Elland Road. First game of the 2010–11 season, and they don't come much bigger than a visit to Leeds United. I'm still not entirely sure who was the most surprised when Nigel Clough stopped our coach a couple of hundred metres away from the stadium and told us to walk it. We looked at him to check he wasn't joking. He wasn't.

So we all climbed out of the bus and made our way through the Leeds fans. They didn't say a lot, to be fair, but they looked pretty shocked. It was a great feeling walking from the bus. We didn't have any fear then, and we didn't have any fear on the pitch when we totally dominated and beat them 2–1. It was my mistake for their goal, so I took even more stick than usual.

There was a lot made about what the gaffer did. People said it was because of a scene in the film *Damned United*, which is about his dad Brian when he was manager of Leeds. I don't know his reasons, but it was typical Nigel Clough and took all the pressure off the lads.

It was a perfect start to my last year at Derby. Winning was brilliant, but what made the day even more memorable was that I went straight from the match to co-present *606* on BBC 5Live for the first time. Yes, I was still a professional footballer. But I was also beginning to settle into my new role as a media pundit, co-commentator and presenter.

To be the first footballer to be asked to do the iconic *606* while still playing is something that will always give me a lot of pride. What began as a stand-in role for Alan Green had become a fantastic opportunity for me with retirement coming ever closer. I've never had a problem facing a baying mob of 30,000 booing supporters, but I have never been so nervous in all my life as that first *606*.

I must have done something right because, on the back of that, the BBC signed me up for the World Cup. Me, Robbie Savage, the boy from Wexham, mixing it with legends in South Africa. My excitement levels took a major hit, however, when it became obvious my mother-in-law, Alice, was losing a long and courageous battle against cancer. The summer of 2010 was a strange roller coaster of emotions.

We – Sarah, the boys and I – had a holiday booked in Barbados in June before I headed off to the World Cup. Unfortunately, my wife had to turn round and go home after only one day because of her mum. I stayed with Charlie and Freddie, and best mate Tuffy came to the rescue by flying out to help with the boys. It must have been so hard for Sarah. Not only did she have to cope with her mother passing away, I was going to leave her alone with the boys for a month.

Four weeks away. I admit it: I got homesick. Missed Sarah, missed my boys. I also had a wonderful time at the greatest football show on earth and learned something new. There are no tigers in South Africa! As someone who likes a big game, I jumped at the chance of seeing some big game and went on safari to Kruger. I was really disappointed not to spot a tiger, though.

It's a 12-hour journey from London to Johannesburg, which tested my fear of flying again. I was travelling alone, but at Heathrow I bumped into Alex McLeish, who was also heading to South Africa. Naturally, I assumed we were on the same plane. So we had a couple of glasses of wine, and I suddenly heard my name on the Tannoy – last call! Turned out that Alex was on a flight an hour after me.

Just imagine if I'd missed my flight? I sprinted to the gate, boarded and we then sat there for three or four hours because something was wrong with the plane, which made me even more nervous than usual. From Johannesburg I flew down to Durban, where I stayed in a fantastic B & B owned by a Scottish guy called Big Davie. He had two Rhodesian Ridgebacks, and I love my dogs. There was a pool, the beach, and we even found a Hooters in Durban.

What a life. I was being paid to cover a World Cup. It may surprise some people to discover that my respect grew for journalists. To see them wait around for hours in the mixed zone and get blanked by players. I've done it to them – walked past after I've lost – and I know now that it's not very nice. People think you just have to turn up, but you have to do your homework and write your report, and try to speak to players and managers afterwards. It's hard work being a journalist.

I was also a professional footballer, coming up to my final season, and determined to report back to Derby as fit as possible. The beach at Durban was my jogging arena, but I was slightly worried when 5Live's John Southall, who does marathons, was outrunning me. I also went out running with David Moyes in Johannesburg, and he pulled his calf. I told him it served him right for not signing me.

While I enjoyed the trip to the game park, and jogging on the beach, and eating out with people like Moyesie, Danny Baker, Chris Waddle and Jan Molby, the real buzz came from co-commentating the matches and seeing the biggest names in the world in action. I was also an ambassador for William Hill and kept a video diary of the World Cup, which went down really well.

The breakthrough in my media career came in a place called Nelspruit. Everyone told me there was nothing to do there, but it was 25ºC every day, we stayed in yet another lovely little guest house and Mike Sewell of 5Live and I went to Kruger. Most importantly, New Zealand held Italy to a 1–1 draw, and I got just a bit excited! I discovered a few months later that it was this match plus my *606* show that led to me being nominated in the Rising Star category of the Sony awards – the equivalent of a broadcasting Oscar.

Chris Evans, who presents the Radio 2 *Breakfast Show*, was in the gym listening to my commentary. He got me on air the next morning, and I was even the subject of his famous 'top tenuous' slot. Everyone loved what I did. You are supposed to be impartial, but I admit I get carried away. I did the same thing at the Carling Cup final when Birmingham played Arsenal. I tend to root for the underdog. But that World Cup game was the day I arrived. The equivalent of making my mark as a player.

And I was still a player and determined to be a big part of Derby's season. Coming off a successful World Cup, I reported back for pre-season training by finishing third in the 'bleep' tests to prove my fitness.

We went cliff jumping in Devon and did the swimming thing again with the help of Olympic swimmer Ross Davenport. I had one more important date before the real action started – the launch of this book in conjunction with the Alzheimers' Association. Mum and Dad came to it at Pride Park, and she stole the show!

There was a massive queue outside the club shop as the fans waited for me to do a signing session. I want to tell you a bizarre story that might give you some insight into what players face these days. I had a photo taken with my arm around a lady, and a couple of days later a letter arrived at Pride Park alleging that I had brushed the head of the person with my arm as I put it round her for the photo, and that subsequently she'd suffered complete loss of hearing in one ear.

I couldn't believe it, but I was horrified to think that I'd apparently and accidentally caused someone an injury – even though I didn't remember doing it. I immediately asked my solicitor, Stephen Lownsbrough, for advice, and he wrote her a nice letter. Letters started arriving, making totally untrue comments about my character, asking for meetings and suggesting the papers were interested in her story. People started getting in touch, claiming to be reporters. In one call to Stephen's firm, Blacks, we were told that it would appear in a paper that week. I was bewildered and a bit scared. I'd suffered six months of worry and potentially significant legal fees for something where I was totally innocent.

And then another letter arrived – the person admitting I had not made her deaf and the incident never took place and she had made the whole thing up. The person also admitted making the phone call supposedly from a reporter and that she was attempting to make money out of me and her story. Incredible! I feel relieved and angry. The whole experience has made me think: if this is what happens to a Championship player who does a bit of media work, what the hell do the likes of Wayne Rooney have to cope with? Thank goodness for my great legal team at Blacks.

Back on the day of the book launch, I had no idea what was round the corner, of course. The same could be said of Derby County, although things looked promising when we chalked off five home wins on the bounce, we were fourth in the League, playing exceptional football, and I also notched up my 600th game. I thought we had a chance of getting promoted. The players were on fire; I was on fire.

Saturday nights I had *606*, and that was an education. I've learned that it takes a certain kind of person to ring up a radio show and that some people are intelligent, some are not as intelligent and some . . . One of the first calls I took was a bloke telling me that David James was hopeless and should retire. I asked him how he'd played that day and the bloke hadn't even been to the game! He saw that Bristol City had lost and rang in with his opinion.

Then there was the famous incident of the seven pairs of trainers. A guy said, on air, that he'd seen me walk into a shop, buy seven pairs of trainers and get a young boy to carry them out to my car. I was yelling, 'Liar, liar,' and the producer was in my headphones saying, 'You can't say he's a liar.' But it was a disgrace. Another guy rang up and said I was wrong about eating pizzas after a game, and I told him that we ate pizzas and chicken curry to refuel. Pizzagate – someone else trying to make an issue out of it.

I also get lots of good, funny calls. I have labelled myself 'the peoples' pundit', and I approach it as if I'm in a pub with my mates. I'm too enthusiastic sometimes. I know I can say a wrong word. I'm not the most articulate and I'm not the brightest, but I say it how it is. If I mess up, it won't be because I've been nasty or vindictive, it will be because I've said the wrong word. Luckily I think I was saying mainly the right words because five months into *606* I was given an award by the Plain Speaking Society. What an honour.

Some plain speaking went on at Derby too, most of it from me whenever I wasn't in the team. I was left out at Barnsley, so I didn't even take my washbag to Crystal Palace. Then the gaffer put the team up and I was in it. We won 5–0, and I didn't look back. I get the hump when I'm not playing. Always have done, and I'm not going to change now. When he dropped me against Barnsley, I understood it, but then he did it to me when we went to Leicester because he thought three games in a week was too much for me.

He told me on the bus, and I admit I reacted badly. I threw my bag down and he said to me, 'Don't you want to be sub?'

I wanted to say, 'No, I don't want to be sub, I want to play.'

We lost the game 2–0, and he should have played me. I didn't need the rest, and I was flying. It was also Leicester, my old club. It was like the beginning of the end. I have never taken being dropped very well and, yes, my reaction was bad. It wasn't the only time. I threw my boots down when he brought me off against Nottingham Forest. Nigel was trying to look after me, and I felt I was one of the fittest players. Against Forest, he said he was protecting me from a possible sending-off.

He was disappointed in me throwing my boots down. I sulked in training too, and he didn't expect that from his captain. I thought that maybe he didn't trust me. He was upset and he's a strong-minded person, so I wondered if I would play again. I apologised to him and I was honest, and I think he realised that it was only because I cared so much.

There was another example. We lost to Crawley in the FA Cup and, once again, I was brought off and Crawley scored. The same thing had happened against Forest. I thought it was wrong to substitute your captain, and when I looked around the dressing room afterwards, I saw players who weren't hurting enough. It hurts me to lose, so it must kill the manager. As a player, you get looked after, but some people weren't showing the faith back.

That night Crawley desired it more than we did. It was January, we were about to lose Kris Commons, and we brought in players for the sake of it to add numbers.

I also had a chance of moving to Canada. I went to speak to Vancouver Whitecaps about a move to the Major League Soccer. They put forward a good proposal and I had to think about it, but I couldn't have left the family for two years.

After the defeat against Crawley, we struggled hugely. The manager didn't change things, but Derby is one of the hardest places to play when things are not going well. I don't know whether it's because fans are living in the past, but the expectation level is too high. Some of the supporters had never taken to me, and I was the first one they would have a go at. You had to play like Real Madrid every week to please them, and we definitely weren't playing like Real Madrid. The crowd were on our backs, we had meeting after meeting, and the gaffer asked, 'Are you still with me?'

'Yes,' was the answer.

We'd been paint balling, had a trip to Cheltenham, gone to Marbella and Amsterdam. The gaffer was trying everything. It was hard for him and it was hard for us. From my point of view, the end of the season was approaching fast, and the way it was looking, it was the end of my final season as a professional player, too. If I hadn't decided on a career in the media, I think I would have played on until I was 40. I wasn't making as much of an impact on the Derby side as the year before, but I could still make a difference.

The media bandwagon was gathering pace. I did a couple of *Question of Sport* roadshows, in Nottingham and Manchester, and I loved them. Sue Barker is like our mum. They had a referee on stage and a sin bin, and if you said anything wrong or derogatory, you ended up in the sin bin. Sue asked a question about a female tennis player, and I said, 'No idea, Sue, but it wasn't you.' She put me in the sin bin!

I had regular gigs on *Football Focus*, *MOTD2* and joined the ESPN pundits team of John Barnes, Steve McManaman and Kevin Keegan. Three Liverpool names, one from Crewe! Ray Stubbs is great to work with. One of my clips found its way to YouTube – I was watching Mario Balotelli warm up and he couldn't put on his training bib. It was hysterical, and I instantly dubbed him 'Bibotelli'! That won me some great reviews.

I also went on a refereeing course. Me! It was part of the FA's Respect campaign. I had the course in the morning and then reffed a kids' game in the afternoon. Has my respect gone up for referees? No! I still think they could use a lot more common sense. But it was one of the hardest things I've ever done. It's lonely and the kids hammer you.

Chris Moyles, the BBC Radio 1 presenter, brought his roadshow to Derby and invited me on. He said I looked like a Barbie doll. I told him that I'd been really excited at being invited to be a guest on the No. 1 breakfast show presented by Chris, but I was a bit disappointed to find that it wasn't Chris Evans! I've got to know people like Chris Moyles and Chris Evans through Twitter. I'm the king of Twitter. I take the mick out of myself, but I've made friends with Rio Ferdinand, Lee Westwood, Ian Poulter, Eamonn Holmes, Vernon Kay, Graeme Swann – the list goes on and on.

You have loads of people hitting on you, calling your family all sorts. They think they are getting at you, and they don't realise I've been battered all through my playing career. They think that calling me 'big nose' on

Twitter will get to me! The only downside about Twitter is that lazy journalists use it for stories, especially the *Daily Star* for some reason. They usually have Katie Price on their front page. I don't want to be the next Katie Price. I cracked a joke about how long my drive was and that I'd put the bins out and 'see everyone in four days', and they took it seriously. At least I can have my say in *The Mirror*.

Twitter is a good laugh. I ran a competition called #savagenight, where I asked people to do impressions of me and Tuffy. This guy called Daniel B. Bacon dressed up his missus as Tuffy and put on a fake nose to be me. He had these raw sausages and told 'Tuffy' to breathe on them and they were burned because of his breath. The prize was a night out with me and my mates.

Talking of laughs, I took part in a video for Comic Relief. It was a spoof of the Alicia Keys hit 'Empire State of Mind' called 'Newport State of Mind'.

As well as laughs, there were tears. My beloved Boxer Naz had to be put down. She wasn't well, weeing in the house, walking into glass and barking into space. Sarah took her to the vet and called me. I got into my car and cried my eyes out as I drove over. I held her while he injected her. It was the worst thing I have ever had to do. The way I look at it, though, she had a great life. My other Boxer, Tai, missed her to start with, but he has a better life now, too, because Naz had become a burden. Sarah doesn't want another dog, but I'm going to take one home one day and she won't be able to do anything about it. I want a British bulldog.

There was also sadness as the end of the season came ever nearer. I have a confession. I was hoping for some sort of offer from Derby. I knew that I was a burden on the wage bill, but I would have stayed for £3,000 to £4,000 a week. I read that the club were looking for a veteran midfielder next season, and if that was true then I would feel a bit miffed. I genuinely thought that there might be a chance of a coaching role or just having me round the place for another year. I knew that my time as a player was coming to an end and that James Bailey would eventually take over from me, but I thought I could still be an influence. The gaffer has been a fantastic manager for me and I admit I'm disappointed that I won't be able to help any longer.

At least I contributed to Derby's survival battle. The heat was off by the time we played Bristol City in April – my last home match for the Rams. It was so emotional. My dad was there, and I hope he understood what it was all about. My life has been about playing football on a Saturday, and I still find it hard to imagine doing anything else. I think back to the letter that Dad wrote as I set off on my footballing journey, all those years ago. He drummed into me the importance of hard work, hard work, hard work.

I have worked hard all my life at football, and now I intend to do the same in my media career. My final game as a professional was on 7 May, away at Reading. I finished up in my vest and underpants after throwing all my kit to the crowd. For anyone interested, no, I didn't have a sock hidden anywhere! I was overwhelmed by all the messages of support, especially one voicemail which I have saved for obvious reasons. I could not believe it when I called up the answer machine and heard another Robbie. Robbie Williams! Ringing to offer me help and advice as well as an invitation to see Take That with Sarah. Unbelievable. I rang him back straight away. I thought it was a fabulous gesture from the second most-famous Robbie in the world!

It would have been hard to top that, but 48 hours after my football farewell I capped it by being voted Rising Star at the Sony Awards. Geri Halliwell was on stage talking about ageing pop stars and I was convinced Ronnie Wood had won it. Yes, that Ronnie Wood! He qualified for the Rising Star category because he was in his first year of radio broadcasting. Amazingly, I won. I hadn't realised originally what an honour it was, but it was like me winning the Premier League player of the year. Fantastic. As I looked around the room and saw all the big names in broadcasting, it dawned on me just how different my life is going to be from now on.

24

MR MARMITE MAN

If twelve people met in a pub to talk football and the name of Robbie Savage came up, then six what would say, 'What a wanker,' while the other six would say, 'We'd have loved him in our team.' I'm like Marmite, which is the description the *Mirror* uses for my column. Hate me or love me and not a lot in between. It seems to be the same for my new media career, and I don't suppose it will change. It's the final chapter, as far as this book and my life as a footballer is concerned, but it's the first chapter of the rest of my life.

The rest of 2011 promises to be a busy one and a very different one. Robbie Savage, ex-footballer, doesn't sound great. But Robbie Savage, award-winning broadcaster, has a ring to it. So does 'Ambassador of Grass Roots Football'. How about possible racehorse owner? Or land developer? Then there is my contract with the BBC to do 45 shows, plus my deal at ESPN, and I am also sports consultant at Blacks. I'm going to be a busy boy. I haven't got enough money to retire. Some of my investments and the financial advice I've received haven't been the best and I need to work. I also want to work.

But first – a holiday. I'll have to start taking them when the kids are off in July and August, and I've never done that before! I will also take my best friends on holiday every year, like always. Tuffy is my best friend and I will so miss going to stay with him a couple of nights a week and having my favourite lamb chops to eat. Don't worry, Tuffy, we'll always be friends.

Yes, my life is going to change beyond all recognition. Even my cars.

I bought a Bentley at the start of the year – second-hand. The bloke who bought it new paid £250,000 and I got it for £130,000. Still, it's going. I shall replace it with a sensible Range Rover. Now I'm in the media, a car picks me up anyway.

Of course I worry about what happens next. First, I'm a worrier. Second, will I be able to jump queues in restaurants, get in free to nightclubs and wipe my own bum now that I'm no longer a footballer? I look around and see players and think to myself, 'How are they still playing?'

I genuinely think that if I didn't have a media career, I could play on until I'm 40. But I don't want to be in League Two on a Tuesday night when I could be doing co-commentary on a Real Madrid or a Manchester United match. I think I will be a bigger star in the media than I was in football. I definitely over-achieved as a footballer but I'd rather have done that than been massively talented and under-achieved.

Mum and Dad are proud of me. I hope that Charlie and Freddie will grow up being just as proud. When I look at my beautiful wife and my lovely angels, I worry that something bad will happen to me because I am so fortunate in my life. 'Misunderstood' would be another word to describe me. People who don't know me just look at the exterior, the cars, the image, the clothes and so on. But I am a nice guy. I'm insecure, and I want to be loved, and if I'm loved, I can do tremendous things. When I take Charlie to Manchester United, I feel as if history is repeating itself.

In April this year, Charlie signed a two-year deal with the United Academy. It's like going back to my youth. He's eight years old, got a great left foot, and he is at United four times a week. He's also clever at school and plays the piano and rugby. Little Freddie has started playing football too. I'm so proud of them.

Dad and the boys were with me on the pitch at Pride Park for my final home game of the season and of my career. There is nothing Dad would have liked more than to have taken his grandson to The Cliff, just as he took me all those years ago. Win, lose or draw, I would pick up the phone or see Dad after a match. His was the only opinion that counted. If he was happy and proud, then I was happy and proud. He never missed a game until he started getting sick. And he will never know how Charlie is doing.

Dad sits at home now. Mum tells him how I'm doing but soon he won't be able to remember. That is the thing that kills me. Even now, I always look up after a match to wave to Sarah and the boys, and there is a gap where Dad should be sitting. No matter how a manager thought I played after a match, the only person who really knew was Dad. We have a long battle ahead with him. His condition continues to get worse, and Mum will have her hands full looking after him.

Mum and Dad always believed in me. I think I've been vastly underrated. If someone had said I would play more than 600 games, then people would have laughed. But I never give up. I've always believed that I should be the best at training and the best in a game. There are far better players than me around, but they haven't all made it. I have a big heart, and I have big desire. I wouldn't have done anything differently. I've always been fair with my contracts, and I've been thankful for what I've had. I've enjoyed buying cars, and I've enjoyed being slaughtered by the fans. And I've been loved wherever I've played.

I have enjoyed my time at every club. At Leicester, I won the League Cup and played under one of the great managers in Martin O'Neill. At Birmingham, I had everything and was at the top of my game. At Blackburn, I had the opportunity to play for my idol, Mark Hughes. And Derby gave me the opportunity to prove how much I love football. At every club I have ever played for, I have given blood, sweat and tears. I have walked away from all my clubs with my head held high.

Football has given me great friends: Darren Eadie, Stephen Bywater, Craig Bellamy, Shefki Kuqi, Paul Devlin, Roque Santa Cruz, Tugay, Geoff Horsfield. I've met some tremendous people, and I've played with some of my heroes. We don't know the meaning of the word 'no', because no one ever says that to us. In football, everything is done for you from the moment you walk into a club as an apprentice. In many ways, it can be quite strange.

I have been accused of trying to get players sent off. I admit it. If I had to dive, then that's what I would do if I could win. I don't give a toss. I'd be happy to be one of the best divers in history, if that's what it took. Mark Hughes always used to say to me, 'Make your mark.' I think I have done that. I had the reputation of being a bad boy on the pitch, but I've been a model professional. I've never been fined. I've never caused disciplinary problems. I haven't been caught in nightclubs. I've worked my nuts off, and I don't think I've always had the credit I've deserved. And I have never lost track of where I've come from.

Football has given me a life, not to mention highlights every four weeks, a fake tan, new white teeth and some seriously nice cars! I have always had an eye for a headline. My scrapbooks prove that. Every time I was in the papers, Dad or Nan would keep the article. I have read everything that's been written on me, and there has been plenty of controversy over the years.

But there's nothing like reading about yourself in glowing terms. There has been negative stuff: headless chicken, no ability, arrogant, big mouth, can't pass the ball. My attitude has been to put two fingers up at everybody, and that's what has driven me on. I know a lot of journalists. I always made it my business to form a relationship with the local paper guy: Bill Anderson at Leicester, Colin Tattum in Birmingham, Andy Neild at Blackburn and Steve Nicholson on the *Derby Telegraph*. John Hartson once told me to stop speaking to the press so much, but I've always enjoyed the banter.

I suppose it's not that surprising that I have started a career in the media. When I was at Birmingham, I had a column with the *Daily Post* in North Wales and also *FourFourTwo* magazine. When I first appeared on Sky, I felt that some of the presenters and pundits looked down on me, didn't think my opinion was worthy. But I take my football seriously. I watch every match that is on TV, and my knowledge is up there with the best. As a media pundit, I want to say it how it is. So many of them are bland and boring. I will probably get myself into trouble more times than not, but I can learn from the mistakes. I will approach being a pundit as I did being a player. I want to get better and better. I want to be the best. I look at what Gary Lineker has achieved since he finished playing, and I would like to be the next Gary Lineker one day.

When I go on TV, my gear gets hammered by the others, but I'd rather be a fashion setter than follower. I have my own style – shirt, tie, blazer, waistcoat, jeans . . . and the handkerchief. That won't be changing.

But I am also very aware that I have changed. Tuffy told me that he had noticed a difference after what happened at Derby. It's made me more determined and driven, because I was given a second chance.

But working every hour that God sends, trying to be the best, is not necessarily the answer. I need to get the balance right, to remember the people who have stood by me in the bad times and not forget where I've come from.

The final whistle has blown. From the age of 14, being a footballer is all I have ever known. I will miss the dressing-room banter. You can hurl obscenities at your mates one minute, and then you're hugging them the next. Waking up in the morning without that worries me. I have thanked Nigel for his understanding regarding my media work, but I must also thank him for giving me the chance to extend my playing career. There are other people who I must acknowledge too.

First, my family. Dad, Mum, Nan, Jonathan, Matt. Especially Dad. I have only now come to realise how much he sacrificed for me. It's hard work making time to take your son to football, as I know with Charlie. Dad never missed a game. He would rush back from business in Holland to make sure I was at Crewe in time for training. He never pushed me, but he was always there for me. Mum is the best, too. She stopped coming to watch me, because she couldn't handle the nasty things people used to say. I've never sworn in front of Mum, but if she agrees to stop smoking then I will agree to stop swearing. Nan is in a home now but still football mad. She tells me off for being booked so often! Jonathan has always been there too.

There are people in football I need to thank. Eric Harrison at Manchester United who taught me morals and the right way to do things, as well as giving me a wonderful footballing education. Neil Baker at Crewe. Neil was the unsung hero, and I think it is a shame he was never given the manager's job when Dario Gradi moved upstairs. I'd like to thank all the managers I played for. I learned from them all, even if I didn't always see eye to eye with them.

Then there are all the club doctors and physios who have had to put up with my hypochondria. Surgeon John Hodgkinson saved my career when I broke my leg, and neurosurgeon Andre Jackowski saved my life when I broke my neck. Thank you, gents.

There are other people who have been important in my life – my mates Tuffy, Nutty, Quags, Hollo, Jim and Jamie. They've always been there for me. I've bought some land with Quags in Swansea and we'd like to build a hotel on it. It's opposite the racecourse, and I would like to buy a horse, too. I have fingers in a few pies.

My media career has really taken off in the last 18 months or so and I have to thank Mark Chapman, Darren Fletcher and Jo Tongue for their support and assistance with *606*. My former agent George Urquhart was like a father figure for years, and I remember those days with affection, and I'm sorry that we drifted apart. Now I have moved on to Paul Mace, Stephen Lownsbrough and Phil Glyn-Smith. I have been with Stephen and Phil for years, and their expertise and advice is invaluable.

Important as Paul, Stephen and Phil are, the most important is the terrific Trish. Trish Braisby has been my PA for the last seven years, and I think of her as a second mother. I couldn't survive without her. She takes charge of everything, from sorting my investments to booking holidays. Everything that needs organising, she organises. Everything that needs sorting, she sorts. Trish has been with me through thick and thin, and without her I don't know how I'd cope. A big hug and thanks, Trish.

The day I crashed my car after being rejected by Manchester United seems a long time ago now. If you'd said then that I would one day be writing a book about my career in football, I wouldn't have believed it. And I definitely wouldn't have believed that Ryan Giggs would write the foreword. Cheers, Giggsy. I'd like to thank Janine Self for listening to my story and helping me put it down on paper. I hope people enjoy reading about my life as much as I have enjoyed living it.